Withdrawn from
Davidson College Library

Library of
Davidson College

Contending Sovereignties

Contending Sovereignties

Redefining Political Community

edited by
R. B. J. Walker
Saul H. Mendlovitz

Lynne Rienner Publishers ■ Boulder and London

Published in the United States of America in 1990 by
Lynne Rienner Publishers, Inc.
1800 30th Street, Boulder, Colorado 80301

and in the United Kingdom by
Lynne Rienner Publishers, Inc.
3 Henrietta Street, Covent Garden, London WC2E 8LU

© 1990 by Lynne Rienner Publishers, Inc. All rights reserved

Library of Congress Cataloging-in-Publication Data
Contending sovereignties : redefining political community / edited by
R. B. J. Walker and Saul H. Mendlovitz.
  p. cm.
  Includes bibliographical references.
  ISBN 1-55587-186-0 (alk. paper)
  1. Sovereignty. I. Walker, R. B. J. II. Mendlovitz, Saul H.
JC327.C66 1990
320.1'5—dc20   90-8109
                                                                   CIP

British Cataloguing in Publication Data
A Cataloguing in Publication record for this book
is available from the British Library.

Printed and bound in the United States of America

The paper used in this publication meets the requirements
of the American National Standard for Permanence of
Paper for Printed Library Materials Z39.48-1984.

Contents

Acknowledgments   *vii*
List of Contributors   *ix*

1. Interrogating State Sovereignty
   R. B. J. Walker and Saul H. Mendlovitz   1

2. Rethinking Sovereignty in a Shrinking, Fragmented World
   Joseph A. Camilleri   13

3. The Reification of Political Community
   Warren Magnusson   45

4. Evasions of Sovereignty
   Richard Falk   61

5. Sovereignty as Transformative Practice
   Lester Edwin J. Ruiz   79

6. Spatiality and Policy Discourse: Reading the Global City
   Michael Shapiro and Deanne Neaubauer   97

7. The Politics of Secularism and the Recovery of Religious Tolerance
   Ashis Nandy   125

8. Beyond Sovereignty: An Emerging Global Civilization
   Mary Catherine Bateson   145

9. Sovereignty, Identity, Community: Reflections on the Horizons of Contemporary Political Practice
   R. B. J. Walker   159

Index   *187*

Acknowledgments

This book grew out of the Workshop on Sovereignty: Integration and Fragmentation, held at the Institute of International Relations and World Economy (IMEMO), Moscow, in October 1988. Energized by the drama of unfolding events, the workshop considered some twenty-five papers on a wide range of themes over a six-day period. The relation between formal claims to state sovereignty and changing conceptions of political community attracted especially intense discussion and debate, and it is this relation we have chosen to examine here.

The workshop was the first of a series of explorations organized by the Global Civilization Project, which involves close collaboration among the following research centers: the Soviet Political Science Association; the Center of International Studies, Princeton University; the Centre for the Study of Developing Societies, New Delhi; the International Peace Research Institute Meigaku, Japan; the Latin American Institute for Transnational Studies, Santiago, Chile; and the World Order Models Project, New York. The workshop involved the joint efforts of many of the individuals associated with the Global Civilization Project. In particular, the planning of the workshop was the responsibility of the senior staff of IMEMO Academician Evgeni Primakov and Dr. Alexander Kislov, Drs. Georgi Shakhnazarov and William Smirnov of the Soviet Political Science Association, and Professors Richard Falk and Saul Mendlovitz of the World Order Models Project. Dr. Vladimir Koptsov and Dr. Lester Ruiz were cheerfully responsible for the smooth and efficient organization of the logistical necessities. We especially want to thank the fifty or so participants in the discussions, half from the Soviet Union and half from different regions of the world, who made it such a demanding and rewarding experience. Financial support for the workshop came from the Miriam and Ira P. Wallach Foundation, and from the Soviet Peace Fund.

The Contributors

Mary Catherine Bateson, Department of Anthropology, George Mason University, Fairfax, Virginia, USA

Joseph A. Camilleri, Department of Politics, La Trobe University, Melbourne, Australia

Richard Falk, Center of International Studies, Princeton University, Princeton, New Jersey, USA

Warren Magnusson, Department of Political Science, University of Victoria, Victoria, British Columbia, Canada

Saul H. Mendlovitz, Rutgers Law School, Newark, New Jersey, USA

Ashis Nandy, Centre for the Study of Developing Societies, New Delhi, India

Deanne Neaubauer, University of Hawaii, Honolulu, Hawaii, USA

Lester Edwin J. Ruiz, Department of Politics and Philosophy, Hofstra University, Hempstead, New York, USA

Michael Shapiro, Department of Political Science, University of Hawaii, Honolulu, Hawaii, USA

R. B. J. Walker, Department of Political Science, University of Victoria, Victoria, British Columbia, Canada

1
Interrogating State Sovereignty

R. B. J. Walker & Saul H. Mendlovitz

The claim that profound structural transformations are undermining the principle of state sovereignty has been advanced by many analysts from quite different theoretical traditions. No longer, it is said, can states pretend to be autonomous or to exercise a monopoly on the legitimate use of violence in a specific territory. The most important forces that affect people's lives are global in scale and consequence. Even the most powerful states recognize serious global constraints on their capacity to affirm their own national interest above all else. In view of capacities for nuclear destruction, the global mobility of capital, and a new awareness of the fragility of the planetary ecology, the organization of political life within a fragmented system of states appears to be increasingly inconsistent with emerging realities.

Although this is a claim about novelty, it is already a venerable part of twentieth century social and political thought. Partly empirical in character, it draws on the interpretation of observed trends and new political practices. Partly speculative also, it has become a vehicle of aspiration and hope as well as a warning of new dangers. Both the interpretation and the speculation have generated considerable scholarly controversy, but the claim itself is only rarely regarded as entirely outrageous.

With the openings and relaxations of the past few years, skepticism about state sovereignty has been advanced with renewed vigor. The sense of frozen inertia inspired by the Cold War has begun to give way to a sense of fluidity, speed, and acceleration. Something is going on, even though we may not be very sure of what it is. The name Gorbachev, for example, has become associated with a new appreciation of interdependence globally just as much as with the need for renewal at home. We may focus on the dissolution of empire in Eastern Europe; or the preparations for "1992" in Western Europe; or the global reorganization of economic life that has been under way during the 1970s and 1980s; or the revitalization of interest in the United Nations; or the demands for some kind of "common security"; or a newly emerging appreciation of the planetary environment; or on innovations in communications technologies: wherever one turns, it is difficult to engage with the unfolding of daily events without sensing the anachronisms and myopias of both academic analysis and public policy. Despite persistent attempts to reify the state as an eternal presence in human affairs, and despite continuing appeals to national identity and the principle of nonintervention, questions about both the meaning and significance of state sovereignty are again firmly on political and scholarly agendas.

Speculation and the interpretation of observed trends, however, are only the beginning of serious reflection about the significance of contemporary transformations. Both empirical analysis and normative aspiration—as well as the policy initiatives and political strategies that flow from them—depend on assumptions about the character of political life, about how political practices are to be understood and how they may be transformed. Most crucially for the chapters in this book, we have become so used to thinking about political life as if state sovereignty is the only guide to what is possible that it even informs our understanding of what alternatives there might be.

Much of the discussion of state sovereignty in a world of flux and transformation has turned on a ritual of affirmation and denial. Despite evidence about how states have changed historically, and about how different forms of the state have emerged in various parts of the world and in relation to different locations within geopolitical and economic structures, the state itself has been treated as either the only possible arena in which serious political life can take place or as a merely transient prelude to a universal community of humankind. Eternally present or imminently absent: these options are deeply embedded in our understanding of what it means to be realistic—or utopian—in political life.[1] They inform scholarly categories and popular rhetoric, the delineation of research strategies, and the search for more effective policy initiatives.

Between these options lies a litany of well-known though notoriously imprecise concepts: we may refer to processes of internationalization or globalization, for example, or speak of interdependence and world politics. These are attempts to give a name to widespread suspicions that—to use a common but telling phrase—state sovereignty offers only a misleading map of where we are and an even less useful guide to where we might be going. Like the term *state* itself, however, now so familiar but once so novel[2]—even heretical—these terms seek to articulate new possibilities in ways that can only be understood on the basis of familiar historical experience.

Such concepts *are* imprecise. This is what makes them interesting, though also frustrating for those who like their concepts to be clearly defined. We sense, for example, that these terms refer to more than just relations between sovereign states. But what, precisely, is meant by this reference to more? Do terms like *internationalization* and *globalization* signify the same supposedly emergent quality? What is at stake when we refer to world politics rather than a world system, global economy, world order, or global society?[3] Is the term *interdependence* anything more than a cliché? And why is it so difficult even to engage with the principle of state sovereignty without becoming ensnared in those obviously unsatisfactory rituals of affirmation and denial, realism and utopianism, the eternal present and the transcendent future?

The terms *interdependence* and *world politics* are especially interesting in this respect. They refer to both the known and the unknown. They slip easily off the tongue, but they also remain treacherous sites of ambiguity. They afford ample opportunity for rhetorical flourish, but also for the deferral of all the hard questions they nevertheless pose.

What, for example, is it that is supposedly interdependent (or even dependent)? It could be states, in which case the term is little more than new packaging for a very old theme. The very notion of a state system implies that states are already interdependent in some sense. Much of the history of the modern state system can be interpreted as a series of responses to new forms of interdependence. The Treaty of Westphalia (1648), for example, affirmed a mutual recognition of the need to prevent religious warfare from overwhelming fragile accommodations between secular states. The formalizations of international law and tacit agreements about the rules of the game; the supposedly responsible behavior of the great powers and the institutionalization of international organizations; structural arrangements such as the balance of power; regional alliances; spheres of influence; diplomatic conventions: these are all responses to the interdependence of states. Yet they are usually understood as the necessary conditions of the interstate order that make state sovereignty possible, rather than as fundamental challenges to state sovereignty.[4] Contemporary forms of interdependence may require more complex forms of cooperation between states, but these will only seem radically novel to those who confuse the history of the state system with abstract models of anarchy or a Hobbesian state of nature.[5]

The term *interdependence* has also come to refer to much more than relations between states. It is used in conjunction with various accounts of economic, technological, social, and cultural interaction, of global networks of communication and exchange that refuse to privilege the territorial boundaries of sovereign states. Yet if it is not only states that are interdependent, it is not at all clear what the other subjects of interdependence might be. One might be referring, for example, to multinational corporations or professional organizations, to money traders, computer networks, social movements, or even individuals.

In this case the claim to novelty is more plausible, as well as disconcerting. For here we quickly run up against the conventional limits of our understanding of what political life can be.[6] What does it mean to speak of all individuals as in some sense interdependent, as part of a common system or even of a global society? What does it mean to speak of the global organization of production, distribution, and exchange, when people's political lives and identities are framed and articulated within particular states, each still jealous of its autonomy and national identity? Because these questions are disconcerting, it is not surprising that many who have spoken about emerging patterns of interdependence in this broader sense have fallen back on a more traditional interest in complex patterns of interdependence between states. It is in this context, for example, that one might compare the literature on international, or at least European, integration popular in the early 1970s with the currently influential literatures on "international regimes" and "cooperation under anarchy."[7]

Even so, the more provocative, nonstatist interpretations of interdependence find a powerful echo in some usages of the term *world politics*. Sometimes this is merely a rather innocuous synonym for interstate or international relations. But interpreted strictly—that is, in accordance with the principle of state sovereignty—it is a straightforward contradiction in terms. One might speak of interstate or international *relations*, but *politics* is supposed to be something that can occur only within the secure boundaries of sovereign states. This is why the history of Western political thought has been written as a tale of two traditions. The most familiar part of the story is a celebration of the polis and, subsequently, of the state. It tells of the establishment of a secure basis for political community—and thus the possibility of freedom, industry, and progress—within states. The less familiar and less edifying part tells us of the consequences of an absence of political community, and thus of mere relations, fragile accommodations, and, inevitably, war.[8]

The possibility of anything that might be called world politics rather than interstate relations is in fact denied explicitly by the principle of state sovereignty. This principle affirms the priority of particular peoples—the citizens of particular states—over any universalizing claims to humanity as such.[9] The implication of this affirmation is already apparent from the infamy that still clings to the name of Machiavelli. Recognizing the incongruity between the demands of statemanship or civic *virtù* and the universalizing claims of Christian virtue, Machiavelli had the temerity to privilege the former over the latter. Machiavelli's reputation still lingers, but his radicalism has become formalized as the taken-for-granted foundation of modern political life.

Both Machiavelli's contrast between *virtù* and virtue—between the ethics of political greatness and the ethics of Christian morality—and the principle of state sovereignty were responses to the specific historical conditions of early-modern Europe. They were articulated as responses to the gradual dissolution of a quite different account of the character, location, and significance of political life, an account framed within principles of hierarchical subordination. The claims of Church and Empire, the obligations of feudal modes of socioeconomic organization, as well as the categories of philosophical and theological speculation all rested on a hierarchical understanding of the relation between the collective and the particular, the universal and the specific. With the massive transformations of early-modern Europe, these hierarchical formulations no longer provided a plausible account of this relation. It is in this context, for example, that we usually understand the emergence of new conceptions of the individual and nature as radically distinct from each other, of the Cartesian ego set apart from the objective world. It is in this context also that the most fundamental questions about political identity had to be posed anew.

The principle of state sovereignty formalizes a specific answer to questions about who we are as political beings that were posed in early-modern Europe. As an answer, it poses new questions—and suggests appropriate answers to them—in turn. Once we affirm that we are citizens first and humans second—and that when push comes to shove, the claims of citizenship (nationalism, national interest, national security, and so on) must take priority over the claims of humanity in general (universal ethics, universal human rights), some way must be found to resolve the contradiction.

In the context of political life *within* states, we now remember various accounts of a social contract or a general will, or concepts of obligation, freedom, and representation, that seek to reconcile particular individuals with the universalizing claims of the state. In the context of relations *between* states, many have sought to reconcile the autonomous claims of states with a cooperative form of interstate order or even with a state system at perpetual peace. All these resolutions have been imperfect, despite claims about democracy everywhere and pieties about a modern community of nations. They have been understood to be especially imperfect in the context of relations between states where the consequences drawn by Machiavelli about the demands of statist community have now come to imply the possible obliteration of humankind as such.

A considerable literature has accumulated on our inability to respond adequately to the questions that are posed by the principle of state sovereignty. If we ask what is to be done about, for example, military insecurities, economic disparities, or ecological disruptions—problems that have arguably become more pressing as terms like interdependence and world politics have become more persuasive—we continue to engage with questions that are already posed in general terms by the principle of state sovereignty. Given the priority of citizenship over any universalizing understanding of humanity as such, how can it be possible to respond to problems we share as inhabitants of a fragile planet, as members of a common species, as participants in a worldwide system of production, distribution, and exchange? The principle of state sovereignty already affirms a restricted range of possible answers to such questions. Within states, it suggests, we may aspire to political community, cultural identity, security, freedom, law, justice, and progress. Between states, we may also aspire to an international community of peace-loving nations. Contemporary controversies about the continuing adequacy of state sovereignty focus primarily on whether these aspirations remain plausible in the face of structural transformations and global dangers.

Yet while there has been considerable interest in the questions posed by the principle of state sovereignty, there has been much less reflection on the questions to which state sovereignty is itself an answer. Who are "we"? What is the political community within which we ought to be thinking about principles of freedom and obligation, justice and democracy? How ought we to understand the relationship between specific communities and other communities, and between specific communities and humanity in general? How ought we to understand the apparent contradiction between the cultural parochialism of state sovereignty as a product of specifically Western experiences and the embrace of state sovereignty everywhere, not least in connection with the mobilization of nationalist resistances to Western hegemonies? How do states manage to sustain their claims to autonomous authority in the face of competing claims to cultural identity, economic interest, and local commitments? What, in fact, is the political status of "humanity"?

These are clearly very difficult questions, and it is easy to see why so many analysts who are nevertheless suspicious of the principle of state sovereignty tend to shy away from them. The rituals of affirmation and denial are not very helpful in this context. And the names and metaphors through which we seek to give some precision to terms such as interdependence or world politics are indeed vague and speculative, mere groping among contradictory evidence and uneven developments. Even so, to talk of interdependence, world order, globalization, peace, or world politics is necessarily to recognize that such questions must be asked. If profound structural transformations are challenging the principle of state sovereignty, if they are making our conventional answers to the problems posed by the principle of state sovereignty less and less convincing, then it is necessary to bring more clearly out into the open the questions to which state sovereignty has been such a persuasive response for so long.

It is often tempting to minimize the significance of these questions, either in the name of immediate policy relevance or of some empirically conceived social science. On the one hand, a sense of fluidity and transition invites questions about what ought to be done. Many things undoubtedly do need to be done, yet demands for policy often become a convenient way of reinforcing the power and legitimacy of existing authorities, not of raising fundamental questions about power and legitimate authority. What is to be done by whom, and for whom? What might it mean to engage in policymaking on behalf of "humanity"? Or, less grandiosely but perhaps more urgently, what might it mean to engage in policymaking on behalf of the world's poorest people?

There are certainly many policy proposals that seek to respond to "the global problematic" or to global disparities of wealth and poverty. Some are even mildly encouraging. Yet even ardent supporters of forms of interstate collaboration such as the United Nations or the Group of Seven will admit, even insist, that there remains a large disjunction between collaborative policies and vague intimations of global polity. Many analysts argue that further interstate cooperation is all we can hope for, and that the principle of state sovereignty does offer a sufficient account of the political practices capable of generating appropriate policy initiatives. This is, after all, a point of view that has succeeded in appropriating the title of political realism to itself. Nevertheless, many of those who have been called realists have also voiced strong warnings never to expect things to remain the same.[10] Policy-making is not a synonym for politics, and no amount of supposedly realist reification can make it so.

On the other hand, questions about the nature of political life and the contours of political community raise matters that have long been of concern to students of political theory. Yet political theory has for some time been in at least partial eclipse because of the overwhelming influence of socio-scientific forms of social and political analysis. In the Anglo-American world especially, sharp distinctions have been made between the scientific and the normative and between empirical explanation and hermeneutic interpretation. Moreover, much of the energy of political theory has been directed toward maintaining a critical stance toward concepts and assumptions—about knowledge and modernity, community and democracy, equality and subjectivity—that social science has preferred to render unproblematic. Understandably preoccupied with reproblematizing the character of political life within states, political theorists have rarely broached with much confidence the transformative implications of interdependence or world politics.

Thus, even if the demands of public policy or social science are tempting, it is difficult to avoid the sense that rather more is at stake in contemporary discussions of state sovereignty. Behind the call for more effective policy lies a significant degree of uncertainty about the character and even the location of political life. Our understanding of power and legitimate authority is contentious. The increasingly global reach of the processes that affect people's lives is increasingly understood to require sustained rethinking of who "we" are and of how "we" might now relate to each other. The extent to which the recent literature on interdependence and world politics has been drawn, for example, to reinvigorate discussions of justice or ethics[11] reflects the degree to which positivistic distinctions between political science and political theory, and statist distinctions between political theory and international relations, have been subject to increasingly vigorous challenge.

Recognizing the lure and the limits of both policy analysis and social science, the authors of the chapters in this book seek to explore the ways that accounts of political community formalized in the principle of state sovereignty are being rearticulated in response to profound structural transformations on a global scale. Recognizing, furthermore, the hereditary ritual of affirmation and denial, these authors seek to explore the multiplicity of possible communities that might emerge from contemporary transformations. Acknowledging the extent to which contemporary political discourse has been shaped by the presumption that state sovereignty provides the only plausible account of who we are as political beings, these essays are for the most part deliberately tentative in character. They seek to develop accounts of how the relationship between state sovereignty and claims about political community might be opened out for further examination in spite of the rituals through which historical contingencies have been described and legitimized as eternal necessities.

The opening chapter, by Joseph Camilleri, perhaps goes furthest in judging the principle of state sovereignty to be incompatible with the way political life is being reorganized. He insists, to begin with, that state sovereignty be understood as a response to specific historical conditions. After surveying the conventional account of how a new understanding of political community was formalized in early-modern Europe, he canvasses a wide range of recent literature on transformations in the contemporary world capitalist economy. Noting how the internationalization of economic activity has been associated with the centralization of state power, he nevertheless concludes that state sovereignty must be understood as merely a transitory phase in an evolutionary process, a bridge between national and world capitalism.

Camilleri focuses explicitly on the tension between state sovereignty and more cosmopolitan claims about humanity as such. His sympathies are clearly cosmopolitan, and his analysis captures a widespread impatience with realist appraisals of the inevitability of statist fragmentation. The following chapter, by Warren Magnusson, develops a rather different reading of the historical record, one more concerned with political community within states. Magnusson is concerned less with a progressive evolution away from fragmentation than with the erasure of the "local" from the agenda of serious politics. In this reading, the principle of state sovereignty formalizes the denial of local community quite as much as the denial of any more cosmopolitan community. Consequently, this analysis suggests, any rethinking of the relationship between state sovereignty and political community cannot simply presume that the problem is fragmentation and that therefore the solution must be some kind of integration. Rather, attention must be focused on the practices through which states have managed so successfully to mediate between the local and the cosmopolitan and to marginalize both from the business of serious political life.

The tensions and counterpoints that emerge from these two analyses are taken up in different ways in the next three chapters. In Chapter 4, Richard Falk stresses both the continuing role of states in the modern world and the different strategies through which some political actors—including states—

have in fact managed to participate in other forms of political community. He sketches a pattern of "evasions"—some across boundaries, some within boundaries, and some beyond boundaries—that, while ambiguous in character, are producing new allegiances and political identities.

Lester Ruiz focuses on recent experiences in the Philippines and looks at how claims about state sovereignty enter into ongoing struggles for liberation. Drawing especially on ideas about communities of resistance and solidarity that have been developed within liberation theology, he argues that state sovereignty can be understood as a potentially transformative practice as well as a reification of statist politics.

Michael Shapiro and Deanne Neaubauer then examine the mediation between local and cosmopolitan politics present in that apparent contradiction in terms, the global city. Although the principle of state sovereignty formalizes a strict separation between local spaces such as the city in and a state system understood to be external to those spaces, a city like Los Angeles is firmly embedded in a global political economy. Urban life is increasingly shaped by global structures, and yet policymakers are forced to respond to pressing problems as if they are part of a purely national agenda. Shapiro and Neaubauer pay particular attention to the discursive politics through which the conventions of national policy debate have been normalized in spite of evidence that a city like Los Angeles is increasingly difficult to locate within a purely national political space.

The principle of state sovereignty was not only articulated against the universalizing and hierarchical claims of feudal order and empire. It was also an expression of a new *secular* understanding of social and political life, a challenge to the subordination of politics to religious authority. The rise of nationalism may have made the cultural dimension of state sovereignty rather more complex, but the explicitly secular metaphysics of early-modern Europe remains crucial. Moreover, religious aspirations and conflicts remain very much a part of contemporary political life. As Ashis Nandy argues in the specific context of South Asia, secular statecraft has itself become a source of religious conflict rather than an escape from it. Consequently, Nandy suggests, a rethinking of political community must be informed by a recovery of religious tolerance, a tolerance based on refusing a hegemonic language of secularism that legitimizes new forms of domination and violence.

Mary Catherine Bateson then counterposes the principle of state sovereignty to speculation about an emerging global civilization. The very term *civilization*, she suggests, still reflects the familiar account of political community expressed by the principle of state sovereignty. By contrast, she speculates, whatever may be eventually described as a new global civilization is more likely to involve a quite different pattern of commonality, one composed of multiple fragments and linkages, and informed as much by pluralism and ambiguity as by shared understandings and authority.

Finally, Rob Walker returns to the ritual of affirmation and denial that has characterized so much analysis of state sovereignty. This ritual, he argues, reflects the specifically modern resolution of philosophical options that is formalized in the principle of state sovereignty. The crucial analytical problem, he suggests, concerns the continuing hold of this modernist resolution on both scholarship and political practice. While this resolution will continue to inform our understanding of political community for the foreseeable future, he argues that the most interesting innovations will necessarily respond to a far-reaching rearticulation of spatiotemporal relations. Consequently, they will be characterized by the search for new understandings of the competing claims of universality and diversity, claims that have been resolved so long on the spatial terrain of the territorial state.

All these chapters speak around rather than directly to the grand substantive problems that have stimulated calls for a reappraisal of state sovereignty. They do not address the meaning of state sovereignty in relation to contemporary uncertainties about security, global economic processes, or environmental disasters. Nor do they offer any clear guide to what the alternative to political life organized around state sovereignty might turn out to be. They do, however, emphasize the importance—and the difficulty—of *prior* questions about what it means to engage in political life in the late twentieth century. Confident assertions that we are indeed what the principle of state sovereignty suggests we are—either citizens or cosmopolitans—must be treated with a sustained skepticism. If claims about interdependence or world politics are to be taken seriously, then questions about who "we" are will be posed in increasingly provocative ways for some time to come.

Notes

1. For a helpful discussion see Steve Smith, "The Fall and Rise of the State in International Politics," in Graeme Duncan, ed., *Democracy and the Capitalist State* (Cambridge: Cambridge University Press, 1989), pp. 33–35.

2. Kenneth Dyson, *The State Tradition in Western Europe* (Oxford: Martin Robertson, 1980); Perry Anderson, *Lineages of the Absolutist State* (London: New Left Books, 1974); Quentin Skinner, *The Foundations of Modern Political Thought*, 2 vols. (Cambridge: Cambridge University Press, 1978); Gianfranco Poggi, *The Development of the Modern State* (London: Hutchinson, 1978); Charles Tilly, ed., *The Formation of National States in Western Europe* (Princeton: Princeton University Press, 1975), Joseph R. Strayer, *On the Medieval Origins of the Modern State* (Princeton: Princeton University Press, 1970); Michael Mann, *The Sources of Social Power*, Vol. 1 (Cambridge: Cambridge University Press, 1986); and John Hall, ed., *States in History* (Oxford: Basil Blackwell, 1986).

3. This question is implicit, but only occasionally the subject of any extended discussion, in a broad range of contemporary literature. See, for example: Mel

Gurtov, *Global Politics in the Human Interest* (Boulder, Colo.: Lynne Rienner, 1988); Lynn H. Miller, *Global Order: Values and Power in International Politics* (Boulder, Colo.: Westview Press, 1985), Samuel S. Kim, *The Quest for a Just World Order* (Boulder, Colo.: Westview Press, 1984); Richard Falk, *The Promise of World Order: Essays in Normative International Relations* (Philadelphia: Temple University Press, 1987); Robert O. Keohane and Joseph S. Nye, *Power and Interdependence* (Boston: Little Brown, 1977); James N. Rosenau, *The Study of Global Interdependence* (London: Pinter, 1980); Ray Maghroori and Bennett Ramberg, eds., *Globalism Versus Realism: International Relations' Third Debate* (Boulder, Colo.: Westview Press, 1982); E. O. Czempiel and J. N. Rosenau, eds., *Global Changes and Theoretical Challenges* (Lexington, Mass.: Lexington Books, 1989); Ralph Pettman, *State and Class: A Sociology of International Affairs* (London: Croom Helm, 1979); Silviu Brucan, *The Dialectic of World Politics* (New York: Knopf, 1978); Georgi Shakhnazarov, *The Coming World Order*, trans. Margot Light (Moscow: Progress Publishers, 1981); Robert W. Cox, *Power, Production and World Order: Social Forces in the Making of History* (New York: Columbia University Press, 1987); Stephen Gill and David Law, *The Global Political Economy: Perspectives, Problems and Policies* (Baltimore: Johns Hopkins University Press, 1988); Dan Smith and E. P. Thompson, eds., *Prospects for a Habitable Planet* (London: Penguin, 1987); James Turner, *The Quest for Peace: Three Moral Traditions in Western Cultural History* (Princeton: Princeton University Press, 1987); Edward McWhinney, *United Nations Law Making* (New York: Holmes and Meier, 1984); Richard Falk, Friedrich Kratochwil, and Saul H. Mendlovitz, eds., *International Law: A Contemporary Perspective* (Boulder, Colo.: Westview Press, 1985); and Richard Falk, Samuel Kim, and Saul H. Mendlovitz, eds., *The United Nations and a Just World Order* (Boulder, Colo.: Westview Press, 1990).

4. See, for example, F. H. Hinsley, *Sovereignty*, 2nd ed. (Cambridge: Cambridge University Press, 1986); Alan James, *Sovereign Statehood: The Basis of International Society* (London: Allen & Unwin, 1986); Hedley Bull, *The Anarchical Society: A Study of Order in World Politics* (London: Macmillan, 1977); Martin Wight, *Systems of States*, ed. H. Bull, (Leicester: Leicester University Press, 1977); John Vincent, *Non-Intervention and International Order* (Princeton: Princeton University Press, 1974); Michael Donelan, ed., *The Reason of States* (London: Allen & Unwin, 1978); Terry Nardin, *Law, Morality and the Relations of States* (Princeton: Princeton University Press, 1983); Stephen D. Krasner, *Structural Conflict: The Third World Against Global Liberalism* (Berkeley and Los Angeles: University of California Press, 1985); and Ingrid Detter de Lupis, *International Law and the Independent State*, 2nd ed. (London: Gower, 1987).

5. Much of the recent literature on international cooperation has been informed by an account of the state system as an anarchy understood as analogous with the "state of nature" that Thomas Hobbes identified with relations between proto-bourgeois individuals, and/or as the negation of the account of a cohesive society presumed to exist within states. See, for example, Kenneth A. Oye, ed., *Co-operation Under Anarchy* (Princeton: Princeton University Press, 1986). For critiques of this tendency, especially as it informs the analysis of state sovereignty as an ahistorical principle rather than as an historical political practice, see Richard K. Ashley, "Untying the Sovereign State: A Double Reading of the Anarchy Problematique," *Millennium: Journal of International Studies* 7, no. 2 (Summer 1988): 227–272; and

Ashley, "Living on Border Lines: Man, Poststructuralism and War" in James Der Derian and Michael Shapiro, eds., *International/Intertextual Relations* (Lexington, Mass.: Lexington Books, 1988), pp. 259–321. See also R. B. J. Walker, *State Sovereignty, Global Civilization and the Rearticulation of Political Space*, World Order Studies Program Occasional Paper No. 18 (Princeton: Princeton University Center of International Studies, 1988); Richard K. Ashley and R. B. J. Walker, eds., *Speaking the Language of Exile: Dissident Movements in Global Political Theory*, Special Issue of *International Studies Quarterly* (1990); and James Der Derian, *On Diplomacy* (Oxford: Basil Blackwell, 1987).

6. See especially John Dunn, *Western Political Theory in the Face of the Future* (Cambridge: Cambridge University Press, 1979); Dunn, "Unimagined Community: The Deceptions of Socialist Internationalism," in Dunn, *Rethinking Modern Political Theory* (Cambridge: Cambridge University Press, 1985); and Dunn, "Political Obligations and Political Possibilities," in Dunn, *Political Obligation in its Historical Context* (Cambridge: Cambridge University Press, 1980).

7. Compare, for example, Keohane and Nye, *Power and Independence*; Leon Lindberg and Stuart A. Scheingold, *Europe's Would-Be Polity* (Englewood Cliffs, N.J.: Prentice Hall, 1970); Johan K. de Vree, *Political Integration: The Formation of Theory and its Problems* (The Hague: Mouton, 1972); and Charles Pentland, *International Theory and European Integration* (New York: Praeger, 1973) with Oye, ed., *Co-operation Under Anarchy*; Robert O. Keohane, *After Hegemony: Co-operation and Discord in the World Political Economy* (Princeton: Princeton University Press, 1984); and with Stephen Krasner, ed., *International Regimes* (Ithaca, N.Y.: Cornell University Press, 1983).

8. Martin Wight, "Why Is There No International Theory?" in Herbert Butterfield and Martin Wight, eds., *Diplomatic Investigations* (London: Allen & Unwin, 1966), pp. 17–24.

9. For a brief sketch see Andrew Linklater, *Men and Citizens in the Theory of International Relations* (London: Macmillan, 1982).

10. Most famously, Niccolo Machiavelli in *The Prince*.

11. See the recent discussion by Stanley Hoffmann, *The Political Ethics of International Relations* (New York: Carnegie Council on Ethics and International Affairs, 1988).

2

Rethinking Sovereignty in a Shrinking, Fragmented World

Joseph A. Camilleri

Nothing is today more greatly needed than clarity about the theory that has come to dominate our understanding of national and international life: The theory of state sovereignty parallels the evolution of the modern state. It formalizes the evolving relationship between state and civil society, between political authority and political community. F. H. Hinsley, one of the foremost contemporary exponents of the principle of sovereignty, rightly reminds us that despite loose talk about the way it is acquired, lost, or eroded, sovereignty is not a fact. Rather, it is an expression of a claim about the way political power is or should be exercised.[1] Given the far-reaching transformation of the social and political landscape we have witnessed this century, and especially these past several decades, it is timely and appropriate that we reconsider the extent to which this claim can be sustained.

The Need for Historical Perspective

The impact of social and economic conditions on the concept and practice of state sovereignty cannot be overstated. Confining, for the moment, our attention to Europe—widely recognized as the cradle of the modern sovereign state—we find that in the medieval period both rulers and ruled were subject to a universal legal order that reflected and derived its authority from the law of God. Medieval Europe comprised a cosmopolitan patchwork of overlapping loyalties and allegiances, geographically interwoven jurisdictions and political enclaves.[2] In the feudal system there was no clear demarcation between the domestic and external spheres of organization, no sharp dividing line between "public territories" and "private estates." Yet this diverse and fragmented system of rule nevertheless enjoyed a considerable level of coherence and unity by virtue of "common legal, religious and social traditions and institutions."[3] Although territorially segmented, the constituent units of the cosmopolitan order did not manifest the characteristics of possessiveness and exclusiveness associated with the modern concept of sovereignty. They saw themselves as municipal embodiments of a universal community.[4]

By the end of the fifteenth century, Europe comprised some five hundred more or less independent political units,[5] but the old feudal order was in visible decline. With the growth of trade and manufacturing, and the introduction of royal taxes, power became centralized in the monarchies. The strengthening of monarchical authority implied a sharp contrast with the medieval past, when the allegiance of individuals was directed primarily to their overlord, their village, their profession, or their class. Monarchies developed central institutions that employed educated and competent civil servants, hired armies of mercenary troops, rationalized the collection of taxes, and dispensed justice.

By the sixteenth century several other movements were contributing to this trend. The achievements of the Renaissance in art, literature, and philosophy were particularly important in the secularization of life and a corresponding decline in the spiritual and temporal authority of the church. The concentration of power in the monarchies gathered pace at the expense of the universal authorities—Pope and Emperor—and of the segmentary fiefdoms that had dominated the feudal period. With the Reformation and Counter-Reformation and the subsequent wars of religion, the emerging authority of the secular state appeared to be the most effective remedy for the widespread religious and political disorder that had engulfed Europe. The economic practices of the merchant and the manufacturer, the scientific discoveries that contradicted longstanding religious doctrines, and the deepening schism in the church further weakened the papacy and the other institutions that had underpinned the ideological unity of medieval Europe.

Once the decentralized political arrangements characteristic of feudal society had been dissolved, they were replaced by a system of territorially bounded sovereign states, each equipped with its own centralized administration and possessing a virtual monopoly on the legitimate use of violence. The consolidation of that system, which saw the development of new administrative mechanisms and forms of political control, coupled with the relocation of population and territory, was in part needed to facilitate the increase in trade and industrial activity during this period. Equally important was the role of the sovereign state in redefining the concept of private property, understood as the right to exclude others from the possession of a commodity, whether it be land, capital, or labor. The public authority of the state was needed to enforce and legitimize a system of domestic and external—national and international—relations based on private property,[6] and territorial expansion. The emergence of the sovereign state was in a sense the necessary instrument of Europe's colonial expansion.

The concept of state sovereignty was shaped by the social and economic environment of sixteenth and seventeenth century Europe. This should immediately raise suspicions about the widespread inclination, shared by Hinsley, to treat sovereignty as an inevitable and virtually irreversible stage in the evolution of political institutions, a necessary culmination of the integration of state and community.⁷ As Harold Laski has argued, the sovereign state represents not an absolute but a historical logic.⁸ Though that logic is powerful and continues to be relevant for an understanding of the contemporary world, there remains a need for sustained inquiry into the congruity or incongruity between historically constituted principles and contemporary conditions.

The Theory of State Sovereignty

The origin and history of the concept of sovereignty is closely related to the nature, origin, and evolution of the state, and in particular to the development of centralized authority and an administrative system of political control.⁹ But the notion of the *state* is itself highly problematic and has given rise to a variety of interpretations. For the absolutist theorists of the sixteenth and seventeenth centuries, notably Bodin and Hobbes, the state refers to those individuals and institutions that exercise supreme authority within a given territory or society. In this account, the state represents the highest power in the land, acting as a court of last resort and holding an effective monopoly on the use of force. The state is identified with the power to make, administer, and enforce laws and with the network of institutions necessary for this purpose. For others, the state represents not just the institutions of government but the politically organized society, the body politic, or the nation. According to this view, associated primarily with traditionalists like Hooker and Burke but also idealists like Rousseau and Hegel, the state is a community of free people based on an implicit or explicit consensus.¹⁰ These two contrasting conceptualizations of the state have deeply influenced the theory and practice of state sovereignty and to a considerable extent account for the tensions and ambiguities that have surrounded the concept since its earliest formulation.

Part of the ambiguity surrounding the concept of state sovereignty also has to do with its complex relationship with two other concepts: power and authority. The concept of authority is itself notoriously elusive. Following W. J. Rees, we may distinguish moral authority (one obeys a rule because it accords with one's conscience) from customary authority (the rule is obeyed for fear of incurring the disapproval of another person or persons, usually associated with the violation of social norms, customs, or conventions), and from coercive authority (where the law is backed by force).¹¹ While conceptually distinct, these three forms of authority often overlap in practice, as is clearly the case with the authority of the state. Nevertheless, it has been argued that what distinguishes the state from other institutions is its coercive authority, or as others have labeled it, *supreme coercive power*.

According to this view, the legal sovereignty of the state, whether it is enshrined in a written or unwritten constitution, rests on the enforceability of the law—either directly by the exercise of supreme coercive power, or indirectly by the threat to exercise such power. This deceptively simple definition of sovereignty is fraught with difficulty, for what constitutes supreme coercive power is less than self-evident. Nor is it entirely clear whether such coercive power is exercised by one institution above all others or shared by a range of institutions. If supreme coercive power is to be vested in one institution, the question arises as to whether such an institution can be readily identified. If, on the other hand, several institutions are said to have a share in state sovereignty, in what sense can they be said to exercise supreme coercive power, especially when two or more of these institutions are in conflict with one another? The latter problem is especially acute in a system based on the separation or division of powers. In this context, reference is often made to the United States, where a delicate system of checks and balances operates among president, Congress, and the Supreme Court, and where even amendment of the Constitution is limited by the provision that no state shall, without its consent, be deprived of its equal representation in the Senate.

The theory of state sovereignty has thus had to grapple with three separate but closely related questions: Are there limits to the exercise of sovereignty? Where is sovereignty located? What is the relationship between state sovereignty and civil society? To appreciate more fully the troublesome nature of these questions, it is helpful to recall answers associated with some political thinkers who have helped to shape our understanding of the theory of sovereignty: Bodin, Hobbes, Locke, Rousseau, Kant, and Austin.

Jean Bodin's *De la République* was first published in 1577, at the height of the civil war between Catholics and Huguenots. His thesis that a central authority should wield unlimited power was in part an attempt to restore order and security to the deeply divided political society in France during that period. His main contention was that such power had to be given legal recognition. It had to be endowed with *sovereignty*. Here he uses the words *souveraineté*, *majestas*, and *summa potestas* more or less interchangeably. For Bodin, sovereignty was "supreme power over citizens and subjects unrestrained by law"[12] and therefore unlimited in extension and duration. God, it is true, was above the prince, and the supreme power of the prince over his subjects was subordinate to the "law of God and Nature." But apart from this limitation, the practical consequence of which remained unclear, the sovereign was above the people, or, as Jacques Maritain has argued, "separate from and transcendent over the people."[13] Subjection to the sovereign became the defining characteristic of citizenship.

Despite the lucidity of his argument, Bodin failed to grapple with several unresolved questions in his theory. The prince is said to be subordinate to the law of God and nature, but what if his commands require absolute obedience? What if the sovereign contravenes the constitutional or customary laws of the land, which Bodin called *leges imperii* and which, he seemed to imply, even the sovereign cannot change? Did the sovereignty of the prince ultimately rest on moral, customary, or coercive authority? These unanswered questions may not have immediately affected the practical impact of Bodin's theoretical contribution, but they have serious implications for the contemporary relevance of the concept.[14]

Though several writers over the next several decades helped to refine the concept and vocabulary of sovereignty, the next major step did not come until *The Leviathan* in 1651. Like Bodin and others before him, Thomas Hobbes sought to eliminate the dualism inherent in the notion of a body politic comprised of prince and people by doing away with every right of the people. He abandoned the idea of a social contract between ruler and ruled and substituted for it a contract in which all individuals agreed to submit to the state. Hobbes describes the outcome of this universal surrender of the right to self-government as a "Multitude united in one Person," a "Commonwealth," a "Leviathan."[15] In this sense, the distinctions between society and state and between state and government are virtually abolished. The omnipotent sovereign is for Hobbes the only alternative to complete anarchy. Natural and customary law have no force of their own; it is only the sovereign's consent or command sanctioned by force that gives either reason or custom its legal status. It follows that neither morality nor convention is a limitation on the authority of the sovereign state.

Although Hobbes spoke of the state as an abstract construction that might be composed of one or any number of men, in practice the sovereign was equated with the existing ruler. Not surprisingly, there developed a reaction to the absolutism propounded by Hobbes on the part of those committed to constitutional theory and other more flexible forms of government. For writers such as John Locke, the answer lay not in rejection of the concept of sovereignty or even of Hobbes' egoistic individualism, but rather in the reinterpretation of natural law as a claim to innate, inalienable rights inherent in each individual. It followed that society and the state existed to preserve individual rights, including the right to property, and that such rights were a limitation on the authority of both state and society. At the same time Locke restored the importance of natural law by reaffirming the medieval tradition that moral laws are intrinsic and superior to positive law, and that governments are obliged to give effect by their laws to what is naturally and morally right. He jettisoned the Hobbesian notion of state sovereignty as supreme coercive power, or at least moderated it by conceiving of government as held in trust for the people, deriving its legitimacy from their consent. Tacit though it might be, such consent could be given only in return for adequate protection of individual rights. By infringing such rights, the offending government forfeited the right and authority to govern.

The Lockean attempt to ground sovereignty in constitutional theory by reviving the idea of a partnership between ruler and ruled posed several problems. Not least among these was the effective division of sovereignty between ruler and ruled, thereby undermining the supremacy of power and authority that Bodin, Hobbes, and others had come to regard as the essential ingredient of sovereignty. In his *Social Contract* published in 1756, Jean-Jacques Rousseau sought to rescue sovereignty from the constitutionalist trap while seeking to avoid the authoritarian implications of the Hobbesian thesis. Like Hobbes, he argued that state sovereignty was unlimited and indivisible, and that the state was the result of a contract in which all individuals had agreed to submit to its will. But unlike Hobbes, he equated the state with the body politic that had been formed by the social contract, "reducing government, the rulership, to a mere commission."[16] Indeed, for Rousseau, the idea of a social contract virtually disappears, for he conceives of the community of citizens as a moral and collective personality in which each member, "while uniting himself with all, may still obey himself alone, and remains as free as before."[17] Having a moral identity of its own, society represented a collective good, separate and distinct from the private interests of its members. It found expression in the "general will" and endowed the body politic with absolute power over all its members. Moral authority (or popular sovereignty), at least of a kind, was reaffirmed as the basis of state sovereignty. Nor could the prerogatives of the sovereign "exceed the limits of general conventions."[18] Rousseau's solution to the institutional dilemma posed by sovereignty was to suppress by the device of the general will the distinction between society and its political institutions, between the community and the state, between moral authority and coercive power. It was but a relatively small step, therefore, from Rousseau's theory to G. W. F. Hegel's idealization of the state as an absolute moral being, which he equated with "the divine will, in the sense that it is mind present on earth, unfolding itself to be the actual shape and organization of a world."[19] Admittedly, in order to elevate the state to this exalted ethical plane, Hegel was obliged to restore the distinction between state and civil society, but only in order to contrast the clash of individual egoistic interests that animate civil society with the raison d'être of the state, which is to safeguard and preserve the common good.

The dangerous implications of Rousseau's attempt to fuse the sovereignty of the people with the sovereignty of the state led Immanuel Kant to reassert the principle of constitutional government. Although he accepted Rousseau's notion of popular sovereignty, he was at pains to stress the practical necessity of political organization. As Howard Williams has suggested, Kant "sought to combine the freedom and consent of Rousseau's *Social Contract* with the domination and absolute authority of Hobbes' *Leviathan.*"[20] Each member of society shares in the law of the sovereign, because, as citizen, he is involved in making the law—through a representative—in the legislature. But once made, the law, as administered by the executive and interpreted by the judiciary, is binding on all citizens.

This attempted reconciliation did not fully resolve the disjunction of state and civil societies, for it did not specify the necessary and sufficient conditions for the involvement of the citizenry in the making of the law. Nor did it address the complex question as to whether—issues of constitutionality aside—the individual is ever entitled to disobey the law. Did the law ultimately rest on moral authority, however defined, or on the state's coercive power? It was in no small measure this unresolved question that prompted several writers to take refuge in the relative simplicity of the legal theory of sovereignty. One of its foremost exponents was the nineteenth century English utilitarian John Austin, whose conception of the law was limited exclusively to the category of positive law. The state, for Austin, was a legal order in which a specific authority is the ultimate source of power. This authority, which issues the commands that are habitually obeyed but which is itself immune to the commands of others, is the sovereign power in the state. Its authority is unlimited. For the purpose of this theory the moral character of the law is irrelevant. What matters is its effectiveness. The legal authority of the sovereign state derives from its supreme coercive power.

Notwithstanding their vastly different approaches, the foregoing accounts of sovereignty are open to interpretation as mere exercises in abstraction. Here lies the revolutionary significance of Karl Marx's contribution to our understanding of sovereignty as a political practice. For Marx, a distinction must be drawn between philosophical formulation and political reality. Though the state may represent itself as sovereign and as the guardian of the general interest of society, this is largely an illusion. Though it may exercise power and subdue both groups and individuals to its will, the state, at least in the context of capitalist society, expresses the will of private property as the highest political and moral reality. The sovereign state is in one sense the "official expression of civil society," yet it reflects the unhampered development of bourgeois society, or the free movement of private interests.[21] This is not to deny the relative autonomy of the state nor the fact that those who exercise state authority often think of themselves as raised above the rest of society. By the very nature of bureaucratization, the state does rise above society and becomes a parasite on it.[22] But even in the case of the Bonapartist state in France, Marx is careful to distinguish between its "political independence" and its role as protector of the socially and economically dominant class.[23] In other words, Marx was intent on contrasting the sovereignty of the state (understood as the expression and instrument of the dominant social order) with the sovereignty of the people, for the unity and will of the nation could be realized only by the destruction of state power, which was "but a parasitic excrescence"[24] of the people's sovereignty.

Theoretical Rationale and Practical Context

Regardless of the intricacies or validity of his class analysis, Marx's great insight was his appreciation of the close relationship between theory and practice. The function of the absolutist state as conceived by Bodin and Hobbes was to impose order in a Europe that had experienced the disintegration of the feudal system and prolonged conflict and civil war. The more democratic versions of state sovereignty offered by Locke, Rousseau, and Kant reflected both the experience of a society increasingly self-conscious of its own history and the emergence of a new economic class. The theory and practice of sovereignty as it evolved in eighteenth century Europe reflected, and in part anticipated, a rapidly changing economic and political environment.

It was the sovereign state that established the legal conditions for property relations, for the circulation of commodities, and for the standardization of the medium of exchange (money). It also provided the necessary material infrastructure for industrial development, and in nineteenth century Europe supplied the military force that would underpin the worldwide expansion of European and especially English capital. The nation-state assumed primary responsibility for regulating the business cycle, overseeing industrial relations, supplying credit and subsidies to industry, funding scientific and technological research, organizing energy, transport, and communications systems, and managing the external relations of the economy. The functions of the state did not derive either from the logic of sovereignty or from the will of sovereigns, but from the needs of national economic expansion, the main beneficiaries of which were the emerging capitalist classes.

But the functions of the sovereign state were not purely economic.[25] It also had to resolve or at least moderate conflicts between opposing economic interests and at the same time maintain the legitimacy of the process, on which depended the stability of the prevailing order. (As part of its legitimation function, for example, it has had more recently to offer a variety of rewards, such as income, education, industrial, and political rights, to compensate those who would not otherwise benefit from the expansion of economic activity.[26]) As part of this stabilizing or legitimating function, the state had to develop an extensive system of political and administrative controls. The power and authority of the sovereign state were thereby reinforced by the very nature of the productive process and technical rationality.

There was also an important cultural dimension, not unconnected with the changing character of economic organization—namely, the growth of nationalism. Some have attempted to locate the origins of the principle of nationality in the achievement of particular dynasties, whether by conquest or other means. Others have laid stress on the role of race, religion, or language. Still others have interpreted nationalism as a quasi-metaphysical relationship to time and space, to the shared experience of past glories, grievances, and sacrifices and of future hopes, dreams, and ambitions.[27]

As part of the development of the nation-state, however, nationalism involved more than cultural experience. It represented a marriage of culture and politics. The creation of the nation-state promised the coincidence of state and civil society.[28] Nationalism was a reflection of the increasing complexity of relationships and needs, of beliefs and institutions ushered in by the Renaissance and Reformation and by the subsequent scientific and industrial revolutions. The rise of the nation was greatly facilitated by the rise of a new individualism,[29] and in particular the emerging Protestant ethic with its stress on literacy, personal achievement, and rejection of a monopolistic priesthood. In the expanding world of knowledge, education became the key to identity, culture the necessary instrument and lifeblood of a shared environment. In this sense, the national principle derived much of its impetus from the combined effect of industrialization and urbanization. The industrial project facilitated the convergence of cultural and political experience, the homogeneity of culture within each political unit, and the increasing role of the state as the main vehicle for the transmission of culture.

In this sense national sovereignty became a defining principle of political organization, and the sovereign state the principal vehicle for managing, if not resolving, class, ethnic, or religious conflict within the nation.[30] But it was also the foundation stone of European international relations. Following the French Revolution and the subsequent downfall of Napoleon, national sovereignty as a principle was applied ever more vigorously in the external conduct of the leading European states. Increasingly, the world was seen as comprising social units (states), each with a supreme authority enjoying the allegiance of citizens and exercising an unlimited capacity to dispose of the territory and resources of that society. Outside of their boundaries, these units might act with restraint, but in no circumstance would they acknowledge an external authority higher than their own.[31] Here, then, was the essence of the state-centric view of the world, or as others have subsequently labeled it, the "billiard-ball theory of international relations," or the "international politics paradigm."[32]

In Hinsley's view, the principle was so firmly entrenched in the organization of the modern state that even when the international system broke down with the outbreak of World War I, institutional attempts, such as the League of Nations, to suppress or limit the principle were bound to end in failure.[33] Yet the theory of state sovereignty has not gone unchallenged. Numerous critics have referred to the emergence of federal systems of government and various checks and balances, all of which are said to contribute to the diffusion of power and authority. Externally, they see sovereignty being constrained and qualified by the growth of international law and organization. Finally, the critique of sovereignty has had a normative dimension arising in part from the largely unresolved tension between democratic principles and absolutist tendencies.

Does the theory of state sovereignty in its various guises reflect the articulation of power in the contemporary world? Much of the discussion around this question has been terribly confused, partly because the implications of the relative diffusion or concentration of power are themselves ambiguous. On the one hand, it could be argued that class conflict and the fragmentation of power are antithetical to the notion of state sovereignty. On the other hand, the centralization of power and authority associated with a ruling elite or ruling class does not sit comfortably with the notion of popular sovereignty, unless we maintain the fiction that the powerful few in some mystical sense represent the will of the entire body politic. The idea of popular sovereignty, which the nation-state is meant to embody, does seem at odds with the concentration of power that typifies the modern industrial state.

An additional dimension of the complex environment within which nation-states have to operate is said to be the expanding role of international law and international organization. Regardless of how it is that treaties, agreements, customs, and conventions arise—normally they come into being by virtue of the decisions of governments acting on behalf of sovereign states—the rapidly developing legal order both reflects the inadequacy of the state as a self-contained unit of decisionmaking and restricts its freedom of action. International law—and the varying degrees of international organization that accompany it—feeds on itself and becomes so closely interwoven with domestic law as to make the dividing line increasingly blurred. In these circumstances it has become progressively more difficult to demonstrate the primacy of domestic law, which is arguably one of the cardinal premises of state sovereignty.

But there is another and more profound sense in which states are often obliged to act in ways dictated by persons and groups that do not come under their jurisdiction. The exercise of sovereignty is limited by the realities of power within and between states. To the extent that the international system normally comprises a few powerful and many weaker states, there inevitably arises a hierarchy of relations that does not easily correspond to the theoretical equality of all sovereign states. Even Austin has to concede that the predominance of powerful states may represent a hegemonic order inconsistent with the sovereignty of weaker states, although he describes such instances as "comparatively rare and transient."[34] Oppenheim postulates that power hierarchies in international relations are contained by the operation of the balancing of power, which reduces the disparities between stronger and weaker states sufficiently to provide all states with the indispensable minimum of social equality.[35] But what is the meaning of such equality? Can an international system that is unable to guarantee the conditions necessary for the self-determination of most, if not all, its members be accurately described as a system of "sovereign" states?[36]

Apart from questioning the descriptive and analytical utility of the concept, the critique of state sovereignty has also contained an important normative element, which stems from the tensions between power and autonomy and between hierarchy and democracy. Many have argued that the principle of state sovereignty, taken to its logical conclusion, undermines or at least grievously weakens the democratic ethic. Maritain, for example, focusing on Bodin's theory and in particular on his memorable phrase "the prince is the image of God," concludes that "the sovereign—submitted to God but accountable only to him—transcends the political whole just as God transcends the cosmos."[37] Rather than being part of and representing the body politic, the "prince" is separate and transcendent. He rules not *at* the peak but *above* the peak. The separation and transcendence of the sovereign state from the political community is antithetical to the democratic impulse. More importantly perhaps, that separation also reflects the legal and political division of one sovereign from another, one society from the rest of the international community. For Maritain this separateness is "all the more questionable as the State is mistaken for the body politic itself or for the personification of the people themselves."[38] Understood in this sense, state sovereignty becomes divorced from popular sovereignty and related notions of pluralism, autonomy, freedom, and accountability. Modern states may have sought to incorporate institutional arrangements consistent with widely shared democratic aspirations, but the attempt to graft democratic institutions on to the sovereign state rests on a fundamental contradiction that in practice is often resolved at the expense of the democratic principle.

A separate but related aspect of the critique—also integral to the democratic tradition—is the emphasis on the individual citizen rather than the state as the ultimate source of moral judgment. No edict, order, or law can be absolved from the scrutiny of the citizen. No action of the state can infringe basic human rights. The real constraining force on the citizen, argues Laski, "is not the legal obligation to obey government but the moral obligation to follow what we regard as justice."[39] For Laski, the individual is the supreme arbiter of human conduct. It is the individual, not the state, that is sovereign.

Finally, it has been argued that the concept of an absolute and transcendent authority that demands an unqualified allegiance from its subjects is not compatible with the interests of humanity, by which is meant the interests of those under the state's jurisdiction as well as those beyond it. The morality of sovereign states is presumably one in which each state is a law unto itself, able to act as it pleases regardless of the consequences for others. If states are to be considered ends in themselves, morally immune from external interference, they are presumably entitled to dispose of their territories and resources without consideration for the welfare of other societies. In other words, their actions are premised on narrowly conceived self-interest much as firms and individuals are supposed to operate in the market system of nineteenth century laissez-faire economics.[40] Clearly, this view has enormous implications for the distributive outcomes of international interaction.

In responding to these arguments, advocates of the principle of state sovereignty have mounted a complex and wide-ranging defense of their thesis. The more sophisticated among them concede that changes in the domestic and external environment have restricted the state's room for maneuver. Hinsley, for example, readily acknowledges the impact of technology in significantly reducing the capacity of states to protect their respective populations. He is equally conscious of the implications of technological, financial, and economic interdependence for the legal and moral framework of international conduct. But for him, none of this invalidates state sovereignty as the central ordering principle of political life. States, he argues, are not any less sovereign because they do not possess unfettered freedom of action.

The constraints imposed by international law, we are told by some theorists, are fully compatible with the exercise of state sovereignty since the state's right to enter into international engagements is itself an attribute of sovereignty.[41] In obeying international law the state is not subjecting itself to the will of another state. In the case of external constraints other than purely legal ones, the defense of state sovereignty again rests largely on the legal definition of the concept, which draws the distinction between legal sovereignty and political independence. Others stress the distinction between de facto and de jure independence,[42] or between relative and absolute sovereignty, or again, between positive and negative sovereignty.[43] Still others go so far as to argue that sovereignty confers "vitality" on the state not simply by virtue of formal independence, but through cooperation with other sovereign states.[44]

The relativity of the principle of state sovereignty, based on the legal definition of the term, has a domestic analogue. The supreme legal authority, which the sovereign state implies, requires a supreme coercive power that ensures enforcement of the law through the use or threat of force. But neither the legal authority nor the coercive power should be confused with supreme political influence. Groups and individuals in society may share in the exercise of supreme political influence to the extent that "they determine in certain intended ways the actions of the coercive and legal sovereigns."[45] The point of such a theoretical construction is that it takes account of the dispersion of power in most complex political systems. It also points to the subtle interaction between the sovereign and political society.

For Hinsley, the coincidence between the territorial state and the cultural community, made possible by sovereignty, constitutes the most appropriate and effective framework for the organization of political, economic, and technical power. The expanded functions and power of the state have paralleled and reinforced the increased cohesion of the community and facilitated the closer association between state and community, as evidenced by the rise of mass politics and popular forms of government.[46] It is precisely the growing integration between the cultural and political aspects of social life that, in Hinsley's view, accounts for the solidity of the modern state and prevents the reversion to segmentary politics often associated with the decline of imperial states. The principle of sovereignty, we are told, has become so widely accepted and so necessary to the operation of an advanced political society that it is no longer an issue of theoretical or practical contention.

These qualifications and refinements are a useful contribution to the contemporary restatement of the theory of sovereignty. They represent a considered response to the criticisms that have been intermittently leveled against the principle on both normative and pragmatic grounds. It is questionable, however, whether the defense can easily rest its case on these arguments. The structural transformation of political and economic life in the twentieth century raises troublesome questions, which require more careful and detailed scrutiny.

The Globalization of Human Affairs

The need to rethink the notion of sovereignty is above all a function of the historical process. It reflects a widely perceived failure of the concept to come to terms with the complexity of an increasingly unified world that, paradoxically enough, coincides with the decentralization of authority and progressive fragmentation of society.[47] Even a sophisticated model that encompasses subnational, supranational, and transnational as well as national actors, while it may more accurately reflect the diversity of contemporary politics, does not necessarily explain the origins, nature, or significance of that diversity. It may not correctly identify, let alone analyze, the interacting dependencies and interdependencies that cut across national boundaries. A new explanatory model is needed to make sense of the emerging global division of labor and of the local, regional, and international conflicts and inequalities that it crystallizes and reinforces.

Theorists of widely diverging ideological persuasions have recognized the declining efficacy of state action, the emergence of new issues, and the advent of new actors. Numerous concepts, including aggregation, interdependence, world society, world order, and world economy,[48] have been advanced as a way of opening a window on the globalization of human affairs, of reassessing the meaning and function of sovereignty. James N. Rosenau, for example, has sought to interpret the process of globalization by tracing a bifurcation in which the state-centric world coexists and interacts with a diffuse multi-centric world consisting of diverse, "sovereign-free" actors largely preoccupied with issues of autonomy in contrast to the traditional security dilemmas of states.[49] Several writers have challenged what they consider to be premature conclusions about the extent of international interdependence or of the state's declining freedom of action.[50] Notwithstanding these reservations, there is now considerable evidence, especially in the light of recent trends, that international and transnational interaction is central to the organization and distribution of economic and political power and greatly compounds the already considerable ambiguity surrounding at every level the principle of sovereignty.

Technical change is probably the most conspicuous symptom and agent of globalization. Since World War II, innovations in transport and communications, coupled with the computerization of knowledge, have drastically affected production processes, enabling large enterprises to move capital and labor at lower cost and at vastly increased speed. The net effect has been a remarkable expansion in transnational production and trade. According to Silviu Brucan, it is the scientific and technological revolution, especially since the middle of the twentieth century, that has made "communication universal, transport supersonic, information instantaneous and modern weaponry interplanetary."[51] The spatial and temporal limits to human interaction have been exponentially compressed, and an intricate web of interdependencies has arisen, whose function it is to integrate and unify the world in a manner that has no historical precedent.

The technological factor is mirrored and strengthened by the ideology of modernity, which rests on the universal goal of economic growth and reduces all institutions—economic and political—to instruments for the achievement of that goal. In this sense the international division of labor and the system of states reflect and nurture that ideology. The world polity and its constituent units, sovereign states, are governed by rules that embody the organizational logic of market-oriented growth.[52] The ideology of modernity is open to varying interpretations. But most characterizations of the phenomenon include growth of codified knowledge as a way of controlling the physical environment; political centralization accompanied by the development of highly specialized bureaucracies; continuous increases in economic production and productivity; rapid rate of technological change; and introduction of social and cultural mechanisms designed to achieve the necessary psychological adjustment to these processes.[53]

The ideology of modernity now permeates the economic and political life of almost every national society. Progress centered on the unifying power of the world market has become the dominant image of change not only in the capitalist world. It acts as the driving intellectual force for the restructuring of the centrally planned economies as well as for the modernization of the periphery. East and West, North and South, despite economic asymmetries and ideological differences, experience the same pull. Individual governments, irrespective of the separateness and uniqueness conferred by state sovereignty, are homogenized by global technological and ideological convergence.

Technology and ideology do not operate in a vacuum. They are grounded in economic processes and institutions that have themselves assumed an increasingly international dimension. The role of the transnational corporation in the internationalization of capital has been amply documented, as have the ensuing quantitative and qualitative changes in the nature and functioning of the world economy. The growth of transnational investment, production, and trade since 1945 has been accompanied by an equally spectacular expansion of international banking, most strikingly reflected in the emergence of the Eurocurrency market. The leading U.S., European, and Japanese banks are now integrated into the international circuit of capital. While there is considerable ebb and flow and significant national variations in the unfolding of these trends, integration and interpenetration have become the distinguishing features of economic organization on a global scale.[54] The growing cross-investment among the principal countries investing abroad and the resultant increase in mergers and takeovers is evidence of the growing international centralization of capital. The development of a private international money market, operating in dollars yet outside the control of U. S. institutions, has contributed to the destruction of the Bretton Woods system, created during the period of U.S. hegemony, and replaced it with an international debt economy that has hastened the integration of the newly industrializing countries and oil exporting countries with the advanced capitalist countries.[55] It has also sharply increased the dependence of many countries on transnational banks and international financial institutions.[56]

Many of the political implications of the internationalization of capital are not hard to understand. There is an increasing divergence between the territorial constraints on the state and the international mobility of capital. As a consequence large corporations have become less dependent on the nation-state for a wide range of economic functions. On the other hand, national governments now operate within a global environment that severely restricts their powers of information, regulation, and taxation,[57] functions that are presumably central to the exercise of state sovereignty.

The web of dependencies and interdependencies mediated by technological change is equally apparent in the military sphere and equally subversive of traditional notions of national sovereignty. National governments no longer have exclusive or even secure access to information of strategic significance. Many corporations and scientific and technical institutions are directly involved in the shaping of defense policy by virtue of their role in the research, development, production, and marketing of weapons systems and their component parts. The preeminence of the state in this area is also under challenge by the activity of guerilla, terrorist, and other dissident groups that have taken advantage of the relative ease with which arms and munitions can be acquired and sophisticated urban and industrial centers threatened with indiscriminate violence.

Perhaps the most important technical military development is the advent of weapons of mass destruction, in particular the nuclear weapon, which can travel intercontinental distances at unprecedented speeds, thereby undermining conventional notions of territorial defense. States are thus constrained by the global nature of security and the mounting cost of advance weapons systems, which even superpowers are finding an intolerable economic burden. Partly in order to contain these costs and to cope with the new uncertainties, great and small powers alike have established integrated military alliance systems in which the legitimizing principle is often international rather than national and in which technical rationality takes precedence over political or moral judgment.[58] Combined military exercises, integrated nuclear planning, joint command systems, standardized procurement policies, and other forms of strategic interaction reflect a technological imperative that greatly circumscribes the state's freedom of maneuver.[59] The state is instrumental in the process since each decision requires the formal approval of one or another arm of the state. Yet the decision responds to a logic that underpins the international economic and strategic system rather than the values or objectives of any one of its constituent sovereign units.[60]

It is not surprising that the combined effect of these technological, economic, and military factors should be reflected in the political sphere. It is not merely a question of the proliferation of international agencies and transnational organizations, but an increasingly complex political division of labor that cuts across national boundaries and blurs the dividing line between foreign policy and domestic politics.[61] For example, the growth of communications technology has greatly increased the level of contact between societies and vastly enhanced the contribution of non-state actors to the global monitoring and dissemination of information. The state continues to play an important part in initiating, organizing, and integrating information linkages, but its responsiveness to a rapidly changing global environment cannot obscure its diminishing capacity to control the movement of messages and ideas.

Though states remain important actors in world politics, therefore, they are nevertheless bound in webs of transactions and organizations that restrict their theoretical freedom to make unilateral decisions. The ties that link states to one another, to regional and international agencies, and to nongovernmental organizations point to a highly complex global system. Formal authority continues to be vested in the governments of nation-states, but effective authority—moral, customary, and even coercive authority—is widely dispersed. It cannot be located in any single institution or even group of institutions. With respect to countless economic, environmental, political, and even military issues, governments increasingly feel obliged to act together, thereby giving rise to an intricate pattern of cooperation and competition, which imposes yet further constraints on the state's freedom of action. The greater the need for policy coordination, the more difficult it is for governments to go it alone, and the greater the tendency for international institutions to place additional limitations on the practical options available to sovereign states. The net effect is a network of contacts, coalitions, and interactions within and between national societies that escape the control of the central policy organs of government.

Globalization and its corollary, domestic fragmentation, shed significant new light on several of the key premises underlying the legal and political theory of sovereignty. First, they challenge the notion that political authority is exercised exclusively or even primarily within clearly demarcated territorial boundaries. Second, they call into question the assumption that within its territory the state's authority is unlimited and indivisible. Third, they suggest a growing disjunction between state and civil society, between political authority and economic organization, between cultural identification and social cohesion.

These conclusions need careful qualification. Notwithstanding the steadily upward curve of globalization, the state remains a critical element in the political equation—but more in the form of a variable than a constant. The equation is complex and in a state of flux. The attempt to make sense of the large and elusive puzzle that is globalization is perhaps the hallmark of Wallerstein's contribution to world system theory.[62] Clearly, the world system has been in the making for some considerable time. Though the date of origin cannot be specified with complete precision, the process has roughly paralleled the growth of capitalism and the formation of the modern state.[63] But whereas in its early stages of development national economies and states were decisive in shaping the system and determining its mode of operation, in the contemporary period it appears to have acquired a dynamic of its own. The system is much more than the summation of its component parts. It influences their behavior as much as it is influenced by them. As Silviu Brucan has put it,

> This is a system encompassing the whole planet and functioning with sufficient regularities to impose certain recognizable patterns of behavior on all its subsystems, particularly nation-states. In fact, international relations are becoming so systemic that the systemic acquires a drive of its own.[64]

This system is essentially the world capitalist system, characterized by a single division of labor and a multiplicity of states.

Although the world socialist system encompasses a significant fraction of the world's population and territory and boasts awesome military power, its role in the world system is very much governed by the world market, which is itself the expression of global capitalist production. Communist states, however different their internal economic and political institutions, have to operate within a larger diplomatic, strategic, and economic framework whose modus operandi is in accordance with the logic of the market. A single division of labor thus cuts across national and ideological boundaries. A distinguishing characteristic of this unified system is a pattern of global stratification, which divides the world economy into core areas (the beneficiaries of capital accumulation) and peripheral areas (which are consistently disadvantaged by a process of unequal exchange). The state system, which institutionalizes and legitimizes the core–periphery division, also organizes the distribution of power within the core through an intricate web of legal, diplomatic, and military relations. Wallerstein has further refined his explanatory model by postulating the existence of a semi-periphery understood as an intermediate link in "the surplus extraction chain,"[65] which enhances the adaptability of the international division of labor by providing for mobility along the vertical organization of economic roles.

The important point to note about world system theory, as developed by Wallerstein and others, is that it ascribes a major role to the system of states. The state system enforces the relationship between capital and labor and permits the extraction of surplus from the periphery to the core. States are the political instruments used by dominant classes to maintain their share of the world surplus product.[66] The use of political power for this purpose combines with efficient production for a competitive world market to produce a delicately balanced system in which the hegemonic core will sooner or later lose its relatively dominant position to more efficient producers.[67] Corporate and financial interests mobilize the resources of the nation-state to enhance their position vis-à-vis their competitors. The state provides the political framework within which is conducted the competition between capitalist classes. Is this not a novel but compelling argument for the continuing centrality of the sovereign state? It is not, for here we need to distinguish between the functionality and sovereignty of the state.

As we have observed, the state has played a critical role in the internationalization of trade, production, and finance.[68] The function of the state may therefore be seen as integral to the world system at every stage of its development. Attila Agh describes the role of the state by drawing attention to the three phases of modern capitalism. The first phase (1789–1872), based on free trade, was characterized by the rapid bureaucratization of nation-states and national economies, with the legal and political infrastructure of the state contributing directly to the accumulation of national capital and the international defense of its interests. In this period claims to state sovereignty were perhaps at their most convincing, at least so far as the internal dimension of sovereignty is concerned. The second phase

(1873–1944) was characterized by the collision of rival national capitalisms and increasing emphasis on the state's external and military functions, which gave added impetus to the principle of sovereignty even though counter-trends were already beginning to emerge. The third phase (since 1945), according to Agh, sees the development of global relations and interactions, of a world system "characterized by an advanced interdependence, increasing autonomy, self-motion and institutionalization."[69] Other writers offer a somewhat different periodization. Mary Kaldor, for example, refers to three eras: the textile era, the railway era, and the automobile era.[70] Here again the object of the exercise is to plot the trajectory of the global political economy by analyzing the interaction between capitalism and the system of territorial states.

World system theory in its various guises sharpens our understanding of the globalization of human affairs and furnishes a more comprehensive and historically grounded interpretation of the state. But there is a tendency in such theorizing to presuppose that the system is a highly integrated one in which the relationship between the world economy and the state system is entirely or preeminently functional. This assumption is not borne out by the evidence. The internationalization of economic activity may be greatly assisted by the actions of the national state, but such internationalization may at the same time severely narrow the range of national policy options, and in the process diminish the efficacy of state intervention and therefore the applicability of the sovereignty principle.[71] The world system approach tends to exaggerate the equilibrium tendencies inherent in the system and to underplay the debilitating contradictions to which both the world economy and the state system are exposed.[72]

To begin with, the horizontal structure of the world market is not neatly matched by the vertical structure of interstate relations.[73] Nor is the domestic political process entirely subordinate to the requirements of the international accumulation of capital. The state does retain a degree of political independence. Its actions are not simply the expression of the general capitalist will.[74] It has to accommodate or reconcile a number of competing interests not only within the dominant class but also between capital and organized labor. It has to contend with the demands of various elements of society on which its legitimacy ultimately depends. This is in no way to minimize the challenge to sovereignty. The relations of global production and the international division of labor they express set the ideological and material framework within which national policy is developed. The modern industrial state, locked as it is in a global competition with growth and productivity as the yardsticks of success, may have an expanding political reach, but only insofar as its actions conform to the logic of global economic stratification. Even when the state acts to extend the scope for national regulation and maneuver, the purpose and modality of such action are shaped by global transactions and ideologies that national political forces have largely internalized.

To put it simply, the last hundred years have seen the emergence of a new form of hegemony that cannot be identified with the position, however dominant, of any one group, state, or group of states. Robert Cox makes an innovative contribution to world system theory when he characterizes the hegemonic or imperial system as comprising the executive bodies within government, in both the imperial and allied states, that are charged with promoting and protecting the expansion of capital across state boundaries.[75] The imperial system consists, then, of a transnational structure that operates simultaneously in the center and the periphery, and reflects the symbiotic relationship between state institutions and international organizations such as the IMF, the World Bank, and the OECD. The imperial system does not include those sections of society or elements of the state, whether located in the center or the periphery, whose interests are separate from or opposed to the imperial system. Implicit in this argument is the fragmentation of both dominant and dependent states and the polarization between hegemonic and antihegemonic social forces.

In the post-1945 period the imperial system that came to be known as *Pax Americana* rested on the undisputed dominance of U.S. capital and the overwhelming military power of the United States. Within the United States, several factors contributed to the creation of a new international order, notably the expansion of the military establishment, the development of institutions for macroeconomic management, and the growth of the welfare state. These trends were replicated in varying degrees in other metropolitan states and reinforced by the emergence of international institutions designed to provide a stable framework for the global expansion of capital. Within twenty years U.S. capital, which had become the main beneficiary of the new order, was strong enough to begin distancing itself from the interests of the home state and the home economy. National capital—not only American but, increasingly, European and Japanese—had developed transnational interests and objectives. In the wake of the serious economic downturn that began to unfold in the early 1970s, transnational capital became less favorably attracted to the restoration of a crude free market ideology encapsulated by the advocacy of monetarist economics and the deregulation of national financial systems.

The internationalization of production and finance, made possible in part by the technological revolution, reflected and gave added impetus to the emergence of an international social class. This global class overlapped with, yet was distinct from, nationally defined social classes. It included the managerial elite associated with transnational corporations, whose function it was to develop the ideological and strategic framework for the development of corporate policies and institutions. The managers of national as well as international government organizations were also an integral part of the global class structure, which highlights yet again the close interconnection between transnational capital and the national state and the complexity of the new form of international hegemony.[76]

Implications for Sovereignty

The internationalization of economic activity, particularly since 1950, cannot be reduced to a simple or single trend. The ideology and political economy of modernization have given rise to a complex and contradictory dynamic with far-reaching repercussions for the state, for civil society, and for the relationship between them. We find, on the one hand, a growing web of international interdependencies and, on the other, increased centralization of national institutions and decisionmaking processes. These two trends are inextricably intertwined and mutually reinforcing. They explain the blurring of the distinction between foreign and domestic policy, and to that extent call into question the traditional understanding of state sovereignty.

The most striking impact of globalization on the state is precisely the integration of internal and external functions, and, associated with that, the increasing interaction between security policy and economic policy, both of which now have an important internal and external dimension.[77] The state is called upon to discharge an ever expanding list of social, economic, and administrative functions, and to this end develops ever more extensive control mechanisms—which the ideology of deregulation only partially obscures. Yet bureaucratization and centralization do not generally carry with them an increasing ability to control internal or external outcomes. This loss of control stems in part from increasing national sensitivity to international transactions, which is itself the result of growing levels of interdependence and integration within the state. To give one example, changes in a country's terms of trade, which are more often than not beyond its control, are likely to affect not only the balance of payments, but the value of the currency, interest rates, the level of employment, and the rate of inflation.[78]

Nowhere is the paradoxical effect of globalization more apparent than in the area of national economic management. During the relatively stable period of the 1950s and 1960s, when *Pax Americana* was almost unassailable and Keynesian policies of aggregate demand pumping remarkably effective, it seemed as if the advanced capitalist state was firmly in control. Yet the fluctuating fortunes experienced by the major Western economies since the early 1970s and the failure of Keynesian remedies have highlighted some serious difficulties. With the gradual dissipation of the technological and organizational impetus that sustained the postwar boom, the state has had to oscillate between economic strategies, each of which risks undermining the relatively stable class coalition that prevailed for nearly a quarter of a century. The factors responsible for the state's declining capacity to manage the economy are not primarily endogenous, but largely attributable to the internationalization of capital, which no national apparatus, however centralized or coercive, can fully control.[79]

But if the national economy represents an increasingly complex, unmanageable, porous, and fragile mechanism poorly suited to the exercise of state sovereignty, so does national security. The limitations on the state's capacity to achieve security are not new, but their magnitude and implications certainly are. For a variety of reasons—many of them related to the nature of technical change—the traditional reliance on the use or threat of force has been subject to diminishing returns. Faced with the impossibility of defense against nuclear attack, states have sought refuge in an elaborate strategic edifice based on the principle of deterrence. Paradoxically, this edifice, by virtue of the logic of the balance of terror and the universal destruction it threatens to unleash, has assumed a global dimension that underlines the obsolescence of territorial goals, at least on the part of rival nuclear powers and their allies.

Changes in the international security system are not confined to nuclear weapons. The state system that has dominated international relations for the last four centuries has rested on the twin principles that the state exercised a monopoly over the use of violence and that governments could maintain armed forces adequate either for territorial defense or territorial expansion. Since the end of World War II, territorial behavior, especially on the part of the most advanced industrial states, has visibly declined, partly because of the decreasing strategic and economic significance of frontiers. An equally important factor has been the diminishing control that states exercise over the use of violence because of the emergence of liberation movements, guerilla groups, terrorist organizations, and mercenaries; the declining ability of states to exercise sovereign jurisdiction by reliance on the use of force is a corollary of this factor.[80]

The consequences of globalization are just as profound for civil society as they are for the state. The global spread of modernity has given rise to a series of continuing upheavals, which is still unfolding. In many parts of the Third World, wars of national independence have been followed by a succession of military coups, civil wars, and violent revolutions, all of which reflect in varying degrees the instability of existing institutions confronting a rising tide of collective discontent. Both factors greatly weaken the efficacy of sovereign rule. Nor has political turbulence been entirely absent from the recent experience of the First and Second Worlds. One need only refer to the periodic convulsions that have marked the Fourth and Fifth French Republics, the protracted conflict in Northern Ireland, ethnic discontent in Spain, Yugoslavia, and the Soviet Union, or racial conflict in the United

States and Australia. These divisions have left a deep scar in the consciousness and institutions of contemporary societies.

The experience of the Third World represents in part a profound conflict of values and interests that, though at times dormant, sooner or later breaks out into the open, often in direct opposition to prevailing conceptions and strategies of modernization. Dissatisfaction with various forms of social and physical engineering has unleashed an increasingly powerful reaction against Western notions of nation-building, as well as a desire to cultivate indigenous values, traditions, and resources that are often antithetical to conventional notions of state sovereignty. To the extent that material and psychological grievances against modernity are most likely to crystallize around shared cultural experience, whether it be on the basis of race, language, or religion, it is not surprising that social discontent should take the form of ethnic separatism. This widespread phenomenon, increasingly prevalent in both agricultural and industrial societies, is a manifestation of a growing demand for autonomy, for a new sense of identity, that state sovereignty can neither satisfy nor contain.

Ethnicity, however, is not the only criterion of fragmentation. Numerous other strata and minorities in society experience a sense of relative deprivation, often accentuated by the visible discrepancy between expectations and the system's lagging capacity to satisfy them. Although organized labor, at least in the capitalist world, appears to have generally shed its former militancy, a great many social movements have mushroomed since the early 1960s, many of them expressing in different ways a profound reaction against modernity, against the abstract process and imperatives produced by the acceleration of bureaucratic and technical rationality. The sovereign state, once the agent of modernity, has now become its victim. Not only has it been overtaken by the globalization of human affairs, but it is subject to increasingly fissiparous tendencies. The resistance to the present political and economic organization of society, expressed by the peace/antinuclear, ecological, communalist, consumer, feminist, gay liberation, human potential/self-awareness and other movements, cannot be overestimated. They represent a multidimensional response to the "colonization of the life-world."[81] Their praxis may not yet pose a decisive challenge to the status quo, but it has already generated within the body politic a readiness to resist existing institutions and their life-eroding consequences. The point about these antisystemic movements is that they often elude the traditional categories of nation, state, and class. They articulate new ways of experiencing life, a new attitude to time and space, a new sense of history and identity. Indeed, it may not be far-fetched to suggest that they are in the process of redefining the meaning and boundaries of civil society. They are reaffirming the priority of civil society over the state, of popular sovereignty over state sovereignty. For them the state retains a positive function only to the extent that it can be used as a vehicle for the realization of popular sovereignty. This function may be especially, though not exclusively, relevant to the Third World, where the state is at times perceived as a useful arena of social struggle and a potent symbol of national liberation, as well as a launching pad for the creation of a more democratic international order. Whether or not, and in what way, the state can be effectively integrated into the praxis of critical movements remains, however, a largely unanswered question.

The growth of these movements is no doubt the most striking response to the global spread of modernity. Yet, the more passive, compliant reactions also have a subversive quality. Indifference, withdrawal, and nonparticipation, to the extent that they have become dominant features of industrial society, greatly undermine social purpose and cohesion. Placed in this context, both resistance and opting out call into question the way political space is presently organized. They both reveal the need to redefine what constitutes a community and the terrain that can sustain it. Already it can be said that many of the economic, political, and cultural developments we have surveyed point toward a reconstruction of the prevailing symbols of identification, to a comprehensive re-evaluation of the divide that separates us and them, the insider and the outsider. In this sense, the moral and even customary authority of the sovereign state is under increasing challenge.

It may be that we are living through a period that is a transition to a new form of civil society with no clearly demarcated boundaries set by notions of national identity. Civil society may come to acquire a much richer meaning grounded in a multiplicity of overlapping allegiances and jurisdictions, in which a local, regional, and global dimension qualifies the principle of nationality and redefines the notion of sovereignty. The re-establishment of local and regional self-reliance may greatly contribute to internal democratization and at the same time facilitate the emergence of a cosmopolitan global culture. This conclusion is not altogether surprising. Even where it is has given rise to effective and cohesive nation-states, nationalism need not be a sufficient let alone a permanent factor for social cohesion. The very centralization of the state and the integration of the national economy into the world economy are making it increasingly difficult for national communities to preserve their sense of identity or independence. One of the dominant features of the contemporary period, especially in advanced capitalism, is the disjuncture between the cultural basis of nationalism and the locus of economic decisionmaking. In this sense the state is increasingly divorced from any notion of popular sovereignty.

If this analysis is at all accurate, then the profound changes that have characterized the organizational and technological basis of production have affected not only the state and civil society but also—and perhaps more importantly—the relationship between them. The internationalization of production and the economic interpenetration that goes with it are experienced differently by different states, but also by different sectors within each state, since the process benefits some sectors and disadvantages others. The emerging international division of labor is therefore a divisive force in domestic society. Insofar as it encourages and accentuates domestic conflict, international integration may provoke national disintegration.

Production and circulation have become so complex, so deeply embedded in the processes and institutions of multiple actors—national and transnational alike—that the state's traditional claim to represent a single national will or collective interest is increasingly divorced from reality. The postulated coincidence between state sovereignty and a single cohesive community bears little relationship to the known facts. Notwithstanding appeals to nationalism or the national interest, modern societies are deeply fragmented, unable to express the underlying unity that gives public authority its discipline and legitimacy, and on which the claim to sovereignty ultimately rests. Far from expressing a national will, the state may simply reflect, or at best arbitrate between, powerful competing interests, some of which may in fact be external to the society.

The progressive militarization of modern society is a case in point. The last several decades have witnessed in several countries the growth of institutions that benefit from high and rising defense budgets. The beneficiaries of this process normally include the armed services (often locked in fierce competition with each other for a slice of the cake), political parties, lawyers, financiers, scientists, manufacturers, security organizations, the media, and even unions. It cannot be stressed enough that these diverse interest groups do not necessarily operate within the territorial confines of the state. Any national defense budget is likely to reflect a complex array of pressures exerted by foreign governments, foreign military and intelligence organizations, transnational corporations, international financial institutions, overseas money markets, and a range of other international networks. Militarization, then, is a transnational phenomenon that penetrates the whole of civil society yet is beyond its control. The net effect of this paradoxical process is that the survival of the state apparatus—or to be more precise, of the dominant political, economic, military, and ideological interests it represents—is no longer compatible with the survival of civil society, of which the state is theoretically the political expression. It is this dramatic disjuncture between the survival needs of the state and those of civil society that forms the basis of E. P. Thompson's theory of "exterminism."[82]

Placed in this context, the rise of various movements of dissent, not least in opposition to the state's nuclear policies, is an entirely natural phenomenon. What is in question is the legitimacy of the state, the validity of its claim to sovereignty. To this extent the crisis of legitimacy may be interpreted as a crisis of sovereignty, for what is at issue is the nature of the state, the interests it represents, its relationship to civil society. The crisis, which has both theoretical and practical ramifications, is shaped by a period of far-reaching realignment of concepts, allegiances, and institutions. It is a period in which appeals to national interest and national loyalties, though still fashionable in many quarters, are generally losing their capacity to mobilize human energies and material resources.

Some Tentative Conclusions

The picture that emerges from this analysis is neither simple nor unidirectional. There are both trends and countertrends. On the one hand, the nation-state remains a highly conspicuous and authoritative entity jealously guarding its territorial boundaries. The centralization of state power goes hand in hand with the internationalization of economic activity. As Heilbroner rightly points out, it is the enlargement of the state apparatus that makes possible the coordination and expansion of the productive process.[83] The state system constitutes the necessary institutional prop for capital accumulation on a global scale as well as for the system of unequal exchange that underpins the international division of labor.

On the other hand, the state's capacity to articulate and satisfy human needs appears to be in relative decline. There is a widening gap between promise and performance, between the power of the state and public participation in the exercise of that power, between the state and civil society. The delicate relationship between the public and private realms that is central to the nature and functioning of sovereignty in a domestic context appears to have been seriously impaired. Similarly, national sovereignty in an international context has been greatly eroded by a web of mutually reinforcing dependencies and interdependencies.

The state continues to perform important internal and external functions, but is it truly sovereign? The principle of state sovereignty can now be seen to have emerged and developed under conditions that are fast disappearing. While some states remain relatively strong and others may become relatively stronger, it would seem that states, weak and strong alike, are becoming less able to modify or preserve the complexion of their internal and external environment in line with the autonomously expressed preferences of the communities they claim to represent. Everywhere the cohesion of national societies seems likely to diminish, and so too the mobilizing efficacy of national governments. Historically state sovereignty may turn out to have been a bridge between national capitalism and world capitalism, a phase in an evolutionary process that is still unfolding.

It is arguable that as time goes on this bridge will prove less and less serviceable either in interpreting or in organizing late twentieth-century experience. The image of a world made up of sovereign states internally supreme over the territory they control and externally unrestrained by outside force is a snapshot of reality that cannot do justice to the passage of time. It does not explain the character of the present world, much less permit an appreciation of its possible future. The sovereign state represents one way in which power and authority may be exercised. It is not the only way. The territorial and omnipotent state was the product of the revolutionary changes that swept across Europe in the sixteenth and seventeenth centuries. The religious unity of medieval Europe and the ill-defined political loyalties that it subsumed gave way to a secularized but fragmented system of sovereign states. It may well be that the capitalist reorganization of the world and the contradictions to which it has given rise point to the re-emergence of a cosmopolitan ethic that coexists with and nourishes a bewildering array of local, regional, national, and transnational loyalties and institutions. It may be that the contemporary period is one of considerable fluidity, when the most fundamental questions regarding the exercise of power and authority have been thrown back into the crucible of history.

At stake is not only the size of political entities or even the demarcation of their boundaries, but the very meaning of boundaries, the very nature of the political domain. In this transitional phase characterized by shifting allegiances, new forms of identity, and multiple tiers of jurisdiction, we are witnessing the growth of a more complex and more variegated, yet more unified world order than the system of sovereign states. The basic contradiction today is not between state sovereignty and the growing interdependence of states but rather between two forms of interdependence: one that institutionalizes the principle of popular sovereignty and another that negates the principle by clinging to the increasingly illusory notion of state sovereignty. The net effect is a deepening contradiction between emerging processes of decentralization and democratization within and between societies and the intensified centralization and bureaucratization of much economic and political life. Needless to say, old habits and old ideas will persist even as new ones develop to cope with the emergence of a pluralistic polity that is at once part local, part regional, part national, and part transnational. What concrete shape the political map of the world will take in the twenty-first century remains unclear. But both objective conditions (i.e., the contradictions we have identified) and the universal revolt of conscience (that is, the impulse for emancipation and legitimacy) already suggest that state sovercignty is unlikely to be the distinguishing principle of political organization.

Notes

1. F. H. Hinsley, *Sovereignty* (London: C. A. Watts, 1966), p 1.
2. These included small kingdoms, principalities, duchies, ecclesiastical estates,

city-states, trading cities, and other political entities. See C. Tilly, ed., *The Function of Nation-States in Western Europe* (Princeton: Princeton University Press, 1975), p. 15; also James Anderson and Stuart Hall, "Absolutism and Other Ancestors," in James Anderson, ed., *The Rise of the Modern State* (Brighton: Wheatsheaf Books, 1986), p. 28.

3. See Perry Anderson, *Lineages of the Absolutist State* (London: New Left Books, 1974), pp. 37-38.

4. John Gerard Ruggie, "Continuity and Transformation in the World Polity: Toward a Neo-Realist Synthesis," *World Politics* 35, no. 2 (January 1983): 275.

5. Garrett Mattingly, *Renaissance Diplomacy* (London: Cape, 1955).

6. See Ruggie, "Continuity and Transformation in the World Polity," pp. 275-276.

7. Hinsley, *Sovereignty*, pp. 8-22

8. Harold Laski, *A Grammar of Politics*, 5th ed. (London: Allen & Unwin, 1967), p. 48.

9. Hinsley, *Sovereignty*, p. 9.

10. For a helpful introduction to a very complex story, see Kenneth Dyson, *The State Tradition in Western Europe* (Oxford: Martin Robertson, 1980).

11. W. J. Rees, "The Theory of Sovereignty Restated," *Mind* 59, no. 236 (October 1950): 508-509

12. Jean Bodin, *The Six Bookes of a Commonweale*, trans. Richard Knolles (London: Impencis G. Bishop, 1606), p. 84.

13. Jacques Maritain, *Man and the State*, ed. Richard O'Sullivan (London: Hollis & Carter, 1954), p. 31.

14. For a more detailed exposition of these questions, see George H. Sabine, *A History of Political Theory* (London: George, Harrap & Co., 1963), pp. 407-411.

15. Thomas Hobbes, *Leviathan*, ed. Michael Oakeshott (New York: Collier Books, 1962), p. 132.

16. Hinsley, *Sovereignty*, p. 153.

17. Jean-Jacques Rousseau, *The Social Contract and Discourses*, trans. G. D. H. Cole (New York: E. Dutton, 1950), p. 14.

18. Ibid., p. 31

19. *Hegel's Philosophy of Right*, trans. T. M. Knox (Oxford: Clarendon Press, 1952), p. 166.

20. Howard Williams, *Kant's Political Philosophy* (Oxford: Basil Blackwell, 1983), pp. 170-172.

21. Ralph Miliband, *Class Power and State Power* (London: Verso, 1983), p. 6.

22. John Plamenatz, *Man and Society*, Vol. 2 (London: Longmans, 1965), p. 371.

23. Miliband, *Class Power and State Power*, p. 12.

24. K. Marx and F. Engels, *Selected Works* (Moscow: Progress Publishers, 1950), p. 472.

25. See R. Little and R. D. McKinlay, "Linkage-Responsiveness and the Modern State: An Alternative View of Interdependence," *British Journal of International Studies*, no. 44 (October 1978): 212.

26. See Jürgen Habermas, "What Does a Crisis Mean Today? Legitimation Problems in Late Capitalism," *Social Research* 41, no. 4 (Winter 1973): 656.

27. Ernest Renan, *Discours et Conférences* (Paris: Calman-Lévy, 1887), p. 300.

28. See Hans Kohn, *Nationalism: Its Meaning and History* (Princeton: D. van Nostrand, 1965); also by the same author, *The Age of Nationalism: The First Era of Global History* (New York: Harper & Row, 1962); Carleton J. H. Hayes, *The Historical Evolution of Modern Nationalism* (New York: Richard R. Smith, 1931); Hugh Seton-Watson, *Nations and States* (London: Methuen, 1977).

29. Ernest Gellner, *Nations and Nationalism* (Oxford: Basil Blackwell, 1983), p. 39.

30. Silviu Brucan, "The State and the World System," *International Social Science Journal* 32, no. 4 (October 1980): 756–760.

31. For a classic exposition of this view see Martin Wight, *Power Politics* (Harmondsworth: Penguin Books, 1979); also Hans Morgenthau, *Politics Among Nations*, 5th ed. (New York: Knopf, 1978). For a more nuanced elaboration of the argument see Hedley Bull, *The Anarchical Society: A Study of Order in World Politics* (London: Macmillan, 1977), especially pp. 101–126.

32. See J. H. Leurdjik, "From International to Transnational Politics: A Change of Paradigm?" *International Social Science Journal* 26, no. 1 (1974): 53; also Oran Young, "The Actors in World Politics," in J. N. Rosenau et al., eds., *The Analysis of International Politics* (New York: Free Press, 1972), pp. 125–144.

33. Hinsley, *Sovereignty*, pp. 210–211.

34. John Austin, *The Province of Jurisprudence Determined* (New York: The Humanities Press, 1965).

35. Cited in Georg Schwarzenberger, "The Focus of Sovereignty," in W. J. Stankiewicz, ed., *In Defense of Sovereignty* (New York: Oxford University Press, 1969), pp. 170–171.

36. See Mary Kaldor, "The Global Political Economy," *Alternatives* 11, no. 4 (October 1986): 439.

37. Maritain, *Man and the State*, p. 31.

38. Ibid., p. 46.

39. Laski, *The Grammar of Politics*, p. 63.

40. See Charles R. Beitz, "Bounded Morality: Justice and the State in World Politics," *International Organization* 33, no. 3 (Summer 1979): 405–424.

41. See, for example, K. W. B. Middleton, "Sovereignty in Theory and Practice," in Stankiewicz, *In Defense of Sovereignty*, p. 153.

42. Ibid., p. 157.

43. Schwarzenberger, "The Focus of Sovereignty," p. 167.

44. J. D. B. Miller, "Sovereignty as a Source of Vitality for the State," *Review of International Studies* 12, no. 2 (April 1986): 79–89.

45. Rees, "The Theory of Sovereignty Restated," p. 514.

46. Hinsley, *Sovereignty*, pp. 226–227.

47. James N. Rosenau, "Muddling, Meddling and Modelling: Alternative Approaches to the Study of World Politics in an Era of Rapid Change," *Millennium: Journal of International Studies* 8, no. 2 (Autumn 1979): 130.

48. For a representative sample of these theories, see James N. Rosenau, ed., *Linkage Politics* (New York: Free Press, 1969); Robert O. Keohane and Joseph S. Nye, *Power and Interdependence: World Politics in Transition* (Boston: Little Brown, 1975); John Burton, *World Society* (Cambridge: Cambridge University Press,

1972); Richard Falk, *A Study of Future Worlds* (New York: Macmillan, 1975); Samir Amin, *Accumulation on a World Scale: A Critique of the Theory of Underdevelopment* (New York: Monthly Review Press, 1974).

49. James N. Rosenau, "Patterned Chaos in Modern Life: Structure and Process in the Two Worlds of World Politics," *International Political Science Review* 9, no. 4 (October 1988): 327–364.

50. See, in particular, Karl W. Deutsch, Lewis J. Edlinger, Roy C. Macridis, and Richard L. Merritt, *France, Germany and the Western Alliance* (New York: C. Scribner's and Sons, 1967); Kenneth N. Waltz, "The Myth of Interdependence," in Charles P. Kindleberger, ed., *The International Corporation* (Cambridge, Mass.: MIT Press, 1970).

51. Brucan, "The State and the World System," p. 761.

52. See John W. Meyer, "World Polity," in John W. Meyer and Michael T. Hannan, eds., *National Development and the World System: Educational, Economic and Political Change 1950–1970* (Chicago: University of Chicago Press, 1979).

53. These characteristics are outlined in Cyril E. Black, *The Dynamics of Modernization: A Study in Comparative History* (New York: Harper & Row, 1967), pp. 9–34.

54. See James M. Cypher, "The Transnational Challenge to the Corporate State," *Journal of Economic Issues* 13, no. 2 (June 1979): 513–542; also Richard Rosecrance, "Interdependence, Myth or Reality?" *World Politics* 26, no.1 (October 1973): 1–27.

55. Michael Aglietta, "World Capitalism in the Eighties," *New Left Review*, no. 136 (November–December 1982): 5–41; also Jerry Coakley, "The Internationalization of Bank Capital," *Capital & Class* (Summer 1984): 107–119.

56. Robert E. Wood and May Mmuya, "The Debt Crisis in the Fourth World: Implications for North-South Relations," *Alternatives* 11, no. 1 (January 1986): 107–132.

57. See Robin Murray, "The Internationalization of Capital and the Nation State," *New Left Review* 67 (May–June 1971): 84–109.

58. Many of these arguments are developed in P. A. Reynolds, "Non-State Actors and International Outcomes," *Journal of International Studies* 5 (1979): 91–111.

59. See Philip A. Reynolds and Robert D. McKinlay, "The Concept of Interdependence: Its Uses and Misuses," in Kjell Goldmann and Gunner Sjostedt, eds., *Power, Capabilities and Interdependence* (Beverly Hills: Sage Publications, 1979), pp. 149–150.

60. E. P. Thompson has labeled this systemic logic as "exterminism" in the sense that it is a cumulative process in which cultural, economic, and political pressures within and between states interact with and reinforce one another. See E. P. Thompson, "Notes on Exterminism, the Last Stage of Civilization," in *Exterminism and Cold War*, edited by the New Left Review (London: Verso, 1982), pp. 1–33.

61. Oran Young, "Interdependencies in World Politics," *International Journal* 24, no. 4 (Autumn 1969): 726.

62. See Immanuel Wallerstein, *The Capitalist World Economy* (Cambridge: Cambridge University Press, 1979), pp. 152–164.

63. Immanuel Wallerstein divides the process into four major epochs starting

with the fifteenth century, when the world system emerged in what was then its predominantly European form. See Immanuel Wallerstein, *The Modern World System* (New York: Academic Press, 1974).

64. Brucan, "The State and the World System," p. 761 (emphasis added).

65. Immanuel Wallerstein, "Semi-Peripheral Countries and the Contemporary World Crisis," *Theory and Society* 3, no. 4 (Winter 1976): 461–484.

66. See Christopher Chase-Dunn, "Interstate System and Capitalist World Economy: One Logic or Two?" *International Studies Quarterly* 25, no. 1 (March 1981): 19–42.

67. Ibid., p. 29.

68. See Christian Palloix, "The Self-Expansion of Capital on a World Scale," *The Review of Radical Political Economics* 9, no. 2 (Summer 1977): 11–12.

69. Attila Agh, "The Dual Definition of Capitalism and the Contemporary World System," *Development & Peace* 4, no. 1 (Spring 1983): 193–204.

70. Kaldor, "The Global Political Economy," p. 457.

71. J. Camilleri, "The Advanced Capitalist State and the Contemporary World Crisis," *Science and Society* 45, no. 12 (Summer 1981): 130–158.

72. For wide-ranging critiques of the world system approach, see Theda Skocpol, "Wallerstein's World Capitalist System: A Theoretical and Historical Critique," *American Journal of Sociology* 82, no. 5 (March 1977): 1075–1090; Theda Skocpol, "The Origins of Capitalist Development: A Critique of Neo-Smithian Marxism," *New Left Review* 104 (July–August 1987): 25–92; Peter Worsley, "One World or Three? A Critique of the World System Theory of Immanuel Wallerstein," in R. Miliband and John Saville, eds., *Socialist Register 1980* (London: Merlin Press, 1980); Vincente Navarro, "The Limits of the World Systems Theory in Defining Capitalist and Socialist Formations," *Science and Society* 46, no. 1 (Spring 1982): 76–90.

73. See James Lee Ray, "The World System and the Global Political System," *Sage International Yearbook of Foreign Policy Studies* 8 (1983): 13–34.

74. Bruce Andrews, "The Political Economy of World Capitalism; Theory and Practice," *International Organization* 36, no. 1 (Winter 1982): 148–152.

75. Robert Cox, "Social Forces, States, and World Orders: Beyond International Relations Theory," *Millennium: Journal of International Studies* 10, no. 2 (1981): 141.

76. See Robert W. Cox, "Gramsci, Hegemony, and International Relations: An Essay in Method," *Millennium: Journal of International Studies* 12, no. 2 (1983): 162–175.

77. Edward L. Morse, "The Transformation of Foreign Policies," *World Politics* 22, no. 3 (April 1970): 371–392.

78. This trend has been recognized for some time. See, for example, Richard N. Cooper, *The Economics of Interdependence: Economic Policy in the Atlantic Community* (New York: McGraw-Hill, 1968), p. 10.

79. For a more detailed exposition of this argument, see James P. Hawley and Charles Noble, "The Internationalization of Capital and the Limits of the Interventionist State: Towards an Explanation of Macroeconomic Policy Failure," *Journal of Political and Military Sociology* 10 (Spring 1982): 103–120.

80. This argument is well made by Reynolds, "Non-State Actors and

International Outcomes," pp. 99–100.

81. For a case study of this process, see my analysis of the antinuclear movement in *The State and Nuclear Power: Conflict and Control in the Western World* (Seattle: University of Washington Press, 1984), pp. 107–132.

82. Thompson, "Notes on Exterminism."

83. Robert L. Heilbroner, *Civilization in Decline* (Harmondsworth: Penguin Books, 1977), pp. 63–78.

3

The Reification of Political Community

Warren Magnusson

Political community has long been conceived as an enclosure, be it in the form of a tribe, polis, or empire.[1] In the first of the canonical texts of Western political philosophy, the polis is presented as the ideal enclosure—indeed, as the enclosure that makes politics possible.[2] Since the sixteenth century, prehistoric, ancient, and medieval reifications of political space have gradually been rejected in favor of the modern state.[3] As a result, political theory and political science have come to be focused on the state, which appears as the enclosure constitutive of politics itself. Such a state-centric conception of politics is deeply problematic, and various modern theorists have attempted to escape its strictures.[4] However, their work has had little effect on orthodox conceptions of the nature and venue of politics.

This chapter explores the reification of political community as the state in relation to two alternatives: localities and sociopolitical movements. *Locality* is here conceived as the venue for everyday life, and *movement* as a process that mobilizes people politically. My claim is that popular politics occurs at the juncture of localities and movements, and that state-centric theories conceal the character of politics by reifying localities and movements as dimensions of the state or of prepolitical civil society. The main object of my critique is not the theory or "science" of international relations, but its "other": the theory or science of domestic politics. Mine is a worm's-eye view, which focuses on realities at the margin between "the state" and "civil society," or between formalized politics and social action. At first sight, these realities seem far removed from international relations, but in fact they are the presence of popular politics in the global domain.

States, Localities, and Democracy

Liberal democracy is now regarded, even outside the West, as the perfection of the modern state. It may not be an achieved reality, in the West or elsewhere, but it is for most people the determinant political ideal. In the circumstances, one might expect to find the place of localities—the venues for everyday life—carefully specified in liberal democratic theory. This should be especially true of the Anglo-American world, where the practices of liberal democracy have been long established. Curiously, this is not the case. One searches vainly in most English and U.S. treatises on democracy for any serious discussion of *local* government, *local* politics, or *local* democracy.[5] The authors nevertheless seem to take for granted some system of local government—something like the one they know. Local government is supposed to be necessary for efficient and responsive public administration, for citizen participation in public affairs, and for an appropriate separation of powers. But—with some notable exceptions[6]—the authors regard the explanation of these matters as superfluous, and pass the reader off to Alexis de Tocqueville and John Stuart Mill[7] (with appropriate warnings not to take their hopes too seriously).

One is left with the impression that something is being hidden: What is this? The answer becomes apparent if we ask what democratic theory would be like if the locality had been placed at the center of analysis. The locality is an obvious analogue to the ancient polis. As the venue for everyday life, it is the site for face-to-face contact, immediate economic and social relations, immediately shared experience and interests. It is on the scale that the Greeks imagined was necessary for politics: not so large as to be beyond the scope of ordinary citizens and not so small as to be absorbed into familial and neighborly relations. It is, rather, of a scale that permits and demands politics as a collective activity involving relations among equals. Thus, from this perspective—the perspective of the original classics of Western political philosophy—the locality appears to have political primacy, in the sense that it demands recognition as the optimal political community.[8]

Of course, there is an argument for enlarging the scale of political community, to ensure self-sufficiency, in economic, military, or cultural terms.[9] Certainly, the modern locality, caught in a web of wider social relations, is not sufficient unto itself, even for the most parochial of its inhabitants. In this light, the state can be presented as the inevitable modern enclosure for politics. Hence, Ernest Gellner:

> The agrarian phase of human history is the period during which, so to speak, the very existence of the state is an option. Moreover, the form of the state is highly variable. During the hunting-gathering stage, the option was not available.
>
> By contrast, in the post-agarian, industrial age there is, once again, no option; but now the *presence*, not the absence of the state is inescapable.[10]

Gellner explains this ultimately in terms of the educational requirements of industrial society: localities are not big enough to have their own graduate schools, so they must be contained within states.[11] This is a variant of the familiar claim that we have no alternative to the state today because only states are large enough to perform such functions as providing for security, managing the economy, or offering the full range of modern social services. Theorists seem to consider it unnecessary actually to explore the smaller-scale options for achieving these state goals: the mere assertion of the state's necessity is enough to set the audience nodding in approval.

Why are we satisfied with such banalities? Why do we accept claims about the inevitability of the state, which, if posed in relation to capitalism or patriarchy, would be set aside in embarrassed silence? Why is the debate about the sources of the state's inevitability rather than about the supposed fact of inevitability?

The assumption of inevitability in contemporary discourse of the state seems curious when we consider the mounting evidence about the insufficiency of states as political communities. This is not just a matter of being too large for politics in Aristotle's sense. It is also a matter of being too small to enclose the most pressing political problems: the control of military violence; management of the economy; redistribution of resources; protection of the biosphere. These are transnational if not global problems, demanding transnational if not global solutions. The state's capacity to act in these matters diminished between 1970 and 1990, and this spawned a variety of ad hoc arrangements. The claim that the state provides the inevitably necessary framework for dealing with the modern world seems therefore unwarranted, even a bit bizarre.

Of course, the implicit argument is not really that the state is self-sufficient. It is rather that the state is big enough to create order within its own bounds: to light a candle in the dark night of international relations. Even this argument is dubious. It ignores the great range in the scale and power of states. The smallest—the microstates of the Pacific, the Caribbean, and the Indian Ocean—are locality-based. The largest and most powerful are great empires. In Anglo-American thought, the paradigmatic states have been Britain and the United States, the hegemonic powers of the nineteenth and twentieth centuries. A convenient elision allows statehood and hegemony to be identified, so that the self-sufficiency of the hegemon is attributed to the state per se. The other states that enter into the mainstream of political theory as implicit models all are potentially hegemonic (or at least counterhegemonic): Germany, France, the USSR, China, India, Japan.[12] These are the states that at least appear to be worlds unto themselves, culturally, economically, and politically. The rest of the world is a nonplace in the theory of the state. Who is thinking of Jamaica or New Zealand when s/he argues for the necessity of the modern state?

The obverse of the mostly unstated argument for the state is the explicit attack on the locality as an appropriate political community. This attack appears mostly in the literature on public administration, rather than in political theory or theories of the state.[13] It has an interesting ideological guise. It is clothed in nineteenth century rhetoric about the necessity of local self-government, but its thrust is to demolish any claim by localities to political autonomy. Instead, means are offered, on the one hand, for more efficient, effective, responsive, and responsible administration of local affairs; and, on the other, for more active citizen participation in affairs of state and a more appropriate geographical division of powers within the state. The locality is deconstructed as a set of autonomous individuals involved in complex social relations of varying geographic scale.[14] Communal loyalties are presented as archaic revivals manipulated by self-interested politicians. The exigencies of the state and the market are accepted as given, and boundary rationalization is conceived as adaptation to these exigencies. In the end, localities disappear except as constructs of the state and the market— and the claims of localities to political primacy disappear as well.

In a curious inversion, the locality (rather than the state) appears as an artificial community. Since everyday life lacks definite boundaries, to impose boundaries for purposes of local administration—to establish a political container and say, "This is the locality"—seems artificial. Communal loyalties have a similar lack of definition. They spread over the region and beyond, but they contract toward the neighborhood and the block. There is no agreed order of priority among these loyalties. Thus, the container chosen for local government and politics is apparently arbitrary or artificial, in terms of both "objective" and "subjective" measures of community identity.[15] On the other hand, both the market and the state are conceived as components of the natural environment, to which local government and politics must adapt. They are as fixed as river basins, and much more important for defining rational boundaries.

Although there are still some adherents to the idea that the rational boundaries of local government are given by the land and the sea, the predominant theories today are either market-centered or state-centered. Public choice is the paradigmatic market-centered theory, for it poses the problem of local government organization as a relation between producers and consumers of public goods.[16] Public choice theory points toward a multiplicity of producers in competition with one another, and various forms of consumer organization to purchase the goods. This organizational proliferation is opposed by state-centered theorists who assert the need for state control over markets in public and private goods.[17] Their preference is for a hierarchy of authorities from center to locality, each with comprehensive jurisdiction within its own sphere and each subordinated to the one above. The ideological quarrel between market-centered and state-centered theorists reflects a familiar difference of opinion about the appropriate relation between the state and civil society. The issues at stake are important enough, but for our purposes the significance of the quarrel is to be found in the common assumptions of the protagonists. Both take the political enclosure of the state/market for granted. The market-centered theorists take as natural a global economy mediated, if not largely constituted, by state action. In turn, the state-centered theorists accept as natural the administrative divisions and functional dispositions given in that global economy. Thus, the organizational possibilities are enclosed in a circle.[18]

The localities that make sense in terms of the state or the market are evanescent. The requirements of public administration are constantly changing, as new services are developed, new technologies introduced, and new ideas about means and ends articulated. The market is even less stable: people move, adopt new fashions, acquire new goods and new tastes. Thus, the local boundaries defined by the state or the market are likely to become obsolete as soon as they are established. This evanescence contrasts with the fixity of the state, whose boundaries appear as natural necessities. In nationalist ideology, the state is the political embodiment of the nation, and has the responsibility for protecting and developing it. This means creating a national market, defining and protecting national rights of citizenship, and providing the public goods and services essential to one nation. Since nation–building requires intense loyalties, the state is accorded a monopoly on the symbols of patriotism, which it invokes against internal and external challenges. This monopoly of patriotic symbolism is the ideological counterpart of the monopolies of political authority and legitimate violence implicit in the principles of state sovereignty.

The circularity of nationalist ideology is evident: the nation needs the state as its political embodiment, so the state has to create the nation to legitimate its own existence. Hence, nation-building is the most glorious of state activities. This circularity has not gone unnoticed, and it has occasioned some ironic comment, but it in no way diminishes the claims of the state in the eyes of most political commentators. As the ancient Greeks recognized, political enclosures had to be created by conscious effort; they were not simply effects of other human activities. Thus, polis-building was both natural and necessary. Indeed, it was the most fundamentally political of all activities.[19] This idea is carried forward in modern theories of nation-state–building. The very capacity of the state to mobilize the resources necessary to effect political enclosure—i.e., to establish sovereignty—is taken to be proof of its claims to political priority. In the rough-and-tumble of modern politics, localities, cities, districts, regions, and international communities, all have lost out to "nations" in the struggle for political supremacy. And *that*, apparently, is all that needs to be said.[20]

The key assumption is that political community requires enclosure—that politics proper is impossible without a protected space where ideals can be realized and interests ideally adjudicated. This protected space has been the subject of political theory, as reified in the tradition.[21] This is the space of liberty, equality, and fraternity; of democracy; of order and moderation; of conservatism and radicalism; of liberalism and socialism; even of revolution. On its borders are the unfortunate necessities of Machiavellian and Hegelian theory: war and diplomacy. The latter normally are acknowledged only to be ignored or dissolved in imaginings about a world-state. Serious thought about the relation between what is contained in and what is excluded from the political enclosures is extremely rare, and is usually distorted by the assumption that political community—and the values associated with it—depend on enclosure. That there might be forms of political community that resist enclosure or are stifled by it is barely considered. How these forms might sustain or extend common political ideals is not a serious subject.

Thus, the theory of democracy is, for the most part, just an aspect of the theory of the state. It offers an ideal of state organization, and specifies the conditions for realizing it. What democracy means as a condition for international relations—rather than as a condition for making foreign policy—is not considered; neither are the conditions for democratizing emergent transnational communities, such as those of feminists, environmentalists, or pacifists. Localities seem to get more consideration, but this is deceptive, for local democracy is usually regarded as an aspect of national democracy. The question raised generally is, "How can local institutions contribute to the democratization of the state as such?" And the answer generally is, "by providing for citizen participation, for an appropriate geographical division of powers," and so on. To the extent that local democracy is considered on its own terms, it is usually within the theory of public administration. State-centered accounts treat the municipality as a ministate, and apply to it the democratic prescriptions—e.g., representative institutions—that have been developed for the nation-state. Market-centered theories, such as those about public choice, subordinate democracy to the satisfaction of consumer preferences. In either case, little remains of *local* democracy as a distinctive political ideal.[22]

Like most other political ideals, democracy has been conceived as an aspect of political enclosure. Thus, the irrationality of enclosing the locality has been taken as a sign of the necessary imperfection of local democracy. The locality, it is thought, can only be democratic as a part of the state, for it is too small to survive on its own. Its democracy, therefore, is only partial: one aspect of democracy within the state. This way of thinking about the locality neatly disposes of its most pressing claims. The venue for everyday life, everyday politics, and everyday democracy fades as an object of political theory, in favor of the state that stands over/against it. Thus, the idea of democracy as an aspect of everyday life also fades, along with the political communities that could sustain or extend it. The latter are unintelligible as aspects of the state, and hence are beyond the ken of political theory as normally conceived. Bringing *them* back in has radical implications for political theory.

Social Movements and Political Communities

Arthur Bentley's famous book, *The Process of Government* (1908), seemed to mark a shift from state-centered to society-centered theories of politics.[23]

The shift has been so well publicized that latter-day political scientists can announce with some pride that they are "bringing the state back in."[24] But the supposed shift is really only a move from one vantage point to another. The object of study remains the same: "societies" are constituted by states, and "politics" is defined by the process of government, the activity internal to states.[25] Groups are deemed to be political insofar as they address themselves to the process of government; i.e., insofar as they seek to influence government policy, to secure representation within the state, or, at the extreme, to take over the government itself. If government is the output, politics is the input that connects civil society to the state. It affords space both for parties that seek to control the state and for pressure groups that want to influence it.

This state-centric conception of politics is the ruling idea, not only in everyday life, but also in the scholarly analysis of political processes. It has been criticized for neglecting political forms and processes that occur outside of the input-output relationship between the state and civil society. When these other forms of politics, which are not centered upon the state, *have* been considered, they have been conceived analogously as activities related to governing processes in the firm, the family, the economy, and society at large.[26] This has resulted in an extension of the conventional idea of politics, but rarely in a critical examination of the concept as it is applied within its home domain. Marxist theory comes close to such a critique, because it identifies and attacks as reification the very division between state and civil society. However, the critique often slides into a reification of state-centered class struggle as the core of politics. The effect is to reconstitute a state-centric conception politics in a different theoretical domain.[27]

The theoretical impoverishment that results from a state-centric conception of politics is illustrated by the conventional treatment of social movements.[28] On the one hand, everyone knows that social movements are important politically. On the other hand, no one is sure how to fit them into state-centric political categories. Clearly, a movement is neither a pressure group nor a political party. Nevertheless, parties and pressure groups are often spawned by movements, and just as frequently attempt to speak authoritatively for them. For the state, the institutionalization of a movement as a pressure group or party is often essential for containing and dealing with the threat it represents. The enclosure of a movement within an established political space allows for regularization of the relations between the state and the group concerned. This regularization may have the effect of stilling the social movement. For the state, this return to calm is usually welcome. For those involved in the social movement, the party or the group remains as institutional detritus from their efforts. The interests or concerns embodied in the original movement are given a form appropriate to the smooth functioning of the state.

From the vantage point of the state (which is the normal vantage point of political analysis), the institutionalization of social movements is simply a matter of regularizing their political form. In this sense, social movements become political actors only when they are institutionalized. Before that, they appear simply as prepolitical disturbances in civil society.[29] This suggests that the collective activities of ordinary people, in working out new understandings of themselves and bringing those understandings into the world, are themselves prepolitical. Thus, the creative social activity in which ordinary people are most likely to be engaged appears beyond or outside politics. In the political sphere proper (as in the governmental sphere) the important activities demand expertise, and afford opportunities for creative action only to the elite. "The people" are just the chorus and audience—and the beast without. Such prepolitical, merely social creatures are best confined to the harmless dramas of local politics—or to "Dallas."

Such an account is a distortion of political reality. It seems natural only because of our acceptance of state-centric conceptions of politics. If we begin with popular political activity, rather than from the enclosure imposed upon it, another dimension of reality emerges.

Politics might be defined as purposive social action directed at the conditions of social existence. From this perspective, social movements are the politics of the people—and government is the politics of the state.[30] Parties and pressure groups are the forms imposed on popular politics, under state hegemony. For the most part, they are forms that quell social movements, and hence still the politics of the people. The fact that movements can and do burst the enclosures of the state is evidence not of their prepolitical but of their political character: their capacity to "found" or create new forms of political community, political identity, and political action.

It is worth considering what democratic theory would be like, if it were a theory of social movements rather than of states. It would have to contend with a number of curious features.[31] Movements tend to be:

1. *Plural*: There is not just one movement in any place, but many; a person may be part of as many movements as s/he has energy for and the number of simultaneous movements is in principle unlimited.
2. *Impermanent*: Movements only last as long as the enthusiasm for them—they become bureaucratized or they disappear.
3. *Inchoate*: Movements have no definite membership, authority relations, purposes, or programs.
4. *Inclusive*: In principle, anyone can be part of a movement, and there can be no definite means of excluding a person.
5. *Unbounded*: A movement takes in as many people, as much territory, as many issues as seems appropriate to the people involved.

Not every movement displays each of these features, but in principle movements are the opposites of enclosures. They lack fixity, boundaries, determinacy. How then can they be conceived in terms of democratic theory?

The perplexity with which we approach this question reflects the hold of state-centric political theory. Don't we need definite bounds for the theorization of democracy? (Or liberty, or equality, or justice?) How can we attach democratic conditions to such inchoate phenomena?[32]

Perhaps we can get at these questions more easily by relating it to a particular example, such as feminism. What must feminism be like to be democratic? Several criteria suggest themselves:

1. The movement ought to address itself to all women, regardless of class, nation, race, or social condition.
2. The movement ought to offer all women the opportunity to participate in defining its goals and carrying out its activities.
3. It ought not to discriminate in favor of some women at the expense of others.
4. It ought not to claim exclusive loyalty, or seal itself off from other movements.

These conditions might be multiplied, and they are by no means definitive. Nevertheless, they are sufficiently clear to suggest that the specification of democracy in relation to a movement is by no means impossible. And, what is true of democracy is likely to be true of other political ideals.

One feature of theorizing movement-democracy rather than state-democracy should be evident. Traditional questions about authority relations, representation, and accountability fade into the background. They do not disappear altogether—they are relevant for any formal organization—but they have dubious relevance to an inchoate movement. If, as suggested, movement politics is the politics of the people—the very core of *democratic* politics—this has profound implications for political theory. It suggests that the key considerations of democratic theory ought not to be the traditional matters of state, but the relations within and between social movements. Indeed, it suggests that, insofar as political theory has become the theory of the state, it serves as a legitimating ideology that obscures the very possibility of politics of, by, and for the people. The effects of this are particularly evident in the United States, where the main principles of the conventional liberal democratic theory of the state are reified as constitutional law. Unfortunately, it is not much of an exaggeration to describe U.S. political theory as a series of footnotes to the Constitution.[33] Although theorists elsewhere lack such a touchstone, the phenomenon of the state still largely determines their expectations of political theory. Good theory is supposed to offer a critique of the modern state and specifications for changing it. What it says about movements is mere sociology.

Obviously, to shift from the state to movements, and to ignore the former as an object of theorizing would be wrong. It would be equally wrong to assume that states and movements are unrelated to one another. Nevertheless, working through the main questions of political theory from the bottom up—from the vantage point of the politics of movements—is extremely important because this aspect of politics has been so much ignored and so thoroughly misconstrued. The misconstructions are especially apparent with respect to political community. The word *community* conjures an image of people in their everyday lives. But the concept of political community, as used in political theory, is one of enclosure.[34] Since the actual political activity of ordinary people is so amorphous, it cannot even be conceptualized in terms of an enclosure. Inevitably the political communities imagined by theorists are reifications of political space that obscure the actual and potential communities that people develop in the course of their political activities. Thus, we have theories of political community that are just theories of the state disguised.[35]

From the perspective suggested here, social movements are, fundamentally, political communities. They originate in localities, but normally spread beyond them. They develop complex systems of communications, and invent new authority relations. They convert masses of people, leading them to re-conceive their own identities and their activities: working out goals, strategy, tactics, and carrying them into effect. They are always in development. They have no necessary bounds in space or time. Their extent and longevity depend on the enthusiasm of their participants, the nature of their objectives, and the conditions they encounter. Some social movements—notably nationalist ones—actually seek their own reification as states, but this is by no means typical. The forms of political community embodied in socialism, feminism, environmentalism, pacifism, or transcendental religion are inconsistent with statehood, and whatever tendency there is to reify these movements as states is a perversion of the ideals and communities they represent.[36]

It is testimony to the creative power of many movements—and to the actual character of political community—that they tend to challenge their own reifications. Liberalism is now reified as a global market economy and a set of democratic capitalist states. Socialism is reified in various political parties and socialist states. Together, these reifications are the most powerful political enclosures of the modern era. And yet, they are constantly challenged by the movements they claim to embody: neither liberal aspirations for individual autonomy nor socialist aspirations for collective emancipation are easily contained. Other movements display a similar creative energy. This energy and the possibilities it represents are missed by the theories that take the major reifications of political community as the forms of politics itself.

The Junctures of Popular Politics

By freeing ourselves from standard conceptions of political community, we can begin to examine politics as people actually experience and practice it. In this sense politics is a matter of everyday life. This does not mean that everything is political (although it may mean that anything is worth examining politically). It does mean that politics involves people's everyday experience of the practices that define their social identities, social goals, and modes of social action. In part, this is a matter of their confronting, challenging, or participating in practices of domination, some (but not all) of which are organized by the state. But it is also a matter of their creative social action: inventions, not just resistances. The most powerful expression of this second dimension of politics is in social movements. Each of them involves a different conception of what is fundamental politically: which human identities are crucial, what forms of social action are necessary, what political communities have to be created. As such, movements are the creative edge of politics as an everyday experience.

Localities are the venues for such politics. They are the places where the various practices of domination meet with the practices of political resistance and invention. Politics as creative popular activity thus occurs at the junctures of localities and movements. These junctures are obscured by the reification of political community as the state and political theory as the theory of the state. To focus on these junctures is to open two analytic dimensions: first, *locality* as the place where movements arise and where they meet; and, second, *movement* as a mode of action that redefines political community, and hence connects localities to one another. In exploring these dimensions, we become acutely conscious of the fact that the state never fully contains the everyday experience of politics or political community.

Movements, like localities (and states), are always partial political communities. They never fully encompass the lives of their members; they never include everyone in a locality. Localities thus are the places where movements meet in people's everyday experience. Relations between movements—and between them and the authorities—are thus at the heart of everyday local politics. Such relations are susceptible to normative theorization, as well as empirical investigation. Obviously, one can also work through the requirements of liberal, egalitarian, democratic, and creative social relations. There is great scope for a political theory of local politics in this sense. Furthermore, there is scope for a political theory of movements that considers not only the way they interact in localities, but also the way they make connections between localities. Clearly, great differences exist between movements characterized by xenophobia, fundamentalism, and imperialism; and movements that establish relations in a temper of openness, mutuality, and respect for difference.

The assumed connection between enclosure and political community has led theorists to conceptualize localities as municipalities and movements as parties or pressure groups. These are the forms in which, it is assumed, localities and movements become significant politically. But, ironically, they are also the forms in which localities and movements become *insignificant* politically, since they are forms subordinate to the state. This rendering into insignificance is, of course, a matter of political practice and not simply of theory, but that practice, which is the one associated with the state, is not the only one we have to understand. Live Aid, Greenpeace, and European Nuclear Disarmament, for example, are organizations produced by movements that defy the normal political containers, act in political spaces of their own invention, and exercise political power. The exact importance of these organizations is difficult to assess, but their presence is a sign of politics uncontained by the enclosures of the state and neglected by state-centric political theory. In movements and organizations such as these we can locate popular politics in its global dimension.

Notes

1. The analysis that follows has been heavily influenced by R. B. J. Walker. See his *One World, Many Worlds: Struggles for a Just World Peace* (Boulder, Colo.: Lynne Rienner, 1988) and *Culture, Ideology and World Order* (Boulder, Colo.: Westview Press, 1984), as well as our joint paper, "Decentring the State: Political Theory and Canadian Political Economy," *Studies in Political Economy: A Socialist Review* 27 (Summer 1988): 37–71.

2. On this point, see especially John G. Gunnell, *Political Philosophy and Time: Plato and the Origins of Political Vision* (Chicago: University of Chicago Press, 1968, 1987).

3. In addition to the works cited by Walker and Mendlovitz in note 2 of their introductory chapter in this book see Andrew Vincent, *Theories of the State* (Oxford: Basil Blackwell, 1987); Frederick M. Watkins, *The State as a Concept of Political Science* (New York: Harper & Brothers, 1934); David Held, ed., *States and Societies* (Oxford: Martin Robertson, 1983); James Anderson, ed., *The Rise of the Modern State* (Brighton: Wheatsheaf, 1986); and Yale H. Ferguson and Richard W. Mansbach, *The State, Conceptual Chaos, and the Future of International Relations Theory* (Boulder & London: Lynne Rienner, 1989).

4. Significantly, most of the interesting efforts to break free from a state-centric conception of politics have come from outside the discipline of political science. See, for instance, the works of Michel Foucault, Manuel Castells, Alberto Melucci, Anthony Giddens, and Michael Mann.

5. See, for example, J. Roland Pennock, *Democratic Political Theory* (Princeton: Princeton University Press, 1979); Giovanni Sartori, *The Theory of Democracy Revisited* (Chatham, N.J.: Chatham House, 1987); Jack Lively, *Democracy* (Oxford: Basil Blackwell, 1975); C. B. Macpherson, *Democratic Theory: Essays in Retrieval* (Oxford: Oxford University Press, 1973); Graeme Duncan, ed., *Democratic Theory and Practice* (Cambridge: Cambridge University Press, 1983); and David Held, *Models of Democracy* (Cambridge: Polity, 1987).

6. The most notable is Robert A. Dahl. See his "The City in the Future of Democracy," *American Political Science Review* 61, no. 4 (1967): 953–970; *After the Revolution?* (New Haven: Yale University Press, 1970); and *Dilemmas of*

Pluralist Democracy: Autonomy vs. Control (New Haven: Yale University Press, 1982). See also Norton E. Long, *The Unwalled City: Reconstituting the Urban Community* (New York: Basic Books, 1972); W. Harvey Cox, *Cities: The Public Dimension* (Harmondsworth: Penguin, 1976); and Stephen L. Elkin, *City and Regime in the American Republic* (Chicago: University of Chicago Press, 1987).

7. Alexis de Tocqueville, *Democracy in America*, 2 vols. (New York: Vintage Books, 1945); John Stuart Mill, *Utilitarianism, On Liberty and Considerations on Representative Government*, ed. H. B. Acton (London: Dent, 1972). On the development of ideas about local government, see Sidney and Beatrice Webb, *The Development of English Local Government, 1689–1835* (London: Oxford University Press, 1963); Jon C. Teaford, *The Municipal Revolution in America: Origins of Modern Urban Government, 1650–1825* (Chicago: University of Chicago Press, 1975); Anwar H. Syed, *The Political Theory of American Local Government* (New York: Random House, 1966); W. Hardy Wickwar, *The Political Theory of Local Government* (Columbia: University of South Carolina Press, 1970); and Gerald Frug, "The City as a Legal Concept," *Harvard Law Review* 93, no. 6 (1980): 1059–1154.

8. Plato and Aristotle, the most renowned of the ancient theorists, were, of course, strong critics of democracy. For a more sympathetic account of ancient practices, see M. I. Finley, *Democracy Ancient and Modern* (London: Hogarth Press, 1973).

9. Aristotle anticipated this argument. Indeed, it was he who insisted on "self-sufficiency" as the criterion for political community. He denied, however, that self-sufficiency was a matter of military or economic necessity alone. The polis had to be of a scale sufficient for the good life. It had to be bigger than a clan or a village, but small enough for people to "know one another's characters." Otherwise, there could not be good citizenship. A citizenry of thousands—not of millions—was thus to be preferred. It never occurred to him that a polis had to be large enough to contain an entire culture. See *The Politics of Aristotle*, trans. Ernest Barker (New York: Oxford University Press, 1962), especially Books 1 and 7.

10. Ernest Gellner, *Nations and Nationalism* (Oxford: Basil Blackwell, 1983), p. 5.

11. Ibid., p. 34.

12. It is in continental Europe that explicit theorization of the state as a hegemonic (or counter-hegemonic) order has been most pronounced. See Kenneth Dyson, *The State Tradition in Western Europe* (Oxford: Martin Robertson, 1980). What Dyson misses is the silent presence of the state in Anglo-American political theory. There is reason to think that Europeans—and now also Asians, Africans, and Latin Americans—have had to be more self-conscious about the state, because it appears as a potential counter to British or U. S. hegemony. Talk of "the state" makes English-speaking people uncomfortable because it draws attention to the force that sustains their ideals.

13. For an overview, see Brian C. Smith, *Decentralization: The Territorial Dimension of the State* (London: Allen & Unwin, 1985). See also Mark Gottdiener, *The Decline of Urban Politics: Political Theory and the Crisis of the Local State* (Beverly Hills, Calif.: Sage, 1987); Lionel D. Feldman, ed., *The Politics and Government of Urban Canada*, 4th ed. (Toronto: Methuen, 1981); Gordon L. Clark, *Judges and the Cities* (Chicago: University of Chicago Press, 1985); Dilys M. Hill, *Democratic Theory and Local Government* (London: Allen & Unwin, 1974); Arthur

Maass, ed., *Area and Power* (New York: The Free Press, 1959); James W. Fesler, *Area and Administration* (Montgomery: University of Alabama Press, 1949); Robert A. Dahl and Edward R. Tufte, *Size and Democracy* (London: Oxford University Press, 1974); L. J. Sharpe, ed., *Decentralist Trends in Western Democracies* (London: Sage, 1979); and Ted Robert Gurr and Desmond S. King, *The State and the City* (London: Macmillan, 1987).

14. Suzanne Keller, *The Urban Neighborhood* (New York: Random House, 1968). See also Manuel Castells, *The Urban Question* (Cambridge, Mass.: MIT Press, 1977); Robert L. Bish, *The Public Economy of Metropolitan Areas* (Chicago: Markham, 1971); Patrick Dunleavy, *Urban Political Analysis: The Politics of Collective Consumption* (London: Macmillan, 1980); and Peter Saunders, *Social Theory and the Urban Question*, 2nd ed. (London: Hutchinson, 1986).

15. This problem is the subject of a vast literature on local government reorganization. See, for instance, Donald C. Rowayt, ed., *International Handbook on Local Government Reorganization* (London: Aldwych Press, 1980) and Arthur B. Gunlicks, ed., *Local Government Reform and Reorganization: An International Perspective* (Port Washington, N.Y.: Kennikat Press, 1981).

16. The classic "public choice" analysis is in Robert L. Bish and Vincent Ostrom, *Understanding Urban Government: Metropolitan Reform Reconsidered* (Washington: American Enterprise Institute, 1973).

17. This state-centered view has been developed with particular sophistication in Britain. See Jack Brand, *Local Government Reform in England, 1888–1974* (London: Croom Helm, 1974); John Dearlove, *The Reorganization of British Local Government* (Cambridge: Cambridge University Press, 1979); and L. J. Sharpe, "The Failure of Local Government Modernization in Britain: A Critique of Functionalism," in Feldman, *Urban Canada*, pp. 321–357. See also Jon C. Teaford, *City and Suburbs* (Baltimore: Johns Hopkins University Press, 1979) and John C. Bollens and Henry Schmandt, *The Metropolis*, 3rd ed. (New York: Harper & Row, 1975). The interdependence of state-centered and market-centered views becomes apparent in works that purport to marry them. See Paul E. Peterson, *City Limits* (Chicago: University of Chicago Press, 1981) or, significantly, Sidney and Beatrice Webb, *A Constitution for the Socialist Commonwealth of Great Britain* (Cambridge: Cambridge University Press, 1975).

18. I have analyzed these matters at greater length in "Community Organization and Local Self-Government," in Feldman, *Urban Canada*, pp. 61–86; "Metropolitan Reform in the Capitalist City," *Canadian Journal of Political Science* 14, no. 3 (1981): 557–585; and "Bourgeois Theories of Local Government," *Political Studies* 34, no. 1 (1986): 1–18.

19. See Hannah Arendt, *On Revolution* (New York: Viking Press, 1965) and *The Human Condition* (New York: Doubleday, 1958).

20. Works that challenge the primacy of the state/nation are extremely rare. Among the few recent examples are Jane Jacobs, *Cities and the Wealth of Nations* (New York: Random House, 1984) and Murray Bookchin, *The Limits of the City* (Montreal: Black Rose Books, 1986).

21. On the tradition, see John G. Gunnell, *Political Theory: Tradition and Interpretation* (Boston, Mass.: Little, Brown, 1979) and *Between Philosophy and Politics: The Alienation of Political Theory* (Amherst: University of Massachusetts Press, 1986). See also Sheldon Wolin, *Politics and Vision: Continuity and Innova-*

tion in Western Political Thought (Boston: Little Brown, 1960) and John S. Nelson, ed., *What Should Political Theory Be Now?* (Albany: State University of New York Press, 1983).

22. The neglect of the local is apparent even in works that emphasize the need for mass democratic participation. See C. B. Macpherson, *The Life and Times of Liberal Democracy* (Oxford: Oxford University Press, 1977); Benjamin Barber, *Strong Democracy: Participatory Politics for a New Age* (Berkeley and Los Angeles: University of California Press, 1984); John Burnheim, *Is Democracy Possible? The Alternative to Electoral Politics* (Cambridge: Polity Press, 1985); and Philip Green, *Retrieving Democracy: In Search of Civic Equality* (Totowa, N.J.: Rowman and Allanheld, 1985).

23. Arthur F. Bentley, *The process of Government*, ed. Peter H. Odegard (Cambridge, Mass.: Belknap Press, 1967). See also David B. Truman, *The Governmental Process: Political Interests and Public Opinion* (New York: Knopf, 1951) and David Easton, *The Political System* (Chicago: University of Chicago Press, 1953). It is hardly an exaggeration to say that these works established the paradigm for "political science." See also David M. Ricci, *The Tragedy of Political Science: Politics, Scholarship and Democracy* (New Haven: Yale University Press, 1984).

24. Peter B. Evans, Dietrich Rueschmeyer, and Theda Skocpol, eds., *Bringing the State Back In* (Cambridge: Cambridge University Press, 1985).

25. On the state-centric conception of "society" among sociologists, see Anthony Giddens, *A Contemporary Critique of Historical Materialism* (London: Macmillan, 1981) and *The Nation-State and Violence* (Berkeley and Los Angeles: University of California Press, 1987).

26. Hence, for instance, the considerable literature on "industrial democracy." See, e.g., Seymour Martin Lipset, Martin A. Trow, and James S. Coleman, *Union Democracy* (Glencoe, Ill.: The Free Press, 1956); Paul Blumberg, *Industrial Democracy* (London: Constable, 1968); Tom Schuller, *Democracy at Work* (Oxford: Oxford University Press, 1985); and Carmen Sirianni, ed., *Worker Participation and the Politics of Reform* (Philadelphia: Temple University Press, 1987). See also Carole Pateman, *Participation and Democratic Theory* (London: Cambridge University Press, 1970); Ronald M. Mason, *Participatory and Workplace Democracy* (Carbondale and Edwardsville: Southern Illinois University Press, 1982); and Edward S. Greenberg, *Workplace Democracy: The Political Effects of Participation* (Ithaca, N.Y.: Cornell University Press, 1986).

27. This is a major theme of Magnusson and Walker, "Decentring the State."

28. See, e.g., Neil Smelser, *The Theory of Collective Behavior* (New York: The Free Press, 1962); Mancur Olson, *The Logic of Collective Action* (Cambridge, Mass.: Harvard University Press, 1965); Anthony Oberschall, *Social Conflict and Social Movements* (Englewood Cliffs, N.J.: Prentice-Hall, 1973); John Wilson, *Introduction to Social Movements* (New York: Basic Books, 1973); and Mayer D. Zald and John D. McCarthy, eds., *The Dynamics of Social Movements* (Cambridge, Mass.: Winthrop, 1979).

29. Hence, the fact that sociologists, not political scientists, have developed the concept and led the study of social movements. See J. Craig Jenkins, "Resource Mobilization Theory and the Study of Social Movements," *Annual Review of Sociology* 9 (1983): 527–553; Ron Eyerman, "Social Movements and Social

Theory," *Sociology* 18, no. 1 (1984): 71–82.

30. The literature on the "new" social movements points toward such a conception. See Alain Touraine, *The Voice and the Eye: An Analysis of Social Movements* (Cambridge: Cambridge University Press, 1981); Manuel Castells, *The City and the Grassroots: A Cross-Cultural Theory of Urban Social Movements* (Berkeley and Los Angeles: University of California Press, 1983); Carl Boggs, *Social Movements and Political Power: Emerging Forms of Radicalism in the West* (Philadelphia: Temple University Press, 1986); Jean Cohen, ed., "Social Movements," special issue of *Social Research* 52, no. 4 (1986); and Alberto Melucci, *Nomads of the Present: Social Movements and Individual Needs in Contemporary Society* (London: Hutchinson Radius, 1989).

31. See Walker, *One World, Many Worlds*.

32. The "post-modern turn" in recent political theory has begun to generate some interesting speculations on these and other matters. See, for example, William E. Connolly, *Political Theory and Modernity* (Oxford: Basil Blackwell, 1988); William Corlett, *Community Without Unity: A Politics of Derridian Extravagance* (Durham, N.C.: Duke University Press, 1989); and Anne Norton, *Reflections on Political Identity* (Baltimore: Johns Hopkins University Press, 1988). See also Charles S. Maier, ed., *Changing Boundaries of the Political* (Cambridge: Cambridge University Press, 1987); Dick Howard, *Defining the Political* (London: Macmillan, 1989); and John Keane, ed., *Civil Society and the State* (London: Verso, 1988).

33. The great footnoter of the seventies was John Rawls. See *A Theory of Justice* (Cambridge: Harvard University Press, 1971). Compare A. Bruce Ackerman, *Social Justice in the Liberal State* (New Haven: Yale University Press, 1980); Robert Nozick, *Anarchy, State, and Utopia* (New York: Basic Books, 1974); Michael Walzer, *Spheres of Justice* (New York: Basic Books, 1973); Amy Gutmann, *Liberal Equality* (Cambridge: Cambridge University Press, 1980); and Michael Sandel, *Liberalism and the Limits of Justice* (Cambridge: Cambridge University Press, 1982).

34. For the most part, this concept is tacit. The literature that addresses it directly is suprisingly sparse. See Eugene Kamenka, ed., *Community as a Social Ideal* (New York: St. Martin's Press, 1982); Robert A. Nisbet, *The Quest for Community* (New York: Oxford University Press, 1953, 1969); Glenn Tinder, *Community: Reflections on a Tragic Ideal* (Baton Rouge: Louisiana State University Press, 1980); and Richard Sennett, *The Fall of Public Man* (New York: Knopf, 1977).

35. In addition to the works cited in n33, see, for instance, Jürgen Habermas, *The Theory of Communicative Action* (Boston: Beacon Press, 1984).

36. One need think only of the Soviet Union and Eastern Europe to recognize the price a movement (in this case, socialism) can pay for its reification in state-form.

4

Evasions of Sovereignty

Richard Falk

As yet nobody has drawn a map that reflects the new order . . .

—Lewis Lapham, "Leviathan in Trouble,"
Harper's, September 1988

Sovereignty and the Coming Global Civilization

We are encountering today an ever more widespread belief that a world map composed of sovereign states no longer provides—if indeed it ever did—a useful conception of how the world as a whole is constituted. In the spirit of popular commentary, Lewis Lapham, the editor of an influential U.S. monthly magazine, suggests that if someone were to try depicting "the new order," "it would look more like medieval France than nineteenth century Europe."[1] Lapham's image of the feudal precursor to the modern state system implies a multitude of overlapping authorities that were both more centralized and less territorially specific than those we tend to associate with our own age. Such a deconstruction of the modern state is a suggestive image of late twenty-first century conditions, perhaps, but it is surely premature and quite misleading as a descriptive basis for recasting our understanding of present international realities. Such an evocation of the feudal order does not help us to grasp what lies just beyond the horizon of an unfolding future. Territorial states remain the predominant political actors in our world, even if their interactions are becoming bewilderingly complex and increasingly extraterritorial in their operational reach, and despite the fact that their capacity for autonomy is being multiplied and cumulatively eroded.[2]

Indeed, a strong case can be made for treating a map of states as more accurate than ever before. The global dynamics of nationalism in the late twentieth century have created greater viability for many weaker states, at least in terms of their capacity to resist the most blatant forms of military encroachment by ascendant states. The actual situation is uneven and complicated, but it has certainly become easier for militarily subordinate territorial governments to organize resistance to interventionary diplomacy, and thereby to safeguard their sovereign character against imperial designs. Even the superpowers have faced increasingly formidable challenges to their respective control over so-called "blocs" or "spheres of interest" in the last two decades. Military superiority is far more difficult to translate into political control than it was in the nineteenth century, when mass mobilization around militant nationalist creeds was unusual. Furthermore, the cruder forms of economic penetration have become more difficult to negotiate, requiring elaborate arrangements to limit or disguise foreign capital. The need for indirection is a tribute to the potency of nationalism as a reigning political ideology. Governments can no longer sustain their full legitimacy—either in relation to their own society or with regard to the outer world—if they grant foreign allies special privileges within their territory. Foreign military bases are increasingly difficult to establish, and most of those that exist are under mounting political pressure from the local population. (There are exceptions, of course, either where a government lacks any autonomy—and any pretense of legitimacy—or where it is faced by a security challenge that makes a foreign military presence appear genuinely necessary to collective self-defense, rather than serving as a platform that serves the wider geopolitical strategy of a distant great power.)

At the same time, however, not all states are adequate vehicles of nationalist claims. Many "nations" (as self-conscious ethnic units) are "entrapped" within a sovereign space administered by a government that is controlled by a different nation. Such a state may be autonomous vis-à-vis the external world, but its internal legitimacy is constantly subject to interrogation, if not assault, by assertive national minorities. In other circumstances, crises of governability are evident. The state lacks the capability to produce either order, justice, or security against unwanted outside interference. Contemporary Lebanon is currently the most aggravated instance, but roughly analogous problems torment many societies to varying degrees, and provide governments with expedient justifications for abandoning democracy and human rights, thus exposing their populations to acute forms of daily insecurity with respect to basic needs.

Can we portray the current shape of world order by a conventional map of states? Or is it better to conceive of the world as a criss-cross of patterns based on different issues, regimes, and perceptions? I would argue that a sophisticated atlas is preferable to a map, that we need many different ways of looking at the planet as a whole, ranging from the photographs sent back from space satellites through geoeconomic presentations of resources, trade flows, arms trade, and military alliances, as well as models that coordinate space with population size and standard of living. Even mapping differing expectations about the shape of the future might be revealing.

Hypotheses about a coming global civilization are often put forward—partly descriptively and partly normatively—as an overlay upon this debate about the role, viability, patterning, and variety of sovereign states. The contention goes beyond either liberal formulations of interdependence or Marxist formulations of global class structure and international division of labor.[3] In effect, a global ethos is emerging that suggests a shared destiny for the human species and a fundamental unity across space and through time, built around the bioethical impulse of all human groups to survive and flourish. Such an ethos has implications for the assessment of problems, the provision of solutions, and the overall orientation of action and actors. For most people and leaders, this shared sense of destiny does not displace a persisting primary attachment to the state as a vehicle for aspiration and as an absolute, unconditional bastion of security. As the imagery of "nuclear winter" dramatizes, leaders of nuclear powers seem prepared to threaten the overall survival of civilization and even risk partial or total extinction, if such a threat seems necessary to uphold the sovereign identity of a particular state, or even, more narrowly, the persistence of a particular regime or governing elite. The logic of war in the nuclear age devours the self that is the object of protection, and holds hostage the entire human race—indeed, the life process as a whole. From a religious perspective, it is a blasphemy to creation, the sacred work of divinity, to contemplate as a deliberate and discretionary undertaking by human agency the destruction of the world; nuclearism is indefensible in both the most fundamental philosophical sense and in its practical relationship to human well-being.[4]

There is thus at the base of our inquiry a powerful set of paradoxical forces at work: even as the territorial state becomes more vulnerable to what takes place beyond its sovereign reach, it acquires a capability that generates many varieties of extraterritorial harm as side-effects of "normality." Such a loss of territorial moorings exposes the problem of political organization of international life from the perspective of state sovereignty.

It is difficult to avoid some degree of conceptual confusion at this point. If sovereignty inheres in the people, not the state, then a delegation of authority can be reinterpreted or even reclaimed by popular action. Sovereignty, according to democratic theory, is not to be automatically identified with the state; yet in modern practice—especially on matters of international policy—the state, even the democratic state, has increasingly operated without encountering substantial challenges from "below," and generally, without significant citizen participation. As such, statist understandings of sovereignty tend to prevail.

In the discussion that follows, the inquiry into "evasions" starts from the empirical reality that "sovereignty" is perceived to be concentrated in states. The recovery of sovereignty through the reinvigoration of democratic practice would work against the current tendency to identify sovereignty exclusively with the central governing process of territorial states enjoying international status. The notion of sovereignty rests on an overall congruence among authority, capability, territoriality, and loyalty. That is, at least conceptually, and to varying degrees existentially, states, often credibly, have claimed the authority and capacity to provide security and welfare for the people within state territory in exchange for expectations of loyalty and obedience by the population. However, such a practical adjustment has been combined with the sense that war and conflict provided both a foundation for protecting diversity (or difference) at acceptable cost and a legislative process for achieving change that was incidentally assimilated into the validating processes of international law by way of "the peace treaty" (even territorial changes achieved by "aggression" were given full legal effect). Today, especially under conditions of democracy where access to damaging information tends to be greater, the accumulating evidence of incongruence —the consequences of nuclear winter, global warming and ozone depletion, rainforest destruction, and air and ocean pollution—suggest, quite literally, a shattering of human prospects.

States will endeavor to fashion responses to these challenges. The state has long displayed a considerable capacity for resilience and adaptation. Leaders of states have already given expression to the growing need for cooperation, including self-limiting standards. The following account of the intergovernmental reaction to the harmful effects of ozone depletion is illustrative.

Once a consensus was formed as to the cause and effects of harm, an international agreement, the Montreal Protocol, was negotiated—swiftly and in a spirit of seriousness. Its central mandate is a commitment by treaty members, starting in 1989, to phase out by the end of the century half of those chemicals (especially chlorofluorocarbons) that deplete ozone. Subsequent to the negotiations but before the treaty was in force, acknowledgments were made in private and in public that even full implementation of such a drastic plan of action is woefully insufficient. Indeed, with the surprising help of Margaret Thatcher, a more stringent supplemental agreement of phasing out CFCs was accepted. Some corporate users have voluntarily agreed, beyond treaty requirements, to use more expensive substitutes for CFCs, and public officials have recently insisted that more rigorous standards are required, calling for a commitment to the total elimination of CFCs.[5]

The regime as negotiated, however, lacks an enforcement capability. The regulatory process will therefore test whether, in the face of vested economic interests unevenly distributed among state actors, it is possible to move toward an effective regime of prohibition for CFCs even in a situation where the evidence of severe harm arising from the prohibited activity is substantially uncontested. States may continue to define their own interests. If other states implement, then a failure to implement will not seem so serious; if others cheat, then additional cheating will not matter that much; and why should some states incur higher production costs than others? The calculus of separate interests is reinforced by the conviction that forgoing certain advantages merely shifts benefits to other state actors.

Can the aggregated thrust of separate and dissimilar perspectives be translated into policies that protect the well-being of the whole (which comprises all the parts, including itself) within existing structures? There is no assured answer at this point. There may never be a clear response. Multiple factors may shape a series of understandings, not necessarily fully consistent with one another. For example, how widely shared is the information about the probable gravity of the harm in the event of persistence in previous practices? How deferred in time is the harm likely to be? How great are the economic costs of adjustment? Can they be shifted, or otherwise offset? How aroused is both world public opinion and the particular climate of opinion in important countries? How easy is it to detect noncompliance with agreed standards? How likely are Third World countries to be guided by cost efficiency factors?

Ozone depletion may be an important test, both because of its own bearing on future health and well-being, and because it presents an adjustment challenge that is significant in its requirements, but not overwhelming. The test has several dimensions. Can commitments of compliance be monitored and upheld in the absence of enforcement mechanisms? Can the commitment be made responsive to the severity of the problem during an interval of time when successful adjustment is still possible? Or, is a regime of prohibition already too late, in the sense that the process of harmful effects cannot be reversed by the time the political will is mobilized to take cooperative action? These are some of the general issues to be considered if our concern is with the adjustment capabilities of the state system by way of cooperative action.[6] There is also the question as to whether the more difficult adjustments required to arrest global warming can be agreed upon, and then effectively implemented in sufficient time. Such an adjustment calls, for example, for a gradual shift away from burning fossil fuels as a primary source of energy for heating and transportation. The very nature of modern industrial society as it has evolved in the West is at issue here, as well as the degree to which it is necessarily associated with the structures of the modern state.

A further dimension of the resilience of states concerns the affective loyalties of peoples. Given the way state and society interact in the modern world, the state is seen, increasingly in the postcolonial era, as a necessary and desirable frame for advancing and safeguarding nationalist aspirations. Those nations with no state (Palestinians, Kurds, indigenous peoples) are exceptionally vulnerable to repressive tactics, as they are necessarily located within a state that is largely a vehicle for a rival "nation." Since all territory belongs to existing states, and the loss of territory is generally considered an unacceptable encroachment on sovereign rights, the existence of rival nations within boundaries is regarded by established governments as an active or latent threat. The effect of nationalist energies is to fragment the world political structure, but resistance of these energies means denials of self-determination and reliance on coercion.

Increasingly, the "self" in self-determination as a political conception is associated with nationhood, not with abstract juristic procedures of statehood. Of course, the idea of self-determination can be manipulated to restrict its relevance to existing territorial units as acknowledged by membership in the United Nations and by other criteria. Conferring "nationality" by legal decree, or by issuing a passport, does not displace or overcome existential feelings of nationalist identity. Emerging nationalisms seem, if anything, to be intensifying, although unevenly. It is primarily to satisfy nationalist aspirations that many people in different state settings are voluntarily risking their lives and displaying courage and commitment to alter existing political arrangements.

Thus many state structures are being challenged by nationalist movements. These challenges are generally resisted by reliance on coercion, for such resistance is considered a sovereign right if exercised within territory.[7] Nationalist movements, on the other hand, often seek the protective and assertive frameworks of the sovereign state, including a reliance on human rights. Although their motivation is concentrated on a territorial project, their political outlook often includes a sense of solidarity with other struggling nationalisms, a dependence for support on international institutions, and can in this sense be understood as a common quest for human rights *within* the existing statist structure. If our concern is with world order values—associated here with acting in response to a global ethos—then many of the various nationalisms are potentially capable of making positive contributions to an improvement of the relationship between human population groups and political institutions.

This contention can be specified further. First, by attaining statehood, certain national movements fulfill the process of self-determination of peoples, itself a normative accomplishment. Second, by increasing the congruence between nation and state, violent conflict would be reduced, and more political attention could presumably be devoted to the global agenda.

But there are severe structural problems. There are in 1990 more than eight hundred nationalist movements in the world, and fewer than two hundred states. Among these eight hundred claimants, many are small, weak, dispersed, and nonviable, but not necessarily resigned to their fate. There is no prospect that all of these nationalisms can be accommodated by grants of statehood. Territorial claims are often layered in such a way that the vindication of one nationalist destiny would displace another. As a result, sovereignty is difficult to evade, even if political self-determination is accepted as an authoritative norm. Its application necessarily involves tensions, contradictions, and conflict. Furthermore, states that are inherently incapable of mobilizing resources to meet the needs of their population present serious problems of viability even if their political structure is accepted as legitimate.

Could one imagine denationalized states as a basis for a more constructive role of sovereignty? Of course, most modern states already claim to be secular entities that confer nationality by legal, not ethnic, criteria, and claim that they govern on a nondiscriminatory basis.[8] This secularization of sovereignty, however, has not succeeded in extinguishing the primacy of nationalist identities or the perception of many existing states as repressive of ascendant forms of nationalism. Hence, unfortunately, at a time of long-range, global-scale challenge, it is likely that the political energies of many states and discontented nations will be focused on immediate struggles over autonomy, human rights, and contested movements for statehood.

What is the overall prospect for cooperative undertakings in a world menaced as a whole by disintegrative forces associated with the limits of "carrying capacity" and with an absence of sufficient capabilities to define and protect global interests? These limits must be tested and stretched; the intellectual and political task of a global integrative process is to identify these limits as they bear upon the capabilities of political actors in our world, a task premised on a shared affirmation of the value of sustaining, and even enhancing, the quality of life for the peoples of the world, including future generations. With such a normative premise, the collaborative work of an emergent global civilization would seek to expand the resources of both citizens and leaders by making public opinion more attuned to dangers and to possibilities for constructive action, by abolishing destructive polarities between "us" and "them" without losing the special qualities of diversity that enhance human existence.

States now participate cooperatively in wider political communities that fall into three general categories: (1) hegemonic "communities" in which most of the glue is supplied by the dominant state, and where the weaker participants have had their autonomy and legitimacy gravely compromised—to the extent that a governing elite in subordinate countries acquiesces in such arrangements; (2) alliance "communities," occurring especially during wartime, during periods of high international tension, and in reaction to expansionist drives of antidemocratic and imperialist states; and (3) cooperative "communities" in which the mutual benefits of economic integration or of common regimes for environmental protection and technical relations provide rational incentives for weakening state boundaries. These arrangements are extensions of ordinary diplomacy, fulfilling goals of state actors. Their scope is normally regional, motivated either by domination, fear of an enemy or calculations of gain. Such patterns do not, as yet, respond directly to either the affirmative reality of a global ethos or the more negative dangers associated with the deterioration of the global commons. From the perspective of world order values, such extended political communities can be either regressive or positive, depending on the circumstances. The normative effects can be complex, as is illustrated by debates about the impact of the "1992" plans for further economic integration in Western Europe or the recently concluded free trade treaty between the United States and Canada. Even when the economic effects suggest mutual benefit, for example, a weaker state that participates in such a widening process risks its autonomy and often gives up political space in which to explore alternative lines of policy.[9] In effect, wider frameworks do not necessarily represent a positive adjustment from the perspective of world order values. Quite the contrary, the most prevalent patterns of "suprastatism" often jeopardize some of the most desirable features of national identity that are preserved when states operate on a secure basis of legitimacy (that is, when they provide their people with human rights, political democracy, and overall security).

One focus of this effort to adapt political behavior to the global setting is to reinterpret sovereignty, weakening its preoccupation with conflict and threats to territorial space, without depreciating its role in safeguarding, to the extent possible, the autonomy of particular nations (or more problematically, of groups of nations joined together as a single state beneath a common flag). By changing perceptions about the character of the threat—that is, in perceiving danger in the currently enfeebled arrangements of "the whole" rather than in "the other" as enemy—the choice of instruments for upholding autonomy (i.e., the exercise of sovereignty) can change, especially if these instruments of political assertion can become denuclearized and demilitarized. Such a process centers, of course, on rethinking the meaning of "security"—shifting the locus from "national security" (part against part) to "common security" or "comprehensive security" (parts depend on the whole). It also involves, however, adapting the agenda and priorities of states so that they respond effectively to challenges directed at their citizenry. The assumptions here are decidedly selfish rather than altruistic, insofar as a response to ozone depletion in this instance is principally for the sake of national well-being. In any case, effective sovereignty here entails establishing an ambitious regime of prohibition, based on negotiation and cooperation among states, rather than on the typical understanding of threat as posed by an external enemy and as requiring, in response, counterthreats and military capabilities. It may be better to grasp the integrative tendencies of international life as a challenge to a militarized and highly spatial orientation toward sovereignty rather than to sovereignty per se. Territorial boundaries, defended by military capabilities, cannot guarantee a given society freedom from external penetration. Increasingly, even the most impressively protected boundaries cannot keep out unwanted drugs, persons, ideas, or polluting substances.

Part of the resilience of political life, in general, is the multiplicity of forms for acting in the world, and their interaction. Reverting again to the instance of ozone depletion, the role of independent voices is crucial in placing problems on the main political agenda, since vested interests are often mobilized to render either invisible or ineffectual challenges to current "profitable" practices. To initiate action requires an acknowledgment of the gravity of a problem, as well as enough time to overcome destructive patterns of practice. The existence of democratic space is indispensable, as is the protection of those who are the messengers of bad news. Individuals who break "the silence" of institutions are vulnerable to severe forms of abuse. Their voices are literally stilled by the oppressive reflex action of even democratic political traditions resorting to slogans such as "treason," "espionage," or "national security." When Mordechai Vanunu disclosed the extent of Israel's nuclear weapons program in 1986, for example, he breached Israel's official silence and was abducted abroad by Israeli secret agents, prosecuted, convicted of treason, and sentenced to eighteen years in jail. Thus, the state, by such bureaucratic reflexes, nullifies its own resilience by trying to constrain challenges to existing patterns of practice, especially those practices associated with "national security," the core of its militarist orientation toward sovereignty.

Exposing the state to such challenges as Vanunu's—on grounds of policy and practice, from within and without (through a kind of transnational democracy)—is part of what might enable sovereignty to become more adaptive, at least potentially. Constitutional conceptions such as "checks and balances," "separation of powers," "inalienable rights," and periodic elections to obtain "the consent of the governed" can be usefully engaged here, for they are part of an effort to make government more flexible in the face of changing conditions and values, but not so fluid as to be able too easily to transgress limits on the exercise of power. Notions of "civil disobedience," and more recently "civil resistance," underscore the relevance of conscience to the assessment of official policy. After World War II, in fact, the notion of moral assessment was given an obligatory character in the course of the Nuremberg trials, and subsequently in the formulation of a concept of responsibility to uphold international law in matters of war and peace, even as against direct commands by a head of state.[10] There are, then, many connections between revitalizing political democracy, positive sovereignty, and a relatively smooth transition to a more integrative, less territorial stage of international relations.

It is these "resources" of sovereignty, often unappreciated and even scorned and suppressed, that I will discuss under the phrase "the evasions of sovereignty." "Evasion" needs clarification: it refers here to political action by nonstate actors that addresses the agenda of global concerns. The implicit argument is both functional and normative, raising issues of practicality and desirability.

Patterns of evasion are increasing over time in frequency and scale for several reasons: the growing complexity and interrelatedness of international life; the failure of states to fashion sufficient responses on their own; and the fact that humanistic convictions in a contemporary context are often broader in scope than the values informing normal state action. One consequence of the cumulative effect of evasion-oriented action is to form political communities that cannot be encompassed by state boundaries and that do not yet appear on world maps designating membership in the world political system. What is emerging are transnational and intranational linkages that build up a body of practice and engender new patterns of loyalty.

Patterns of Evasion

By patterns of evasion, I refer to a locus of action distinct from the state, but not necessarily in opposition to it. Indeed, many of the most ambitious patterns of evasion have been initiated and managed by concerted state action, including the formation and operation of the United Nations. Those who act within these patterns draw their inspiration, in part at least, from a nonterritorial outlook that embodies in some form a cosmopolitan ethos. Their intention or influence may be directed toward the state, and to this extent can be perceived as an additional or complementary resource by states confronted with challenges on a global scale. In this reinforcing role, patterns of evasion are an expression of the adjustment capabilities of states, and hence manifest the resilience of the state and the state system. As such, their relevance is mainly stabilizing, at least in the short run, and they can be regarded as efforts to fulfill the order-producing and justice-realizing potential of the state system.

But, as we shall see, these patterns of evasion are often ambiguous in intention and effect, and can highlight not only the strengths but the shortcomings of the state. The transformative implications of patterns of evasion can flow from interpretations of a global ethos that reject basic characteristics of the modern state. These include fundamental behavioral traits of statism—for instance, domestic jurisdiction, violence, and militarism; its basic organizational features—for instance, subordinating global claims to the assertion of territorial supremacy; and its psychopolitical priorities—for instance, favoring territorial and fragmentary loyalties and putting patriotism ahead of the global ethos. In this regard, it is natural to perceive the state in opposition to patterns of evasion, seeking to constrain, or even eliminate, such fields of action.

Both perceptions of reinforcing and antagonistic roles are accurate, making an overall evaluation of evasive tendencies confusing and controversial. The proper assessment of a particular "evasion" depends on a convincing interpretation of its project for the future and its actual role in relation to the state, as well as some judgment of its relation to world order values. To extend the argument, three principal patterns of evasion will be briefly discussed: evasions *across* boundaries (transnational); evasions *within* boundaries (internal); and evasions *beyond* boundaries (supranational).

Evasions across boundaries

Let us now try to indicate a concrete instance of "evasion"—the Great Peace Journey (GPJ), conceived and implemented in the 1980s by a group of Swedish women, and culminating in a First Global Popular Summit held at the United Nation Headquarters in New York City during several days in late September 1988. As a tactical mechanism, the GPJ posed to governments belonging to the United Nations five questions embodying the ideals of the Charter—on matters of nuclear weaponry, foreign bases, disarmament, arms sales, development assistance, and governmental accountability under international law.[11] The composers of the questions adopted the formulation, "Would your government agree if all other governments agree . . . ?" Multinational delegations traveling throughout the world attempted to obtain "Yes" or "No" responses from the most prominent government representatives to whom they were able to arrange access, which ultimately included several heads of state and senior ministers. In the course of three years, most major countries were visited, more than a hundred in all, with "Yes" responses obtained from ninety-one. The organizers were aware that these responses were not in themselves real political commitments, but only endorsements of a common and hypothetical vision of one understanding of the measures needed to overcome the militarism, tensions, and mass poverty of present forms of geopolitics.

While the GPJ questions gave embodiment to one conception of the path to a peaceful, just, and sustainable world, the main impulse of the project was to reverse two features of modern political participation: the passivity of the citizenry in relation to the attitude of foreign governments on issues of world policy, and the presumed territorial character of state/society relations. GPJ proceeded on the basis of transnational democratic convictions, asserting that governments in an interdependent world were accountable not just to their own citizens but to all peoples, and to other governments and international institutions as well. In effect, by their action the entire planet, including those portions governed by principles of sovereign control, was converted into a global commons whose well-being was the responsibility of all peoples.

The GPJ was aware of its dual role: to motivate governments to renew and express their attachment to a vision of a more desirable world order, and to expose the extent of their unwillingness even to affirm the imperative of drastic global reform. More to the point, the GPJ devoted a considerable portion of its limited resources and energies to working with local and regional peace groups and grassroots initiatives, both to build a global network of activists and to establish a foundation for a *transnational* political process. This process combined local, regional, and global priorities, and was kept coherent by the vision of transforming "Yes" answers into a "Yes" world.

The GPJ by itself does not possess the means to transform world order or even to evade sovereignty. Its main "weapon" is to mount verbal, symbolic, and normative challenges to established forms of state power and militarism. At the same time, GPJ is exploring and prefiguring a new sovereignty-evading politics: a community of adherents that is transnational; a commitment to nonviolent practice; an emphasis on feminist insight and leadership; a combining of "gentle anger" with songs of celebration, with flowers and art; and an image of peace that encompasses social justice and ecological priorities. For such adherents, territoriality is not synonymous with loyalty, nor does an outsider lack standing to challenge governments. The delegations that circled the globe included regional and extraregional members, making the double point that there persists a special relationship of rights and duties to one's government (citizens should expect greater access and accountability from their own government), but that in a planetary context all people everywhere have a right to seek out any government to act for peace, justice, and environmental quality.

Another apparent "evasion" of sovereignty is related to the use of information as a base of power. Groups like Amnesty International and SIPRI gather information on crucial issues of international policy, build a reputation for integrity, and then disseminate materials that speak to policy issues with a certain transnational authority. The potency of such actors arises, in part, because the allegations of governments can often be dismissed as propaganda or ideological slander, whereas these transnationally funded and staffed associations disseminate their information across boundaries. Part of the effectiveness of such information arises because virtually all modern governments are concerned about their normative reputation at home and abroad. Governments do not want to be perceived as perpetrators of torture or as suppliers of forbidden weaponry (for example, biological or chemical weaponry), and therefore exposure by an objective source is itself a sanction, and even a deterrent. The strength of the deterrent in any given instance is difficult to gauge, however, since governments are reluctant to acknowledge the effect of moral or legal censure, especially when it exerts influence.

Often transnational information is used by activists to put pressure on particular governments to take action against a pariah state. The antiapartheid campaign is an excellent example. Without transnational networks with access to information damaging to the South African regime, it would be impossible to mount an antiapartheid campaign throughout the world. This is especially true in the United States and Great Britain, where patterns of economic and strategic interests are linked to maintaining the status quo. A related initiative can be identified in efforts by groups seeking to achieve improved standards of corporate accountability, for example in transnational campaigns to boycott products. The recurrent campaign against Nestlé's for its effort to promote infant formula in impoverished regions of Africa is illustrative.

Sovereignty is also "evaded" by transnational environmental groups that disseminate information about and offer symbolic resistance to nuclear testing, to whaling and sealing, and to activities dangerous for the future of polar regions. Greenpeace is the best known transnational actor in the environmental sector. Its effectiveness is difficult to assess or measure, but its obstructive activities often capture the imagination of peoples throughout the world and win their gratitude for opposing practices that states carry out, or allow, beneath the banner of sovereignty.

States may clearly feel threatened by such transnational groups. French official complicity in the operation that destroyed Greenpeace's ship *The Rainbow Warrior* while docked in Auckland, New Zealand, constituted an extraterritorial act of war against a nonviolent group of militant activists motivated by a global ecological ethos. The ship's activist crew was pursuing tactics that were dramatic and confrontational, challenging both the capacity and legitimacy of state action, especially as it relates to nuclear testing in the Pacific. It is this pattern of motivation, reinforced by antistate militancy, that connects such forms of "activism" with more cosmopolitan conceptions of political identity.

We can refer to a wide range of transnational undertakings of a more or less specific character. Their programs of action and tactics help shape responses by states, as well as perceptions as to whether the "evasion" is tolerable or not. These perceptions are also closely linked to varying attitudes toward democratic opposition and to the role of civil society. If the transnational initiative challenges state sovereignty in the national security sphere, responses are likely to be hostile and suppressive. Even democracies with decent human rights records claim virtually absolute control in this sphere, including their prerogative to restrict information via procedures of secrecy, classification, and espionage laws. In the setting of nuclear weapons policy this tendency is maximized.[12]

To the extent that the traditional prerogatives and legitimacy of a state are not called into question, political democracies tend to be generally tolerant of criticism and opposition. However, to the degree that controversy exists about those prerogatives, the transnational identity of an initiative can be used to imply a lack of patriotism on the part of citizens who join in the activity. Often "laws" are invoked by governments to constrain transnational initiatives that challenge state policy. The imprisonment of members of the sanctuary movement by the U.S. government is a case in point. The tactics of the sanctuary movement involve using the established institutional resources of civil society, especially churches, to protect the human rights of vulnerable people. The particular beneficiaries of this initiative were the thousands of refugees from El Salvador threatened with deportation from the United States and with persecution upon return to their country of origin. The imprisonment of sanctuary militants was noted critically in 1988 in the Annual Report of Amnesty International, a respected publication that monitors human rights abuses throughout the world. Such antigovernmental criticism amounts to a normative endorsement on a transnational level of the sanctuary movement. The degree of latitude allowed by governments to such evasions depends on the issue, the precariousness of the existing political arrangement, and the political style adopted by state leaders, especially their sensitivity to international and domestic criticism. Long-range abstract issues with less immediate policy implications tend to be more tolerated, even if their substance is subversive of state power, than do transnational challenges to concrete policy that is already in place.

Evasions within boundaries

Here the denial of sovereignty can be direct or indirect, but its essence consists in acts by citizens against the governing process in their own state. The initiative can have as its goal the change of a given policy or a much broader revision of official policy, practices, and even institutional arrangements (for example, a call for constitutional amendment or even for a constitutional convention). The focus in this inquiry is upon evasions within that respond to the call of a global ethos, and circumvent to some degree control over civil society by the state.

These evasions can involve the formation of permissible political vehicles for the promotion of a global ethos, as in the example of the Green Parties in West Germany, Sweden, and elsewhere. The status of this phenomenon is problematic, especially in regard to whether the particular green political formation is committed to a reforming or transforming mandate, or some mixture.[13]

We have referred to the Vanunu case earlier, an instance of evasion generating a suppressive backlash by the state in the form of prosecution for treason. Vanunu disclosed sensitive information—previously publicly disseminated in its broad contours—on Israel's nuclear weapons program, but in an atmosphere of persisting tension that justified for many Israeli observers strong procedures to limit dissent and opposition.[14] Most expressions of sympathy and appreciation for Vanunu derive from outside of Israel, especially from transnational sources avowedly dedicated to a stateless global ethos (e.g., Vanunu was the recipient of the Right Livelihood Award of the Danish Peace Foundation, and received nominations for the Nobel Peace Prize).

The encouragement of whistle-blowers in the modern state seems of great benefit even if it appears as an "evasion." Society is given information about matters that may concern the well–being of its members in fundamental respects. Secrecy is often used by governments to hold back information from their own citizenry that undermines societal confidence in official competence and integrity. As the effects of interdependence continue to stretch the capacities of states to, or beyond, their limits, an increasing official impulse to withhold damaging information is likely to ensue, making evasions more functionally necessary than ever before—both as a safety valve or early warning system, and, more fundamentally, as an exposure of structural defects in the governing process.

Often the circumstances are mixed. We now know that in several instances governments have withheld from people in their own society damaging information about nuclear reactor accidents and about problems of public health and safety, often over a long stretch of time.[15] We also know that local officials have failed to inform national officials of hazards, for fear that their own competence would be questioned, as in the case of serious nuclear reactor accidents at the Savannah River Plant, where nuclear weapons were produced.[16] Yet the implications can be read narrowly or broadly, either as showing the need to expose specific harm at particular reactors or to confirm those who oppose reliance on the particular technology.

The underlying observation holds: when legitimacy rests partly on competence, and competence is eroded by new challenges, then the impulse to deny the magnitude of the challenge grows strong. Those that question the denial will be generally treated as "enemies" even if their intentions and the effects of their actions are constructive. Often they must accept personal costs and risks to get the story out. The life of Karen Silkwood is emblematic of these costs and risks, but also of the importance of the information.

Evasions beyond boundaries

There are two forms of "evasion" at issue here: behavioral patterns located beyond the reach of a state that impact significantly upon it, e.g., a nuclear accident in a foreign country or the overseas production for export of hard drugs; and transfers of authority to international institutions and regimes, e.g., entrusting regional and global dispute settlement procedures with certain categories of claims, as in establishing international regimes to prohibit commercial whaling and to set quotas on "research."

The first type of evasion involves a loss of control by states in the face of many varieties of interdependence, including those that threaten health, agriculture, climate, and financial stability. The rise of these evasive patterns tends to foster perceptions of limits to state power, as well as to erode claims of competence and adequacy. The magnitude of evasiveness encourages the search for alternative, or at least supplemental, forms of order. For instance, Bangladesh is especially vulnerable to the effects of global warming because it possesses densely settled low-lying coastal lands, yet its contribution to the greenhouse effect is virtually nil. Bangladesh's sovereignty is of no help if it is conceived in territorial terms. Only by entering external arenas to strengthen attempts to reduce reliance on fuels that produce carbon dioxide could Bangladesh apply its sovereign status to limit the damage done to its society by global warming.

In this regard the first form of evasion leads to the second form—that is, states use their discretion to extend their reach by transferring authority to institutions and regimes. Such "exercises" of sovereignty are also "evasions" in the sense that the state gives up discretion and transfers authority in the hope of restoring claims to competence and safeguarding legitimacy. Only by institutionalizing adequate nonterritorial regimes of cooperation can territorial well-being be safeguarded.

Conclusion

As interdependence grows more salient, the competence and confidence of the state tends to be eroded unless it can facilitate the development of innovative and imaginative formats for problem solving. In a sense, the state must learn to get out of its own way if, over time, it is to retain and regain the full plenum of its legitimacy. Cumulatively, however, this sort of adaptation is likely to be consistent with a global political system that appears far less state-centric. The three categories of "evasion" considered above are producing new allegiances and establishing nascent political communities of local, transnational, regional, and global scope. Paradoxically, in order to remain effective, the state must give way to a variety of such alternative ordering frameworks; the more willingly and forcefully it does so, the more its legitimate sphere of authority can be sustained.

The state has demonstrated a remarkable degree of resilience over the several centuries of its existence. Whether it can significantly reorient its sense of sovereign prerogative from space (protecting territory) to time (contributing to a viable and desirable future) is uncertain in the extreme. Only if specific persons, acting on behalf of the state, can develop the sort of understanding and backing needed, can states be led away from their boundary-obsessed territorialism to a more formless contouring of authority that responds to the bewildering array of dangers and opportunities that exist today in the world.

To make this shift at all viable requires an active civil society that gives its citizens "the space" to explore "adjustments," including transnational initiatives, and that depends on the secure establishment of human rights and democracy, including the internal accountability of leaders for violations of international law. Citizens need an enforceable right to a lawful foreign policy if initiatives from below are going to be protected in sensitive times. The natural flow of political life in response to the agenda of global concerns is to encourage "evasions" as a matter of deliberate tactics. Is the state flexible enough to preside over its own partial dissolution and circumvention? This is the veiled question that underlies an inquiry into the overall effects of "evasions" of sovereignty. It would help us decide whether these evasions will gradually crystallize awareness of a global ethos into an effectively global civilization. Such a process would almost certainly substantially reintegrate and redistribute sovereign authority in a manner quite different than the neat territorial allocations of the modern state system that took shape in Europe over the course of several centuries.

If "sovereignty" persists as an important political idea, its content is likely to grow decentered and dispersed, although horizontal linkages of a variety of nonstate actors and formats could establish regional, transnational, and global capabilities of almost indefinite variety, complexity, and potency. An emergent global civilization (of indefinite normative contour) does not at all imply the extinction or the obsolescence of the territorial state or the state system, but it does appear to necessitate challenging the earlier statist monopoly over the symbols and practices of sovereignty that has existed for the past several hundred years.

Notes

1. Lewis Lapham, "Leviathan in Trouble," *Harper's*, Sept. 1988.
2. The quality of political independence has become quite confusing. Third World countries are recipients of modern arms, and have an increased political and military capability to resist overt forms of intervention. At the same time, the interdependent character of international life makes weaker states especially vulnerable to various forms of unwanted penetration.
3. See Richard Ashley, "The Poverty of Neorealism," in Robert O. Keohane, ed., *Neorealism and its Critics* (New York: Columbia University Press, 1986), pp. 255-300.
4. For a more extended argument along these lines see Robert Jay Lifton and Richard Falk, *Indefensible Weapons: The Political and Psychological Case Against Nuclearism* (New York: Basic Books, 1983); see also, of course, Jonathan Schell, *The Fate of the Earth* (New York: Knopf, 1982).
5. *New York Times*, Sept. 27, 1988, p. A20; see also Cynthia Pollock Shea, "Protecting Life on Earth: Steps to Save the Ozone Layer," *Worldwatch Paper* no. 91 Worldwatch Institute, 1988.
6. In theory, there are no impediments to agreements by states to establish supranational institutions with funding and police authority, or to strip themselves of capabilities and prerogatives. In practice, states have been reluctant to diminish their discretionary space, despite the weight of functional considerations. The main obstacles to structural adaptations of sovereignty are best explored in the domain of psycho-politics.
7. The international law of human rights is an explicit intrusion on the domestic

territorial authority of states in the sensitive area of governmental treatment of citizens and of other persons subject to jurisdiction. The intrusion is mainly symbolic, although it can have consequences as when foreign governments withhold benefits or impose sanctions. In its trading relations with the Soviet Union the United States has for years tied most-favored-nation treatment to the issue of the Soviets' alleged failure to allow freer Jewish emigration.

8. Religion, class, race also provide a governing elite with the basis for coercive and exploitative rule that discriminates against excluded minorities.

9. Among such alternative policy paths are the following: neutrality and nonalignment; "soft" energy paths; smaller economic units with various forms of social accounting.

10. For a fuller discussion of the Nuremberg tradition see Richard A. Falk, Robert Jay Lifton, and Gabriel Kolko, eds., *Crimes of War* (New York: Random House, 1971), pp. 73–176.

11. The text of the GPJ questions is as follows:

1. Are you willing to initiate national legislation which guarantees that your country's defense forces, including "military advisers," do not leave your territory for military purposes (other than in United Nations peacekeeping forces)
    • if all other Members of the United Nations undertake to do the same?
2. Are you willing to take steps to ensure that the development, possession, storage and employment of mass-destruction weapons, including nuclear weapons, which threaten to destroy the very conditions necessary for life on this earth, are forbidden in your country
    • if all other Members of the United Nations undertake to do the same?
3. Are you willing to take steps to prevent your country from allowing the supply of military equipment and weapons technology to other countries
    • if all other Members of the United Nations undertake to do the same?
4. Are you willing to work for a distribution of the earth's resources so that the fundamental necessities of human life, such as clean water, food, elementary health care and schooling, are available to all people throughout the world?
5. Are you willing to work to ensure that any conflicts, in which your country may be involved in the future, will be settled by peaceful means of the kind specified in Article 33 of the United Nations Charter, and not by the use or threat of force?

12. See Richard Falk, *The Promise of World Order* (Philadelphia: Temple University Press, 1987), pp. 77–116.

13. For a wider assessment of the progressive potential of environmentally based political coalitions see Robert C. Paehlke, *Environmentalism and the Future of Progressive Politics* (New Haven: Yale University Press, 1989).

14. For a descriptive account, see *Israel's Bomb. The First Victim: The Case of Mordechai Vanunu* (Nottingham: Spokesman Books, 1988).

15. For news accounts see *New York Times* Oct. 1–3, 1988.

16. Cf. *New York Times*, Oct. 5, 1988, pp. A1, A26.

5

Sovereignty as Transformative Practice

Lester Edwin J. Ruiz

Integration, Fragmentation, and Unevenness

The question of sovereignty remains especially critical for peoples and states of the Third World. Liberation movements have anchored their struggles for freedom and justice against colonialism and neocolonialism on the principle of state sovereignty. As the experience of the Non-Aligned Movement has shown, states have secured their claims to self-determination against Northern hegemonies on the assumption that state sovereignty is a morally defensible, even nonnegotiable foundation. Yet, the practices of social and political transformation in the last twenty years, especially in the Third World, have begun to cast doubt on the absolute claims of sovereignty as a principle for grounding and ordering human life. For my present purposes, two sources of doubt have been especially important.

First, the absolute claim to state sovereignty asserted by the dominant powers has received relentless criticism from within the state system itself. Implicit in the quest for a new international economic order, for example, is not only a recognition of the claims of the so-called underdeveloped nations to an equitable share of the resources of the earth, but also a repudiation of what is perceived to be domination under the guise of, and in the name of, state sovereignty.[1] Second, from the margins of the state system, the practices of what R. B. J. Walker identifies as critical social movements—particularly those that cut across political, economic, religious, and gender lines—challenge the dominant logic of statist political practice, as well as underscore the poverty of prevailing ideas in a system of states that is unable to offer meaningful alternatives to the dilemmas of present political theorizing and practice.[2] By refusing the boundaries of conventional institutional politics, and by generating political practices that are often local in origin yet global in trajectory, these movements pose an antisystemic challenge to forms of social and political life rooted in state sovereignty.[3]

Analysts who seek to explore these processes are confronted by at least three difficult and interrelated problems. In the first place, historical conditions have changed. International finance capital, the worldwide reach of multinational corporations, and modern science and technology are generating movements toward global integration and claims about a global commons and even a universalizing humanity. At the same time, the proliferation of states, peoples, and movements, often local in orientation, is generating a countervailing movement not only toward fragmentation but also to an appreciation of plurality, locality, and particularity. These new patterns of integration and fragmentation challenge the resolution of the relation between universality and particularity that is inscribed in the principle of state sovereignty.

In the second place, state sovereignty has become an increasingly contested concept. While a general agreement holds that the notion of sovereignty embodies a claim that "there is a final and absolute political authority in the community,"[4] agreement is decreasing even at the theoretical level as to what constitutes political authority, in whom it resides, and what its limits and prerogatives are. This lack of agreement emerges, in part, from the different theoretical and practical contexts in which the notion of sovereignty has come to be situated—contexts that are themselves undergoing profound transformations. When appropriated, that is historicized, by peoples and movements, the principle of state sovereignty is often severed from its moorings in seventeenth century metaphysics. The way is opened both to its use as a principle of critique—as it often is in the hands of revolutionary movements—and to its transformation into an historical principle and thus into an Archimedean point from which all "sovereignties" are evaluated. Both the reification of and critical challenge to the principle of state sovereignty provide grounds on which serious questions about the nature and character of political community, of human relationship, and of social and political change, may be raised.

In the third place, it is difficult to speak about the notion of state sovereignty given what elsewhere has been called the "unevenness of development." The problem of unevenness does not lie only in the recognition of the widely different contexts and situations that give rise to different interpretations of common symbols and myths. Nor does the problem of unevenness emerge only as a question of the redistribution of resources, whether of a theoretical or practical character. The problem of unevenness also raises uncertainties about the commensurability, applicability, and translatability of questions about political identity and community, questions that cannot be resolved by retreating into pregiven definitions of sovereignty. The "grand narrative" of state sovereignty, elusive at best and illusory at worst, is being challenged by multiple historical narratives.[5] In fact, the question of state sovereignty is thoroughly practical, and must be comprehended at the level of specific social and political practices.

In my view, it is not possible to examine the contemporary significance of state sovereignty without attending to these problems. It is thus necessary to refuse the temptation to start with a grand narrative of state sovereignty and to examine the social and political practices in which the notion of state sovereignty has come to dwell. The interrogation of sovereignty must be contextualized.[6]

Contextualizing the Interrogation of Sovereignty

Political observers have suggested that the Philippines is the quintessential Third World. Indeed, the Philippine experience encompasses a number of historical processes and structural transformations that so-called Third World states have undergone: colonialism/imperialism under Spain (1521–1898) and the United States (1898–1945); a brief period of independence (1945–1972); and a process of political modernization ranging from liberal democratic rule (1945–1972), elite authoritarian liberalism (1972–1986), a popular democratic interlude (February–November 1986), to the restoration of authoritarian rule in the form of bureaucrat authoritarianism (November 1986–). Largely parallel to these political events, a sequence of patterns of economic development/underdevelopment can be distinguished: feudalism; laissez-faire capitalism; bureaucrat ("crony") capitalism; dependent peripheral capitalism. Finally, there is an ongoing nationalist and democratic "people's war," as well as the Muslim secessionist movement in the south.[7] Viewed primarily as a metaphor, the Philippine experience can provide insight not only into the experience of the so-called Third World, but especially into the contours and dynamics of state sovereignty itself.

The so-called February 1986 Revolution—which must be understood in relation to the larger history of the peoples of the Philippines—left a contentious and ambiguous legacy that is reflected in the language that has been used in political analysis. Those who have called it a revolution, in particular Cory Aquino's Revolution, underscore the overturning of what seemed then to be an entrenched dictatorship as a direct result of "people power."[8] Those who have called it an uprising or an insurrection affirm the same emergence of "people power" but qualify it as only a temporary, and tenuous, unity around antifascist sentiments.[9] Still others have called it a coup, emphasizing the overthrow of the Marcos dictatorship and the ascendancy of the Aquino government as nothing more than a change of guard within the same political, economic, and cultural structures, which have their origins in the colonial and neocolonial experience of the peoples of the Philippines.[10] Of course there are also those who have remained faithful, if not to the Marcoses themselves, then to the legacy of "constitutional authoritarianism" whose *basso firmo* is statist, bureaucrat capitalist, and militarist.[11] For them the Cory Aquino Revolution is a betrayal of their political, economic, and cultural interests, a real hindrance to the creation of a polity dominated by elites and characterized by the peaceful, if competitive, coexistence of clans as the generative center of social and political life. Closely related to this faction are those who refuse to subordinate their military prerogatives to civilian authority.[12]

These different terminologies are significant. They embody logics or metanarratives that shape an understanding not only of past and present, but also of the prospects for social change and a future of justice and freedom in the Philippines. In addition they shape social and political practices and trajectories, symbolize the rather complex discursive terrain that characterizes Philippine politics, and imply options for furthering political activity. Thus, those who understood the events of February 1986 as part of Cory's Revolution today continue to support her, if critically, believing that she represents a perspective that can move the Philippines beyond the Marcos legacy. The logic of their analyses revolves around the liberal democratic legacy of the Aquino government that privileges the Corazón Aquino of late 1985 and early 1986 as the paradigm for social change. The growing authoritarianism of the regime is explained as an aberration, the overtaking of Corazón Aquino by conniving loyalists and entrenched militarists. And as if to add insult to injury, the logic relegates "people power" to nothing more than a source of legitimation for the state apparatus.

In contrast, those who understood the events of February 1986 as an uprising or an insurrection within the larger political terrain of revolution have abandoned—at least as early as the infamous 1986 assassination of the labor leader Rolando Olalia, and as late as the massacre at Mendiola Bridge of nineteen protesters in early 1987—any substantive hope in the capacity of the Aquino government to carry forward the process of social change. The surpassing of the Marcos regime's record of human rights violations, the inability to effectively address the external debt, the difficulty of controlling landlord interests that defend an iniquitous land tenure system, and now what appears to be the acceptance of the retention of the U.S. bases, serve only to confirm, proponents of such a perspective argue, the restoration of an authoritarian regime within a still semifeudal, semicolonial political economy. Advocates of this perspective see the "broad Filipino masses," particularly the organized poor who are oppressed, as the real heirs to the nationalist and democratic revolution, compared with which the Cory Revolution was, at best, an inspiring respite, and at worst, an insidious interruption. Those who oppose the present government seek to establish a broadly based, highly disciplined, and profoundly committed movement in order to advance a national democratic revolution.

In my view, what is occurring in the Philippines today is, in the main, an attempt by ruling elites to restore the tradition of liberalism inherited from the West as the foundation for Philippine social and political life. This political tradition valorizes the state as the *locus politicus*, upholds the "possessive," self-interested bourgeois individual as the primary unit of politics, and understands the Western democracies as the exclusive bearers of modernity.[13] In the face of increasing domestic and global contradictions, these liberals opt for the more authoritarian legacies of liberalism, conflating Hobbesian and Lockean logics in order to defend and preserve the status quo. This process of restoring a liberal authoritarian regime is happening in the face of a growing resistance movement that includes nationalists, communist and Marxist revolutionaries, Muslim secessionists, indigenous peoples struggling for self–governance, and an "open Left" mass movement composed of labor, peasants, women, youth, and professionals.

This fundamental political contradiction between the ruling elites and the broad resistance movements, particularly those that are characterized by a liberal democratic and national democratic orientation, underscores not only the contentious character of social and political discourse, but, more importantly, problematizes the meaning of state sovereignty. Indeed, the widening gap between ruler and ruled, the disintegration of the relationship between state and society, calls into question those fundamental claims about legitimacy, authority, tradition, and people that are formalized in the principle of state sovereignty. At least at the level of social and political practice, sovereignty is less a question of the "right of a people to self-determination" and more a practice that gathers together fundamental presuppositions about the character of human dwelling, that is, about how peoples are constituted as historical and political communities.

Legitimacy, Authority, Tradition, People

The relationship between legitimacy and sovereignty is especially problematic in periods of political crisis. One of the first challenges posed to the Marcos regime, for example, was a twofold questioning: first, of its claim of political legitimacy, and second, of its promise of economic development.[14] For liberal democrats, this question of legitimacy, or the normative (legal) acceptability of a political institution or leadership, is based on a particular interpretation of the "rule of law" that emphasizes a juridical and procedural perspective. Thus, critics of Marcos, and to a lesser extent those of the Aquino government, questioned his interpretation of the law while presupposing the normativity of law as such, casting suspicion especially on Marcos' attempt to identify the "rule of law" with the laws of his regime.[15] While this reveals a serious legitimation crisis, it remains a partial challenge insofar as it assumes the unquestionability of the rule of law. The notion implies an acceptance of a particular vision of how political life should be organized, namely, that state and society must be subject to the law, which is the objective expression of the "will of the people." Thus, the question of whether or not a positive relationship exists between the law and the people does not arise. Where the law has become an Archimedean point, critical appraisal of the adequacy of the rule of law is closed off.

This juridico-procedural perspective was gradually tempered by an extraparliamentary cry for substantive change. The challenge that the Aquino opposition then posed to Marcos was based on the conviction that legal considerations must give way to the larger commitment to the will of the people. The so-called February 1986 Revolution was an expression of this conviction. Formal/procedural legitimacy was relocated within the context of substantive legitimacy. Constitutional legitimacy, it was argued, rests on the will of the people. Yet, this view is also open to criticism. While it permitted challenges to the Marcos regime in the name of the people, its commitment to the rule of law still constrained the search for alternatives within the framework of the rule of law itself. For the Marcos regime, and not surprisingly for the Aquino regime as well, legitimacy was not only a function of consent and/or representation, but it was interpreted as a condition of order.[16] Thus, when the Aquino government invited the so-called insurgents to rejoin the wider society in early 1986, it insisted that this return be premised on the adherence to the rule of law, the interpretation of which was the prerogative of the new government. This meant the delegitimization of genuine criticism and the de facto acceptance of the government's legitimacy—the very issue that was at stake for the so-called insurgents.

In contrast, the National Democratic Front (NDF), the main revolutionary formation in the Philippines, has consistently challenged the legitimacy of both the Marcos and Aquino governments. Their lack of legitimacy, the NDF argues, rests on the betrayal by both governments of the peoples of the Philippines, particularly by their adherence to antinationalist, imperialist, and bureaucrat-capitalist principles. Going beyond the liberal democratic notion of constitutional legitimacy, the NDF challenges the legitimacy of these governments on the basis of their politico-economic illegitimacy. Such a challenge frees the question of legitimacy from its juridico-procedural moorings and seeks to locate it on the substantive level. It identifies the importance of the politico-economic structure for the legitimacy of any regime, thereby underscoring how the state-society relation—the proper relationship between political legitimacy, political economy, and the people—is the critical element of all claims to legitimacy, and consequently, to the principle of state sovereignty.

Questions about legitimacy lead on to questions about political authority: the triadic relationship among the people, their government, and the normative goals they share. Indeed, it may be argued that the crisis of legitimacy is symptomatic of a fundamental loss of political authority. When critics of the Aquino government ask on what basis it continues to rule, presupposing thereby an understanding of legitimacy that goes beyond its identification with the existing government, they are challenging both the legal basis of its claim and, more importantly, the very relationship between the Aquino government and the people in the context of the commonly held values of the nation.

For liberal democrats, authority is meaningful only if it is acknowledged. Something is authoritative insofar as it is able to freely generate a person's confidence and commitment on the basis of its normative claims. This is the sense in which authority is said to reside in the people and to be vested in the law. Authority, in other words, is not primarily the prerogative of a ruler but a relationship of participation, authorization, and representation between ruler and ruled. Much like "constitutional authoritarianism," liberal democrats identify this relationship as being structured by the juridico-procedural mechanism of the law and its underlying legal mentality. Unlike the Marcos government, however, which emphasized authorization, the Aquino government emphasizes representation. Both locate the center of authority, be they domestic or international. State sovereignty becomes the Archimedean point against which competing claims are evaluated. Statist logic ultimately remains unchallenged.

Central to both the liberal democratic and national democratic conceptions of authority is the notion that political authority is relational and dialogical. Authority is the giving and receiving of confidence and commitment between persons who recognize and affirm a common community; it is not an independent variable that creates or imposes the values that constitute this common community. The dissolution of this triadic relationship signals the loss of authority. Legitimacy, in brief, is conferred by authority, not the reverse. Authority precedes the law. Relationality precedes authority. Legitimacy rests ultimately on the existence of a political community with commonly held values.

The question of political authority cannot be abstracted from the reality and concept of a tradition. Traditions, as Hans-Georg Gadamer understands them, are the horizoning prejudices that shape and guide human thought, feeling, and action.[17] They provide the sources for norms and values within the political community. For this reason, the question of authority is fundamentally a question of tradition. Here, jurisprudence, religion, culture —the cumulative historical experience of peoples—become the critical sources of authority.

Moreover, the question of tradition is inextricably related to the question of *the people*. This is not simply a matter of concretely specifying who embodies truth and gives consent, but also of defining the character and significance of the people: how peoples are constituted as historical and politi-cal communities. Thus, ideology, socioeconomic location, the peasant and proletarian interest, as well as constitutional law, bureaucracy, and political charisma—all of which involve claims about tradition—come to rest on the question of the people. As the Minjung theologians of Korea have insisted, traditions are borne by the people.[18] Fundamental assumptions and normative visions are embodied in political and historical communities. I want to suggest, against those who view tradition simply as dogma or orthodoxy, that in its widest sense tradition is politicized because it is borne by a people. As it is borne by a people, it becomes concrete reality; that is, more truly historical.

This question of the people has become especially difficult in the Philippine case because the fundamental presuppositions that have shaped Philippine society, and that have been institutionalized, are breaking down. Not simply a crisis of institutions, as both Marcos and Aquino supporters want to argue, the question of the people has to do with what it means to be *subjects of history*. Perhaps, more important, it is a profound crisis of the meaning of community, a crisis of political identity.

The precise contours of the crisis of political identity are complex. In the 1950s and 1960s, claims about political identity were formulated in relation to nationalism. Against the imposition of a Western bourgeois vision, nationalists like Renato Constantino counterposed values rooted in the rich and diverse heritage of the peoples of the Philippines. They emphasized how Philippine historical experience was largely a struggle against Westernization and modernization. More recently, Reynaldo Ileto, radicalizing Constantino's nationalist argument, has stressed a rather different understanding of political identity, one more concerned with the interplay of religious traditions and political projects, particularly among peoples who have traditionally fallen outside the orbit of the dominant Western liberal democratic assumptions of the ruling elites. For these peoples, sovereignty as self-determination is alien to their experience; their primary political reality was community and participation.

In the late 1960s and early 1970s, the question of the people was articulated in terms of the question of development and liberation. Presupposing normative values of humanity and community and drawing from the social teachings of the church, the notion of people was posited in terms of the values of equality and participation, setting the religio-cultural perspective of people within a modernizing politico-economic horizon. Identity became understood in terms of *populus* rather than *ethnos*. This dilemma is especially important for the indigenous Cordillera peoples of the northern Philippines, and the Muslims of the south. Here, the gradual transformation of their political horizon from a religio-moral to a politico-economic one—effected through the practices of modernity carried by the dominant culture—tends to eclipse aspects of human identity that naturally dwell in the religio-cultural domain. In many instances, the logic of modernization has overcome the latter, rendering human identity truncated and incomplete. The struggles of indigenous peoples for self-determination and sovereignty are often struggles against what Mircea Eliade called, in another context, the eclipse of the sacred.

With the intensification of the crisis brought about both by the United States and the Marcos government, and the shifting trends in the global political economy, the question of people was radicalized into the question of liberation, already presupposed, though not thematized, in the earlier discussions of development. Developmentalism was repudiated, and the centrality of the politico-economic understanding of people was established. This understanding of people, drawing much of its inspiration from

Philippine Marxism, and set within a liberation perspective tempered by a non-Western, indigenous proletarian/populist commitment, led to a radicalization of the crisis of political identity. While this understanding signified the rejection of the bourgeois interpretation of national self-determination, popular sovereignty, and liberty, it also affirmed a critical solidarity with the Marxist-Leninist-Maoist project of revolution.

It is precisely on this question of the people that liberal democrats and national democrats are most sharply divided. It is here, too, that the principle of state sovereignty reveals itself to be profoundly contested—despite political agreement on the centrality of the people and the shared sense of the need of social and political transformation. Indeed, there are real differences about who the people are, and therefore, what direction the process of social change must take. Who, for example, are the bearers of the possibility of transformation and how does fundamental change come into being?

On the one hand, for liberal democrats, claims about the people are largely understood in terms of citizenship, that is, in terms of individuals whose identities are constituted mainly through their rights and obligations vis-à-vis the state and that are guaranteed by law. "Parliamentary struggle" is the main paradigm for social change. On the other hand, for national democrats, *the people* is largely understood in terms of class formations: workers, peasants, petty bourgeoisie, national bourgeoisie, and indigenous peoples. As classes, most of these groups have been excluded not only from the decisionmaking process of the state, but more significantly, from the fruits of their labor that, together with their capacity to create and recreate species life, constitutes their identity. Thus, any fundamental change, national democrats have argued, must begin by affirming the constitutive character of these classes for social change, and by an unequivocal commitment to the transformation of the relations of production and reproduction, returning to these classes their original unity with the products of their labor. Since the majority of these classes, particularly the workers and peasants, have been systematically excluded from participation in the legal process, and since the ruling elites have consistently refused to share or surrender power, the main form of struggle for social change is armed revolution.

Thus, coming to a meaningful consensus about what or who the people are is a difficult task. Debate has emphasized two distinctive positions. Some have argued that the reality of people is to be construed mainly as primarily religio-cultural. Others insist on a politico-economic perspective. Perhaps more significantly, both positions have become wedded to assumptions about liberal democracy, as the ruling elites have demonstrated in their politics. In my view, the bifurcation is misconceived, and the uncritical appropriation of liberal democratic assumptions is dangerous. Reductionist construals of the people can lead to disastrous consequences, not least of which is the failure to comprehend the depth and multi-dimensional character of political identity. Moreover, an uncritical appropriation of liberal democracy is likely to reinforce the already profound domination of the state over society.

When ceasefire negotiations were held between the National Democratic Front and the Aquino government, for example, one of the reasons for the collapse of the talks was the declaration by the government that it was the sole possessor of legitimacy, and its insistence that the framework of the negotiations be what was then the 1986 Draft Constitution, thereby overtly asserting its legitimacy over the protests of large sectors of society. Similarly, one of the major obstacles to the satisfactory resolution of the ongoing struggles of the indigenous Cordillera peoples for autonomy in the north and the Muslim secessionist movement in the south is the insistence by the Aquino government, reminiscent of the attitude on autonomy advanced by the Marcos government, that the indigenous peoples respect the state's right to the region as public domain. In effect, this subordinates the indigenous peoples' right of ancestral domain to the state. The Bangsa Moro peoples, while divided into secessionists, autonomists, and pragmatists, are of one mind that their 450-year struggle for self-determination is grounded in the recognition of their particular culture as normative for political life. Like the Native Americans in the United States, the Dene in Canada, and the so-called aborigines of Australia, the Cordillera and Muslim peoples have a rich and diverse heritage different from the majority culture. They continue to insist that the state respect and recognize their right and obligation to organize their lives according to these traditions. State sovereignty, in brief, is re-stated as a question of identity.

Quite clearly, discussions of the meaning of state sovereignty in the Philippines, and I suspect in other Third World states, have revolved around the notion of state sovereignty as a question of legitimate public authority, grounded in the experience of a people struggling for freedom and justice. Consequently, appeals to self-determination and state sovereignty function less as a substantive definition of political identity and more as the site both for affirming the uniqueness of particular peoples and as a line of defense against hegemonies at the domestic and international levels. Since the state remains a crucial political actor—often the only bulwark against hegemonies at the international level—state sovereignty has almost invariably been construed within the parameters of statist logic. Moreover, this logic both expresses and is reinforced by those specifically modernist narratives that seek to overcome what Richard Bernstein has called the Cartesian Anxiety.[19] Against ambiguity and uncertainty, just as against the proliferation of identities and political communities, state sovereignty promises order, a promise that ruling elites are quite willing to fulfill.

Transformative Practice and the Future of Sovereignty

Nevertheless, states and revolutionary movements do not monopolize contemporary social and political practice, especially in the Third World. The emergence of antisystemic movements—"people's power" in the Philippines, the Chipko Hug a Tree movement in India, the global feminist movement, the peace movement in Western Europe, the popular movement in Chile that repudiated Augusto Pinochet, and converging human rights movements all over the world—are testimony not only to the changing contours of social and political life, but intimations of a different, qualitatively new, politics. Perhaps it is here that the theory and practice of state sovereignty is most profoundly challenged.

In an earlier work, I argued that critical social movements are the enactment of a drama of liberation and transformation toward a future of freedom and justice.[20] What is decisive in this drama is the priority of liberation and transformation that is implied in the practices of these movements. It is important to recognize, as Andre Gunder Frank and Marta Fuentes have, the difference between social movements in the West and in the South. The latter tend to be largely popular and working class, the former mostly middle class.[21] What is often ignored, however, is that the vitality of critical social movements depends, to some degree, on the linkages that are made between them and revolutionary movements. Indeed, the conjoining of critical social movements and the revolutionary project of justice and liberation is giving birth to what Sharon Welch calls communities of resistance and solidarity.[22] While both critical social movements and revolutionary movements address common concerns, they operate within a plurality of social and political spaces. In many instances, they provide mutual criticism in the spirit of critical solidarity. Here the challenge of critical social movements is fundamental, particularly in the context of the dominant statist tradition of modern politics. For these movements not only articulate a different understanding of political and ideological space, they keep these spaces open for transformation. This is crucial, since that state system, particularly in the post–World War II era, has tended toward greater authoritarianism and centralization, contracting political space, and, depoliticizing the masses. "The space of action of the new social movements," Claus Offe has argued, "is a space of noninstitutional politics which is not provided for in the doctrines and practices of liberal democracy and the welfare state."[23]

> Whereas the neoconservative project seeks to restore the nonpolitical, noncontingent, and uncontestable foundations of civil society (such as property, the market, the work ethic, the family, and scientific truth) in order to safeguard a more restricted—and therefore more solid—sphere of state authority . . . the politics of new social movements, by contrast, seeks to politicize the institutions of civil society in ways that are not constrained by the channels of representative-bureaucratic political institutions, and thereby reconstitute a civil society that is no longer dependent upon ever more regulation, control, and intervention.[24]

Because of their marginal relationship to the doctrines and practice of liberal democracy and the welfare state, critical social movements, particularly those that are not only "class conscious" but are also "class aware," offer the possibility of a much broader movement of resistance to domination. Because of their multifaceted forms of political practice, they are able to refuse the modernist temptation to heroize or to reduce the responsibility for change to an elitist vanguard or managerial class. They remind us that politics cannot be reduced to economics. For as long as they uphold the priority of justice and equality, refuse the illusion of nonideological politics, and remain in solidarity with authentic revolutionary movements, critical social movements offer the possibility of a more radically democratic and participatory politics that can avoid the pitfalls of modern political strategies.

Such movements also pose challenges to the modernist epistemological assumptions that inform these strategies. Communities of resistance and solidarity embody what Michel Foucault called "subjugated knowledges" that challenge dominant political and epistemic practices.[25] Indeed, the possibility of new knowledge and/or new experience, and therefore of transformation, rests to a large degree on a certain marginality or exteriority and negativity.[26] Speaking of this relationship between knowledge and experience (historicality), Gadamer writes:

> Experience in the real sense is always negative. If we have an experience of an object, this means we have not seen the thing carefully hitherto and now know it better. Thus, the negativity of experience has a curiously productive meaning . . . a comprehensive knowledge that we acquire.[27]

To affirm historicality, and the celebration of plurality and difference it presupposes, is to invite the charge of moral relativism, since, as Walker points out, difference in the modernist narrative is always defined as relativistic in the context of presumed guarantees of unity and identity.[28] The central objection to the historicization of truth is the belief that it rests on a *fundamentum inconcussum* that transcends any and all contingent realties. This, in fact, is an historically and culturally contingent framing of the options. In the first place, any form of domination rests on values assumed to be universal, unchanging, and exclusive. Hegemonic discourse that emerges from this needs to be challenged by insisting on its temporal and spatial limits. In the second place, moral inquiry infected by this modernist and logocentric disposition assumes the moral superiority of the inquirer, from which it follows that any challenge to the latter is ipso facto false and thus deserving of condemnation. From an ethical standpoint, it is important to cast suspicion on this logic, since the claims that it makes are based on an unquestioned but unwarranted and untenable moral superiority; and more importantly, because it refuses to recognize the moral claims of the other. Without such claims there can be no transformative politics.

This is where the question of epistemological and political location becomes decisive. Transformation requires that one be located within a particular historical social formation, not only to assert the normative priority of this social formation, to explicate its religio-moral challenge, or even to appropriate its values, but in order to articulate a perspective open to the variety of peoples' histories that constitute our pluralistic world. Criticism articulated from a particular social formation exterior to the totalizing pretensions of the system becomes a disruptive/irruptive site that opens the dominant system to reflection and action. The conjoining of this epistemic and political challenge leads to the transformation of a history of thought into the knowledge of struggle. Indeed, location is less a theoretical position and more the site of deliberative, communicative action.[29]

The Politics of Communities of Resistance and Solidarity

What kind of political communities are envisioned—indeed, presupposed—by these communities of resistance and solidarity? In the first place, they are political communities that are committed to deliberation as constitutive of their existence. Deliberation cannot be reduced to mere speech. It encompasses the whole range of participative practices that Jürgen Habermas, at least when disciplined of his flirtations with "ideal speech situations," is pointing to in his theory of communicative action.[30] It is Paulo Friere's dialogics of liberation.[31] These communities presuppose a recognition and affirmation not only of the plurality of human life, celebrating difference as constitutive of political life, but also of meaningful and direct participation in the governance of the community—at whatever level is called for. As Charles Taylor puts it, though in a different context, "it is not enough that a given (political) regime take account of my values, which it might do without thought or action on my part. . . . What is important is that I play a part in a common deliberation.[32]

This practical activity of participation and solidarity challenges the statist, bureaucratic, and hierarchical structures of domination. This is the significance of the *communidades de base* in Central and South America, the Philippines, and elsewhere. These communities of resistance and solidarity are models of radically democratic, participatory political communities. They are not only reversing hierarchic and bureaucratic structures of religious and political institutions, shifting the locus of power from these dominative centers and restoring it to those who are struggling for liberation and transformation, but they are also retrieving the meaning and significance of popular participation, which has largely been eclipsed by formal representation in liberal democratic regimes. In short, not only are they political events that mark the rediscovery of democracy, but they are deepening democracy as well.

Of course, deliberation, when located within the historical framework of domination, becomes deliberation about and toward liberation. It becomes part of the struggles for liberation while refusing to be reduced simply to a tool for attaining the goals of revolution. Using the analogy of speech, one of the practices of domination is the refusal to allow the voices of the people to be heard. Deliberation is the restoration of speaking to the speechless, of power to the powerless, and the nurturing and protection of these voices from those who would silence them.

As deliberating communities, communities of resistance and solidarity point to the creation and preservation of what Hannah Arendt called "the common," that is, the public realm.[33] Contrary to those dominative practices that reduce the common to a pregiven structure of reality, or even to an ethnocentric project given universal status through its imposition worldwide, the common is the space for difference carved out by deliberating communities as they seek meaningful consensus. Political communities committed to the critical retrieval and preservation of the common, particularly a global common, cast suspicion on the logocentric and totalizing dispositions of the modernist narrative and undermine its hegemony. They also redefine the common beyond the boundaries of the present state system, recognizing not only our shared global context, or our profoundly pluralistic existence, but what Saul H. Mendlovitz calls our *human specie identity*.[34]

Communities of resistance and solidarity reflect a notion of political community that is largely a regulative ideal rather than a description of a future society. It is a point of entry, a beginning, but not a final solution. This is not a deficiency, however. Such a construal of political community celebrates the simple fact of its historicality, i.e., of its spatiotemporal configuration, which is always in the process of being created and re-created toward a common goal of justice and freedom. There are given limits to political communities such as these, since communities of resistance and solidarity are rooted in their own space and time and culture and society. This necessary limitation, however, is transformed into a practical critique that, in the language of Foucault, makes transgressions possible, makes it possible to undermine, subvert, put into question, those dominative practices —particularly of pseudo-universals and false dichotomies—that discipline present-day political experience.[35]

Moreover, such political communities cannot be limited to one historical expression, such as an encompassing political subject, a universal class, or the rational state. This is not a refusal to identify which historical communities bear the possibilities of transformation. Rather, it is a recognition that struggles for transformation may require different understandings and practices that acknowledge but do not totalize racial, sexual, and class categories. These communities of resistance and solidarity throughout the world are characterized by their linkages to each other through proximity as well as through comportment, their unequivocal commitment to the struggles of the poor and the oppressed—who are the "bearers of the battle between freedom and order, justice and law, humanization and dehumanization, true and false piety, in the world"[36]—and their dreams for a truly just and humane global civilization.

A politics of struggle is concerned with truth. But truth is always located truth. Perspective is critical. Context is crucial. Since communities of resistance and solidarity engage in a politics of struggle that is situated within a context of domination, their struggles become activities of clearing. A politics of struggle seeks not only to open up intellectual, moral, and political space so that the "fundamentally new and better" can emerge, but it also seeks to deliberate on the character of that space—what it means, for whom it is space, which spaces are important. The political practices of communities of resistance and solidarity, unlike the more conventional—indeed, dominant political and social preparty and party formations—are concerned not only with change but are committed to changing the way we change.

Notes

1. Archie Singham and Shirley Hune, *Non-Alignment in an Age of Alignments* (London: Zed Books, 1986), pp. 13–32, 57–76.

2. R. B. J. Walker, *One World, Many Worlds: Struggles for a Just World Peace* (Boulder, Colo.: Lynne Rienner, 1988). See also Carl Boggs, *Social Movements and Political Power: Emerging Forms of Radicalism in the West* (Philadelphia: Temple University Press, 1986).

3. Giovanni Arrighi, Terence K. Hopkins, and Immanuel Wallerstein, "The Dilemmas of Anti-systemic Movements," *Social Research* 53, no. 1 (Spring 1986): 185–206; Charles Maier, ed., *Changing Boundaries of the Political* (Cambridge: Cambridge University Press, 1987); John Keane, ed., *Civil Society and the State* (London: Verso, 1988).

4. F. H. Hinsley, *Sovereignty*, 2nd ed. (Cambridge: Cambridge University Press, 1986).

5. See, for example, Sharon Welch, *Communities of Resistance and Solidarity: A Feminist Theology of Liberation* (New York: Orbis Books, 1985); Cornel West, *Prophesy Deliverance! An Afro-American Revolutionary Christianity* (Philadelphia: Westminster Press, 1982); Richard Shaull, *Heralds of a New Reformation: The Poor of South and North America* (New York: Orbis Books, 1984); Gustavo Gutiérrez, *We Drink from our Own Wells*, trans. Matthew J. O'Connell (New York: Orbis Books, 1983); Forum for Interdisciplinary Endeavors and Studies (FIDES), *Religion and Society: Towards a Theology of Struggle, Book I* (Manila: FIDES, 1988); Virginia Fabella and Sergio Torres, eds., *Irruption of the Third World: Challenge to Theology* (New York: Orbis Books, 1983).

6. Matthew Lamb, *Solidarity with Victims: Toward a Theology of Social Transformation* (New York: Crossroads, 1982), pp. 61–99; Gustavo Gutiérrez, *A Theology of Liberation: History, Politics, Salvation*, trans. Sr. Caridad Inda and John Eagleson (New York: Orbis Books, 1988), pp. 3–12. Compare with the essays in

James Der Derian and Michael J. Shapiro, eds., *International/Intertextual Relations: Postmodern Readings of World Politics* (Lexington, Mass.: Lexington Books, 1989); Saul H. Mendlovitz and R. B. J. Walker, eds., *Towards a Just World Peace: Perspectives from Social Movements* (London: Butterworth Scientific Limited, 1987); and Gayatri C. Spivak, *In Other Worlds: Essays in Cultural Politics* (New York: Routledge and Kegan Paul, 1988).

7. The scholarship in this area is voluminous. The following are only suggestive: Teodoro Agoncillo and Milagros Guerrero, *A History of the Filipino People*, 5th ed. (Quezon City: R. P. García, 1977); Miguel Bernad, *Christianization of the Philippines: Problems and Prospects* (Manila: The Filipiniana Book Guild, 1972); Renato Constantino, *The Philippines: A Past Revisited* (Quezon City: Tala Publishing Service, 1975); Onofre Corpuz, *The Philippines* (Englewood Cliffs, N.J.: Prentice-Hall, 1965); Cesar Adib Majul, *Muslims in the Philippines*, 3rd ed. (Manila: St. Mary's Publishing House, 1973); Reynaldo Ileto, *Pasyon and Revolution: Popular Movements in the Philippines, 1840–1910* (Quezon City: Ateneo de Manila University Press, 1979); Amado Guerrero, *Philippine Society and Revolution* (Oakland, Calif.: International Association of Filipino Patriots, 1979); José María Sison, *The Philippine Revolution: The Leader's View* (New York: Taylor and Francis, 1989); David Schirmer and Stephen Rosskamm Shalom, eds., *The Philippines Reader* (Boston: South End Press, 1988); William Chapman, *Inside the Philippine Revolution* (New York: Norton, 1987); Raymond Bonner, *Waltzing with a Dictator: The Marcoses and the Making of American Policy* (New York: Times, 1987); Glenn Anthony May, *A Past Recovered* (Quezon City: New Day Publishers, 1987); Stanley Karnow, *In Our Image: America's Empire in the Philippines* (New York: Random House, 1989).

8. Sandra Burton, "Aquino's Philippines: The Center Holds," *Foreign Affairs* 65, no. 3 (1987): 524–537.

9. Francisco Nemenzo, "A Nation in Ferment: Analysis of the February Revolution," in M. Rajaretnam, ed., *The Aquino Alternative* (n.p.: Institute of Southeast Asian Studies, n.d.); Lester Edwin J. Ruiz, "The Prospects for Democratization and Social Change in the Philippines: Two Years After the February Revolution (Lecture delivered at Harvard University, February 18, 1988); Ricardo Ferrer, "The Political Economy of the Aquino Regime: From Liberalism to Bureaucrat Authoritarianism," *Economic and Political Weekly*, July 30, 1988.

10. Renato Constantino, *The Aquino Watch* (Quezon City: Karrel, 1987).

11. Lester Edwin J. Ruiz, "Philippine Politics as a Peoples' Quest for Authentic Political Subjecthood," *Alternatives* 11, no. 4, 505–534; See also Lester Edwin J. Ruiz, "Towards a Transformative Politics: A Quest for Authentic Political Subjecthood" (Ph.D. diss., Princeton Theological Seminary, 1985).

12. The November 30, 1989, coup d'état attempt led by Col. Gregorio "Gringo" Honasan very clearly suggests the continued existence of this perspective. Indeed, it is interesting to note that despite their denials, the so-called Marcos loyalists and this faction of the Armed Forces of the Philippines are tacitly, if not openly, supportive of each other's views and political ambitions.

13. I adopt Richard K. Ashley's definition of modernity as the "multifaceted historical narrative rooted in the Enlightenment, dominant in western society, expressed in rationalist theory, and centering on the progressive unfolding of universalizing reason and social harmony via science, technology, law, and the state."

See Richard K. Ashley, "Living on Border Lines: Man, Poststructuralism and War," in Der Derian and Shapiro eds., *International/Intertextual Relations*, 259–321.

14. Walden Bello and Elaine Elinson, *Elite Democracy and Authoritarian Rule: The Crisis of the Political Regime of US Intervention in the Philippines and the Third World from the Kennedy Years to the Reagan Era* (San Francisco: Solidarity Network, 1981).

15. Jovito Salonga, "Reflections on the Constitution, Human Rights, and the Rule of Law: After Martial Law" (Speech delivered at the Symposium of the Greater Manila Region of the Integrated Bar of the Philippines, Manila, Philippines, February 10, 1981); see also, Jovito Salonga, "The Democratic Opposition and its Vision of the Society the People Want" (Speech delivered before the Manila Rotary Club, Manila, Philippines, October 9, 1980).

16. This argument is not new. In fact, it is the linchpin for the entire argument of "Philippine Constitutional Authoritarianism." See Ferdinand E. Marcos, *The Democratic Revolution in the Philippines*, 2nd ed. (Englewood Cliffs, N.J.: Prentice-Hall International, 1979); Ferdinand Marcos, "The Philippine Experience: A Perspective on Human Rights and the Rule of Law" (Manila: National Media Production Center, n.d.); Ferdinand Marcos, "Martial Law and Human Rights" (Manila: National Media Production Center, n.d.); and Ferdinand Marcos, Blas Ople, Onofre Corpus et al., *Toward the New Society: Essays on Aspects of Philippine Development* (Manila: National Media Production Center, 1974). Compare the ideas articulated in these essays with Samuel Huntington, *Political Order in Changing Societies* (New Haven: Yale University Press, 1968). For a critical analysis of this topic see my "Constitutionalism and Foundational Values: Philippine Constitutional Authoritarianism Revisited," in Richard Falk, Robert Johansen, and Samuel Kim, eds., *Constitutionalism and World Order: Essays in Honor of Saul H. Mendlovitz* (forthcoming).

17. Hans-Georg Gadamer, *Truth and Method*, trans. Garrett Baarden and T. Cumming (New York: Seabury, 1975).

18. Yong Bok Kim, ed., *Minjung Theology: People as the Subjects of History* (Singapore: Christian Conference of Asia, 1981).

19. Richard Bernstein, *Beyond Objectivism and Relativism: Science, Hermeneutics and Praxis* (Philadelphia: University of Pennsylvania Press, 1983), pp. 1–50.

20. See Note 11. Also Lester Edwin J. Ruiz, "Towards a Theology of Politics: Meditations on Religion, Politics, and Social Transformation," in Feliciano Cariño, ed., *Theology Politics and Struggle* (Quezon City: National Council of Churches in the Philippines, 1986), pp. 1–46.

21. Andre Gunder Frank and Marta Fuentes, "Nine Theses on Social Movements," *IFDA Dossier* 63 (January/February 1988): 27–44.

22. Welch, *Communities of Resistance and Solidarity*.

23. Claus Offe, "Challenging the Boundaries of Institutional Politics: Social Movements since the 1960s," in Maier, ed., *Changing Boundaries of the Political*, pp. 63–106.

24. Ibid.

25. Michel Foucault, *Power/Knowledge: Selected Interviews and Other Writings, 1972–1977* (New York: Pantheon, 1980).

26. Jacques Derrida, *Margins of Philosophy*, trans. Alan Bass (Chicago:

University of Chicago Press, 1982), pp. 1–28, 207–272; Emmanuel Levinas, *Totality and Infinity: An Essay on Exteriority*, trans. Alphonso Lingis (Pittsburgh: Duquesne University Press, 1969); Theodor Adorno, *Negative Dialectics*, trans. E. B. Ashton (New York: Continuum, 1973); Marc Ellis and Otto Maduro, eds., *The Future of Liberation Theology: Essays in Honor of Gustavo Gutierrez* (New York: Orbis Books, 1989).

27. Gadamer, *Truth and Method*, pp. 316–321.

28. Walker, *One World, Many Worlds*.

29. Calvin O. Schrag, *Communicative Praxis and the Space of Subjectivity* (Bloomington: Indiana University Press, 1986).

30. Jürgen Habermas, *Communication and the Evolution of Society*, trans. Thomas McCarthy (Boston: Beacon Press, 1979), pp. 1–68.

31. Paul Friere, *Pedagogy of the Oppressed*, trans. Myra Bergman Ramos (New York: Seabury, 1968).

32. Charles Taylor, "The Philosophy of the Social Sciences," in Melvin Richter, ed., *Political Theory and Political Education* (Princeton: Princeton University Press, 1980), pp. 76–93, especially p. 79.

33. Hannah Arendt, *The Human Condition* (Chicago: University of Chicago Press, 1978), pp. 52–53.

34. The notion of "human specie identity" is being developed by Saul H. Mendlovitz. Similar images include Richard Falk's "citizen pilgrim" and Manfred Halpern's "pilgrim warrior."

35. Michel Foucault, "What is Enlightenment?" in Paul Rabinow, ed., *The Foucault Reader* (New York: Pantheon, 1984), pp. 32–50.

36. Paul Lehmann, *The Transfiguration of Politics: The Presence and Power of Jesus of Nazareth in and Over Human Affairs* (New York: Harper & Row, 1975), p. 258.

6

Spatiality and Policy Discourse: Reading the Global City

Michael Shapiro & Deanne Neaubauer

The Spatialization of the City

In every age, the city has been a domain reflecting spatial strategies. For example, the medieval city was among other things a fortress. At least from the point of view of defense, it was less appropriate to ask about policymaking *in* the city than to think of the city itself as policy. Its walled perimeter constituted a defense against predation from groups as diverse as outlaw bands and the mercenary armies of the great dynasties. When someone was in the city they were safer than when they were outside its walls, and discourse about the "city"—understood as protected space—was to a large extent oriented by the shape of the walls. In connection with war policy, then, there was relatively little mystification involved in speaking about the inside versus the outside of the city, for protective strategy was relatively visible.

Although there are still connections between warfare and the modern city, today they are difficult to discern not only because the contemporary state has displaced the ancient and medieval city's dominant position in the warfare nexus but also because the connections are less available to the gaze. In the present condition, the economic, social, political and administrative spatial practices constituting the modern city are not represented in the form of visible structures, and, in general, the connections between policy discourse and the spatial strategies are less clear. As Paul Virilio has noted, it is no longer appropriate to think of the metropolitan agglomeration as in possession of a facade or a definitive spatial demarcation vis-à-vis the periphery. In effect, the city as geographic space has been replaced by a series of nodalities based on electronic modes of transmission. Man–machine interfaces of communication and surveillance have produced a city based more on temporality of transmissions than on immovable facades.[1] Thus, spatial strategies (understood as the practices that give places their meaning and value and create the boundaries that separate activities) have undergone

---

Reprinted with permission from *Alternatives: Social Transformation and Humane Governance* 15, no. 3 (July 1989).

dramatic changes that challenge even the simplest grammatical proprieties such as the statements, "X is in New York," or "X is in Los Angeles."

For example, a recent article on the style pages of the *New York Times*, "The Los Angeles Life on New York Time," describes "a small army of Los Angeles residents" who awake at 3:00 am in order to be at work at 5:00 am."[2] The rest of their schedule is similarly out of synch with that of other LA residents—lunch at 9:00, happy hour at 2:00, bed at 8:00. These people are "stockbrokers, bankers, lawyers and news and entertainment people whose professional lives are keyed to New York and other Eastern cities." That they can operate in a geographically remote area is of course a function of modern technology, the increasing extent to which social, occupational and other aspects of human relations are based on rapidly deployed electronic connections. To the extent that work relations depend on speed and the timing of communications, geographic space dissolves in favor of what Virilio has called chronospace.[3] In this kind of space, in which geography and temporality are imbricated, A's distance from B in work- or war-related functions becomes a question of the speed of travel, of weapons or information. Among other things, this new form of spatialization invalidates both the traditional discourses related to work and commerce and those related to international politics in general and the discursive clusters such as those surrounding the concept of "security" policy in particular. Below, we address a variety of implications of modern spatial practices, particularly as they help one construct the city of Los Angeles as policy space, for in many ways Los Angeles is an exemplar of modern spatiality. But for the moment our attention is on the New York end of this "style" story.

What should not be lost in this story is the meaning of the *textual* space where these "Los Angeles residents" working in "New York" are described. The style pages of the *New York Times* are part of the relatively modern space within which buyers and sellers encounter each other. They are a symbolic extension of the display spaces produced by the age of merchandising in that they reproduce the social codes found in store windows and other advertising spaces, the codes within which consumers learn to locate themselves. Indeed much of New York City is constituted as merchandising space though often disguised as something else. For example, even the artistic space of the museum functions as an indirect form of merchandising space, for as Jean Baudrillard has pointed out, it serves as the "public backing" of the process of art consumption. "Museums play the role of banks in the political economy of painting."[4]

The discursive deficits

This kind of spatial practice is rarely available as part of political understandings because in most contemporary policy talk, the shape of the arena in which policy is conceived is taken for granted. These arenas, which are constituted by spatial practices among other things, are not an audible part of policy talk. Rather, they exist at a silent level. Or, to turn to a lexic metaphor, they are a series of power inscriptions that do their effective work without being read. They belong, in effect, to a political rhetoric that is implicit in a society's spatial practices, as part of its "ground plan," that situates the sets of eligible speaker/actors who can produce meaningful and effective policy utterances and actions.[5] And, in general, they contextualize and thus render coherent the discourses that bestow meaning and value on things, actions and relationships.

The shape of a society's spaces—leisure space, work space, public space, military space—tends to remain largely implicit for a variety of reasons. One is, of course, the relatively long duration of that shaping process so that few can discern a process of actual boundary shaping or movement. However, part of the inattention to spatial predicates of policy discourse is positively administered. Dominant forms of social theory, for example both liberal and Marxist, fail, with some exceptions, to encode the spatial dimensions of human association.[6] For the dominant tendencies in both these theoretical traditions, space is either natural or neutral; it is either the empty arena within which political association and contention develop or it is the sanctified, historically destined places whose boundaries and internal configurations should remain inviolable.

There are good reasons to resist this naturalizing of space. At a minimum, a careful attention to the irredeemably contextual contribution of a speaker or writer's situation to the meaning of utterances should suggest why. Intelligibility is intimately connected to standing, to the sites and locations from which meanings are shaped. And, the spaces from which discourse is produced are just as much constituted as sets of practices as the discourses themselves; social relations thus form a complex in which topological and discursive practices are inseparable.[7]

But those who use a discourse—an institutionalized practice through which meaning and value is imposed, reaffirmed and exchanged—generally fail to discern the historically developed, presupposed practices, spatial among others, that ventriloquate themselves through the discourse. This is the case, in part, because, as Jacques Derrida has pointed out, our utterances seem to be wholly present to us: "The subject can hear or speak to himself and be affected by the signifier he produces without passing through an external detour, the world, the sphere of what is not 'his own'."[8] Nevertheless, the rhetorical contributions of space can be registered; at least their indirect effects are available to the gaze. What is often required is that one manage to suspend the usual aggressive practices through which everyday life is constructed.

For purposes of analysis, it is useful to distinguish two levels of spatiality shaping the modern city, one that is relatively visible once it is conceptualized and one that is more remote. To focus first on the former, we can consider today's urban pedestrians who conform to a spatiality that shapes their everyday lives while, at the same time, their movements constitute a space-shaping practice. To compare this level with that of the second, more remote level, we can turn to Anthony Giddens' conception of "time-space distantiation," where distantiation refers to "the processes whereby societies are 'stretched' over shorter or longer spans of time and space."[9] Giddens goes on to elaborate on how aspects of power which reproduce structures of domination are closely tied to the spatio-temporal extension of activities. What happens within a society or locale is shaped in part by the forces operating at the extremes of its extensions. For example, part of temporality is "the grounding of legitimations in tradition,"[10] and part of spatiality is the current set of "regularized transactions with others who are physically absent."[11] Thus, the greater the spatio-temporal distantiation of a domain, the more its activities defy visibility. Therefore, pedestrians can be read in two ways—in terms of the presently operating forces whose effects they reinscribe or resist; and in terms of the more remote forces that continue to shape their movements.

In developing a perspective that fits primarily into the first aspect of the reading, Michel de Certeau has emphasized the extent to which New York pedestrians translate the more visually available dimensions of spatiality, those belonging to the effectivity of everyday life. But while one could say that New York pedestrians are engaged in spatial practices, to say this is not to say that they are initiators of such practices. As de Certeau has noted, New York City's pedestrians are "the City's common practitioners . . . whose bodies follow the cursives and strokes of the urban 'text' they write without reading."[12] Certainly there are subversive or insurrectional aspects of "pedestrian utterances" and "perambulatory rhetorics," in that some who are on foot in the city (e.g. children) move in ways that create a counter-rhetoric to that produced by city planners and architects.[13] But most intelligible pedestrian utterances serve to rationalize and even mythify the city, to deepen the boundaries of its spatial arrangements.[14]

To understand how this is the case requires both a particular conception of space and some historical distance. As a conception of space, what one needs is a recognition that, as Edward Soja has put it, "The spatial organization of human society is an evolving product of human action, a form of social construction," not just a neutral context in which human action is deployed.[15] And to gain some historical distance, we must recognize that one group of New York pedestrians (the shoppers as opposed to the "street people") move, conceptually speaking, in a part of a commercial space that was developed in the late 19th century. The most notable venue for this development was 19th century Paris that witnessed the development of the large department stores such as Bon Marche, and along with the development of such stores came the development of merchandising, which represented a radical shift in the terrain connecting entrepreneur and buyer.[16] Whereas before, transactions were a process of bargaining between salespersons and customers (goods were not displayed with price tags), with merchandising came the production of browsing space, the right of customers to return purchases, and an ever-increasing amount of display space. Through merchandising, entrepreneurs shifted from merely announcing the availability of their goods to an activity which sought to stimulate an interest in them.

The space of shopping thus underwent a revolutionary change. No longer seen as the haggling or transaction, the face-to-face contention between buyer and seller, the new commercial space involved the construction of a code or discourse for representing consumable objects, a code connecting the objects to a desired social space. Shoppers in arcades and on shopping streets could peer into store windows with goods displayed in a way that connected those goods with representations of social relations, and similar displays were erected within the stores. Shopping thus became the consumption not of an object designed to meet a need but the consumption of a social code which the consumer was encouraged to associate with displayed objects.

In its initial form the department store democratized social space, and to that extent was a social invention consistent with late-19th century liberal democracy. The standardized presentations served to lessen significantly the social control role of the clerk in the presentation of goods. The movement of customers from one department to another made possible the co-mingling of social classes. With considerable rapidity the form of the department store itself became standardized (and later reproduced in the supermarket and other mass marketing enterprises). Class distinctions remained, but they were not encoded in the classifications of goods. Coding goods by social class and in broader cultural messages became the duty of mass advertising. Training in the creation and utilization of these codes has become in turn a necessary function of the schools and the formal education process.[17]

This different concept of selling goods and the social space which its conception created has endured. Contemporary New York City's pedestrians still occupy such a space. They consume a code with which the objects they see are associated and in connection with which they take on their meaning and value. What directs their steps is not the need for a particular object but the historical production of a commercial space in which merchandising connects desiring with social relations and thus with all the complexities involved in such relations—e.g., the libidinal and other economies of the family, the work place, public space. The disposition of shoppers, which helps to constitute the value of consumable objects, thus requires a decoding that turns our attention to a social space constituted within a still dominant discourse in which valuing and the social are complexly interwoven.

This complex commercial/social/desiring space extends from the street to museum displays, "style pages," and other spaces for artistic representation. Thus consumption fantasies of New York shoppers are provoked by the exhibitions and other "high culture" displays as well as what is represented in the so-called "popular culture" domain (television, newspapers, magazines, etc.). The spatial practices of the sidewalks are therefore connected with a social space that constitutes much of New York City as display space. Moreover, this commercial/social space in which shoppers move has venerable historical roots.

The remote forces shaping pedestrian utterances

For conceptual purposes, it is useful to take this story of the modern/social/commercial space back further to the footfalls of a 17th century pedestrian, for the world made in part by modern commerce is powerfully foreshadowed by a brief vignette in the life of Father Joseph. Aldous Huxley's *Grey Eminence,* an account of the production of the Thirty Years' War through the machinations of Cardinal Richelieu and his foreign emissary, Father Joseph, begins with a trek to Rome. As the barefoot Capuchin is walking toward Rome he is involved at once in a worldly and other-worldly activity. Although his mission is primarily political—he is carrying a message to the Pope from the King of France—his inward disposition is spiritual. From the historical archive, Huxley constructs the inner life of Father Joseph as a spiritual practice of the self that was a form of "personalistic pseudo mysticism," an "active annihilating by means of which he hoped to be able to disinfect his politics."[18]

> "love, love, love, Christ's love . . . " the little flame was alight again. He kept it burning unwaveringly, while he walked a quarter of a mile. Then it was time to pass on to operation—the repudiation of distracting thoughts and the resolve to banish them from the mind.[19]

Father Joseph's practice of the self is reflective of the shape of the medieval world from whence his mentality derives. This mentality, along with the fact that he is a part of a religious order involved in mundane political affairs, reflects the persistence into the 17th century of the religious, vertical spatialization of the world. As Foucault states in his rough retracing of the "history of space," "The Middle Ages . . . was a hierachic assemblage of places."[20] There was the sacred and the profane, the celestial and the super-celestial, and, what was most important for church authority, the earthly world was to be read as a symbolic reality with referents in the transcendent, heavenly world.

In Huxley's telling, Father Joseph, a representative of this medieval spatial mentality, is finally enlisted by Cardinal Richelieu in a struggle that both produces the Thirty Years' War and represents the triumph of a modern, geopolitical spatialization of the world. Despite Father Joseph's predilection for a holy war against the Protestants as well as non-Christian "heretics," he helps Richelieu put France on the Protestant side of the war in order to ensure French control of the European Continent against the challenges of Catholic Spain and Austria.

Certainly major aspects of the geopolitical spatialization have persisted into the present, for the nation-state system, which Richelieu's policy helped to produce, has endured. But it should be noted that those involved in commerce have had an effect and a stake in the nation-oriented centralization involved in the turn toward state control. Historically it was the development of the nation-state that helped to protect and sustain commerce, and, in turn, it was commercial interests that helped to support state authority against the divisive pressures of the great landed estates. Huxley seems to be offering a subtle premonition of this future mutual facilitation, for he has Father Joseph pass another kind of pedestrian on his trek to Rome. This is the passage immediately after the one above reflecting his practice of the self: "Headed in the opposite direction, a train of pack animals from the city jingled slowly past him."[21]

Father Joseph was on his way to participate in an exchange of commitments, which were connected to the old hierarchical arrangement of spaces. The pack animals and merchants were involved in an unmistakable journey. As the jingle attests, it was trade, and such travels helped to etch a world with a different shape. They operated on behalf of a horizontal, desacralized world, and this world, which was to triumph over the sacred, vertically oriented social space, would produce an ever-increasing traffic of commercial travel and a corresponding rearrangement of international, national and various forms of domestic spatialization.

Of course to emphasize the domination of the horizontal world is not enough, for within the horizontal are a variety of contending spatial practices —struggles between proximate and distant forces, different nodalities as municipal authorities and distant economic forms of power struggle to control urban space. For example, with the more horizontal articulation of space in the present, there exists a critical intersection of distances or proximities with systems of calculation. This intersection forms what Foucault has called "the forms of relations among sites."[22] One can easily exemplify such a critical geography in connection with "conventional weapons" whose impact on understandings of geopolitical space involves the numbers held in relation to their proximity to variously strategically understood locations. And, of course, temporality is part of this calculation-oriented demography, for it brings into view the issues of the mobility of weapons and their speed of delivery.

A Modern Version of Sacred Spatialization: The Liberal Discourse

We have lost the vertical, medieval world, but we must not imagine that modern social space is wholly desacralized. Although the grand narratives belonging to ecclesiastical authority have been largely discredited and have thus lost their ability to produce the world's spaces, their replacements have had their sacralizing impetus. One of the major ones has been what can best be termed the liberal discourse on space, which has recently been reasserted by Michael Walzer. Characterizing liberalism as "the art of separation," he describes the shift from the medieval, "pre-liberal maps" as a shift from a conception of society as an organic whole, wherein political, civil society, church and commerce are all interdependent, to a conception in which society is like a house with a modern floor plan. There are walls separating church, state, university, etc., and this creates a politics in which people are free from unwarranted intrusions.[23]

In what is perhaps the most revealing statement in his narrative of the reconceptualization of society's spaces, Walzer states: "Liberalism is a world of walls, and each creates a new liberty."[24] This common liberal view is a remarkably depoliticized narrative of the production of modernity's spaces. A dramatic contrast is provided in Gilles Deleuze and Felix Guattari's counterliberal narrative, influenced by Marx's notion of the counteracted tendency. Deleuze and Guattari figure the counteracted tendency in spatial terms, arguing that with every deterritorialization, such as the sundering of the space of dominance/subjection involved in the medieval Church's control over both territory and the codes giving territory its significance, there are liberated new possibilities for economies of desire and energy to flow across old boundaries and reshape the world. But each deterritorialization is accompanied soon after by a "reterritorialization" in which there is a "mobilization of dominant forces to prevent the new productive possibilities from becoming new human freedoms."[25] This reterritorialization is conducted, they assert, by the ". . . apparatuses" of the capitalist machine—government bureaucracies, legal structures, city planners, etc.[26]

Walzer is not insensitive to the counter-narrative, and his celebration of the liberal "art of separation" contains a dialogue with what he calls the Marxist gloss which he construes as an argument to the effect that the liberal separations are a pretense. Walzer assumes that Marxism is constituted simply as a desire to efface the separations, to tear down the walls and reinstitute the organic connections of the "pre-liberal maps."[27] Apart from the impoverishment of the political conversation that results from this anaemic representation of Marxist theory, what are evident from Walzer's discussion are the discursive economies of his liberal talk. His liberalism consists in legitimating the arrangements produced by political contention by treating them as wisdom rather than political victories. Politics can go on once people have secured their holdings, and we can forget about the political process involved in establishing such holdings, the equivalents of what Foucault has called "the blood that has dried on the codes of the law."[28] We can render boundaries innocuous by speaking unproblematically about "public" or "private" spheres, the "work place," "recreational space." What is left of the political process in this model is a more or less policing function that consists of the prevention of intrusions from one institutional setting to another.

Clearly, there is a significant operation of power and authority in the *production* of those domains whose inviolability Walzer seeks to preserve. This form of the liberal discourse depoliticizes modernity's contemporary ground plan and thereby serves as a legitimation rhetoric; it distributes discursive assets to those who control the flow of goods, commitments and, in general, all valued outcomes.[29]

Walzer's view of the liberal discourse, which is obtuse to the politics of the production of modern spaces amounts to a resanctification of the ground that the Church lost to capitalist activity. "How do we draw the map," asks Walzer, "of the social world so that churches and schools, states and markets, bureaucracies and families each find their proper place?"[30] In this kind of account, where a narrative of institutions locates existing arrangements within a sanctified space of historically destined proprieties, there is no place to register a politics concerned with how institutionalized spatial arrangements deploy power and control.

It was undoubtedly the Walzer-type discourse that Foucault had in mind when he remarked that "contemporary space is perhaps still not entirely desanctified." He was referring to the oppositions representing contemporary *practices* of space taken as simple givens, for example, "between private space and public space, between family space and social space, between cultural space and useful space, between the space of leisure and that of work."[31] Rather than sanctifying what are politically relevant practices, one could turn to a variety of politicizing modes for extracting the political tendencies that inhere in the spatializing of modernity.

Most politically perspicacious are those modes that register spatializing practices. Walzer assumes that critical discourses (e.g. Marxism) simply represent a desire for reproducing an "undifferentiated organic whole," but what critical analyses provide, rather, is a way to encode, among other things, how modernity produces space or the boundary-maintaining practices and the discursive legitimations aiding and abetting the control practices constituted by these spaces. For example, Foucault has shown how the development of a delinquent milieu, part of a new domain of the social, cannot be separated from the system of rules, penalties, and law enforcement practices that had a role in constituting such a domain.[32] While Walzer celebrates a system of laws, a distribution of legalities and illegalities, as a liberating phenomenon insofar as it protects individuals from intrusions into their private lives, Foucault understands that such "private lives" are created by among other things the structure of penalties and their enforcements. Penalties are nested in a web of spatial practices organized around the primary opposition of public space versus private space, which is immanent in any understanding of "property crime." In addition, Foucault recognizes that the system of legalities not only reinforces certain dominant and morally approved social practices but also creates some stigmatized and disapproved but nevertheless useful social spaces.

For example, from whence do these marginal social types who provide a ready source of information and instigative activity for law enforcement officials come? The prison, a relatively recent aspect of society's production of penal spaces, "has succeeded extremely well in producing delinquency, a specific type, a politically less dangerous and on occasion, usable, form of illegality."[33]

A Political Mapping of Urban Policy

Once we have such a politicized view of spatial practices, that we recognize that spaces are produced by various forms of power and authority, that, finally, the liberal "art of separation" is a mythifying, depoliticizing discourse serving to legitimate existing power arrangements, we are prepared to produce a political form of policy analysis. What is liberated is inquiry aimed at a politicizing view of the production of the boundaries and nodalities that create spaces. Such boundary creation is best viewed not as an art, because space is not politically neutral. Henri Lefebre, perhaps the theorist most responsible for politicizing modernity's spaces has put the matter simply, ". . . There is a politics of space because space is political."[34] It only appears to be politically neutral, he notes, because the production processes going into shaping it are no longer in evidence; what is left is space that seems natural because it has been used in familiar ways for some time.

> If space has an air of neutrality and indifference with regard to its contents and thus seems to be purely formal, the epitome of rational abstraction, it is precisely because it has already been occupied and used, and has already been the focus of past processes whose traces are not always evident in the landscape.[35]

The spatial constitution of Los Angeles

We now turn to the Los Angeles side of the New York–Los Angeles nexus in order to explore the practices shaping Los Angeles. In so doing, we want to repoliticize what now appears bland and normal by recovering its historic production. For purposes of analysis, an advertisement for the Sports Channel (ESPN) provides an insight not only into contemporary Los Angeles but also much of modern America, for its rhetoric has remote and significant origins that register themselves in the piece. The advertisement shows defensive back Lester Hayes of the Los Angeles Raiders football team. He is kneeling in the middle of the Los Angeles Coliseum while facing the scoreboard which shows that it is at the end of the third quarter of a close contest. The main caption reads, "Join our congregation this Sunday for an Inspirational Experience." The advertisement is a virtual jumble of codes that bespeak modern spatial practices. To address these it is necessary to address what has been involved in the historical commodification of sport.

The development of the modern stadium has played a role in this process similar to that connected to the development of the concert hall. In the case of the concert hall, the enclosure for performing music represented a significant change, which is described by Jacques Attali as one from music as dialogue to music as monologue, for the concert hall performance increasingly replaced the music associated with popular festivals, in which there was not a separation between performer and audience.[36] Apart from the social and economic implications of confining musical space and controlling entry, the concert hall had a powerful political semiotic. According to Attali, it created an audience that affirmed by their silence "their submission to the artificialized spectacle of harmony—master and slave, the rule governing the symbolic game of their domination."[37] Of course in the case of music, the development of the phonographic record, the next important stage in the production of modern musical space, had an even more dramatic impact on the space of music.

Among the effects of such commodified forms of musical repetition has been the delocalizing of the power configuration that had developed around the concert hall. Music is now an intimate part of other spaces, not the least of which is the merchandising space discussed above.[38] Similarly, the sporting stadium as an enclosed arena for sport is part of a historical rearrangement of playing space, which is connected to what Norbert Elias has called the "sportization of pastimes."[39] Just as the concert hall represents the diminution of the more participatory festival, the stadium represents the diminution of village play, a process which accelerated in the 18th century in England when bourgeois and aristocratic classes feared the insurrectional effects of folkish pastimes. Games like Shrove Tuesday football, in which one village would try to kick a soccer ball through another, frequently ended in mass political protests against local extensions of centralized authority.

At one level, "sportization" meant creating and enforcing strict rules of the game in order to bring bourgeois notions of justice and fairness to the rough and often injurious village games. However, at another level it meant delocalizing the control of games in order to moderate the political effects of mass gatherings. The development from game to sport and the concomitant rearrangements in the formation of playing space were thus intimately connected to policing peasant classes.[40] Of course not incidental to the development of this new overlap between legal and playing space were gambling interests which needed "fair" contest in order to encourage and control betting.[41] The stadium is thus an enclosure that represents a concrete version of the enclosing of playing space for political and commercial reasons. The replacement of broad-based forms of play and the concomitant radical separation of player and spectator is of course part of a long story that is incidental to the present point. More to the point is the next step in delocalization that ESPN's invitation into the Los Angeles Coliseum reflects. Most of the viewing audience will visit the Coliseum from their living rooms. Control over playing space in modern professional sports is inextricably connected to the modern aspect of the commodification of play, its electronic transmission to remote audiences.

Thus the invitation to join ESPN's congregation, an obvious reference to the competition that a Sunday telecast has with Sunday church services (and even Sunday televised church services), is an invitation to a remote kind of solidarity, a feeling of oneness with people at a distance, all involved in a modern Sunday ritual. What is perhaps most ironic about the transmission of sporting activities to passive and isolated spectators referred to as a "congregation," is that the age of remote transmission is in effect an age that is effacing the ritual spaces in which people used to congregate. The kneeling, prayerful football player is a pale attempt to evoke this lost ritual space.

To be invited into ESPN's congregation is only symbolically to be invited into an arena (whose seemingly long expanse is attractive compared to the confined home and work spaces of most viewers). Professional sports activities developed most in urban areas because these were the only places able to draw large audiences. But now this aspect of urban space is being effaced in favor of broadcasting space, and the delegating power of this new space remote from local political and legal authority is clear.[42] For example, even the timing of sporting events now relates not to local work and traffic patterns but to the viewing patterns of a variegated, nationwide audience. All of this represents a new form of power that operates at the increased level of spatio-temporal distantiation that Giddens has described. It is the power connected with control over space of communication and transmission, a form of control connected to the globalization of the modern city.

Remedievalization in the Global City

The spatial strategies of the modern city incorporate those dimensions of modern communications which have contributed to the creation of the modern global economy. We have noted that it was appropriate to speak of the medieval city as policy in that it functioned as a fortress, constituting a policy of defense by its very existence. In a similar manner the modern city reflects aspects of this medievalism but in two distinctly opposed manifestations. Through its location in the modern global economy, the modern city, of which we will continue the example of Los Angeles, is policy in that increasingly its primary function is to sustain those aspects of the international economy with which it is linked. That which we conventionally regard as "policy"—and mean by it a self-conscious act on the part of government (or the state) to utilize public power in a distinctive fashion—is subordinated in a literal sense to the demands of the international economy. By opening to the world in a primary sense the city is acted on, but has limited capability in turn to act on those forces which generate the initiations to which it must respond. Thus, the impoverishment of policy discourse in its liberal and decisional forms.

In the other manifestation the city becomes the site of a respatialization based on segmentalized identities. The medieval city, while not completely isolated from its surrounding space, was nevertheless a center of vertically informed identities providing the dual securities of protection against physical assault and the grossly polluting effects of the unfamiliar. Its walls symbolized the city's relations to its surroundings, functioning as a membrane filtering passages between inner and outer worlds, permitting measured routines conjoining time and space into carefully sustained rituals of association, obligation and identity. The decline of medieval society was due in part to increased commerce, literally a traffic with the outside world. These commercial activities in turn produced new codes for the organization of both time and space which increasingly came to be expressed in the universalizing values of monetary exchange.[43] In part this decline was also due to the massive destruction of primeval forests which converted their densities into the relative openness of agricultural spaces and in the process rendered these spaces suitable for the ordering strategies of newly developing centralized nation-states, which for their part became the new guarantors of security. The associated and interdependent verticalities of medieval society (linking church, administration and commerce within the medieval city) progressively gave way to the identities promoted by the emerging nation-states and the redefinition of group and self which attended the impositions of labor, ownership and wealth codes as ingredients of the industrial order. Whereas the medieval city incorporated by taking into its walled confines, its successor incorporated by creating new economies one of which was built-space itself. Coupled with the phenomenal increases in human population attendant to industrialization and the powerful horizontalizations of extended control exercised by centers over their peripheries, the modern industrial city comes to define a relentless incorporation by continued expansionary inclusion. Of modern cities Los Angeles with its 464 square miles of area is the archetype.

The global city imposes reverticalizations on the grid of horizontalizations typical of the industrial era city. As Christopherson and Storper have suggested in their analysis of the Los Angeles film industry, this reverticalization is the product of a novel disintegration of the older verticalizations of monopolistic industrialism which followed its initial stages of horizontal expansion.[44]

> In the contemporary motion picture industry by contrast production is carried out primarily by independent production companies which subcontract direct production activity to small specialized firms. The industry is vertically disintegrated and its production process is nonroutinized and designed to maximize variability of outputs and flexibility with respect to inputs. The numerous transactions required to produce a film product now take place on the market rather than within a firm.

As the site of international capital which comes to dominate the city, its center constitutes a literal verticality, a concentration in skyscrapers of those global firms which control the economic activity which radiates from the center to the various peripheries. Ownership of the modern city center by international capital is a key marker in identifying the extent to which an economy is internationalized.[45] Ownership of the vertical center permits the controlling groups to share the intense psychological and social experience of a common lifestyle, including the electronic rearrangement of the workday which everywhere links the modern global financial community. It also permits a subtle but compelling demonstration to local political authority of the extraordinary economic power of foreign capital. Surrounding city government with its continuing murmuring presence, it attenuates the "policy process" with an irresistible context.

Verticalization also comes to characterize settlement patterns. Middle-class and upper-class (and predominantly white) groups segregate themselves into armed and closed communities, from the fortified high-rise with its armed guards and security systems to the walled, guarded communities atop hills, down canyons or situated astride ocean view bluffs. Segregated at least by income, these communities often also provide other "attractions" such as age cohorts (in retirement communities) which act as protections of the familiar against the strange. At the other end of the scale, increased migration, much of it from the Third World, flows into the older areas of the city creating poor ethnic settlements. W. C. Baer indicates that fully 83% of immigrant households settle in the urban core area of Los Angeles with the remainder being distributed to the urban core areas of surrounding counties.[46] These populations come to constitute much of the non-familiar from which those with wealth are fleeing.

In some respects these segregations of spatiality by wealth, class and race or ethnicity have been constant features of the modern city. Their global city counterparts differ precisely by the retreat to verticality represented by these segregations. The ethnic ghettos of the late-19th century and early-20th century American city created strong boundaries of effective inclusion and exclusion, but they were impinged on by the prevailing liberal ethos of social integration, public education, civic participation and social mobility. The single most important countervailing force to the exclusionary/vertical structures of the ghetto was the intergenerational pressure for social and cultural assimilation. Central to the relative success of this assimilation was the socializing force of the economy: to escape the ghetto one required the currency of the dominant economy.

These forces appear to be less strong in the global city. International capital supplies a significant alternative to participation in the nexus of domestic capital/wealth/political power. Within upper class segmentalized social groups, identifications with external sources of power and wealth rival those of the domestic site. In previous historical national and local arenas, the translation of economic power into political power or vice versa had both instrumental and intrinsic value in that success meant a greater capacity to control and shape the relatively all-important local environment. Among other matters such success led to programs of "civic improvement," however they were defined, in large measure to preserve the security, well-being and happiness of local wealth-holding elites. Identifications in the global city are more highly instrumentalized. The local environment has the primary purpose of serving as a "capital farm," whose returns are to be maintained at a steady and growing pace. Foreign elites resident in the city are likely to be transient, posted by their corporations for a relatively brief stint of duty. Satisfactions to be drawn from the local environment are focussed on the pleasures of an enclave existence: secure and pleasant accommodations, recreational luxuries, the accoutrements of "high culture." Domestic elites satisfy the same needs by purchasing an identical life-style complemented by the mobility provided by their wealth. Their capital, achieved in large measure from the sale of domestic assets, is converted into international economy assets, or channelled into more highly concentrated national assets. This extension of investment and asset identification contributes strongly to an increased horizontalization of economic activity (as did the initial spread of capitalist activity throughout the nation-state), while producing strong social verticalization within the city itself.

The rapidity and variation of immigration into Los Angeles (signified by its more than 90 language groups) create forces which compete successfully with the dominant cultural program of assimiliation, acculturation and socialization. The city is more than a repository of a Third World labor force; parts of it become virtual extensions of the Third World. Not unlike Brazil, where tendencies toward integration into the global economy are responsible for a reculturation into subnational primary identity groups, the rapidly developing ethnic settlements of Los Angeles distribute islands of cultural particularity across the familiar plain of Southern California America. Entire communities previously populated with "fully integrated" immigrated Americans have been transformed into ethnic enclaves, speaking a primary language other than English and importing political culture and expectations from outside the conventional American idiom. These Third World communities gain their raison d'être in relation to the global city as a labor force willing to tolerate working conditions which their US counterparts have come to reject. Exposed daily to the consumption code of the American dream they are programmed by the predominant civic culture toward conventional goals of assimilation and acculturation. But for this generation, and some would argue subsequent generations as well, these goals are increasingly problematic. The vertical walls of cultural particularism and primary language identity direct them as much inward as outward. Their primary indentifications are with the cultural groups which provide basic meaning to their daily existence.

The modern city is, to employ Foucault's term, a simultaneity. "The present epoch," he writes, "will perhaps be above all the epoch of juxtaposition, the epoch of the near and the far, of the side-by-side, of the dispersed."[47] Its horizontalizations, fueled by investment capital from abroad, simultaneously confront its vertical segregations. They are linked by communications activities which symbolize a presumed neutrality in the muted conflicts between the interests which produce both horizontal expansion and vertical contraction. The "freeways" of Los Angeles, for example, once so named to differentiate them from toll roads and arterials full from cross traffic, now have the additional connotation of ways free from the social and cultural content of the spaces they traverse. A quantum of the fear which attached to the random Los Angeles freeway shootings of 1987 stems from the violation of these neutral spaces. A characteristic modern fear is to be forced from the freeway onto a strange exit, to be removed from the familiar and safe into the unknown and dangerous (the dramatic premise for Tom Wolfe's recent savage novel of New York).[48] Random freeway violence escalates those fears, threatening the routes of safe passage between islands of cultural familiarity and presumed safety.

The ubiquitous commercial culture transmitted by the mass media channels another stream of horizontalism through the islands of vertical particularity. In the approved version of the American dream the immigrant masses are able to internalize the strivings located within these consumption messages to organize progress through assimilationist activities, resulting in an increased identity with the dominant culture, its values and political authority. Historically, this is a generational process in which the accomplishments of the immigrating generation are realized in its successor, in large measure a product of formal educational socialization. The commercial rhythms of the global city, enforcing a code of status based on immediate consumption, are in direct conflict with the implied deferred gratifications of the assimilationist program. The gigantic power surges of foreign capital rolling through the global city produce shock waves which impact on all the islands of cultural verticality. What were formerly the excesses of domestic wealth pale beside these new and competing demonstrations of affluence. (A pattern of wealth impact which American capital itself initially distributed throughout the postwar world.) The result is an inflation of value in the new which devalues time (unless it becomes a reclaimed time and reinterpreted as an "antique" past), precisely that commodity which traditional culture has in abundance.

The global city becomes a lattice work of time and space in which time is hyper-valued in direct proportion to its commercial achievements. International capital culture literally pulsates with global exchange rates and a process of change so compressed that minute time increments "drive" large capital programs.[49] Time is so much of the essence that key decisionmakers must never be separated from the worldwide communication system which links them to their investment decisions. (A new traffic problem on the Santa Monica Freeway—and doubtless others—is congestion among cellular phone users calling from their automobiles while stalled in the daily vehicle congestion.) For the middle classes the value of time is in part determined by the styles and fashions assigned to objects and practices which provide a sense of meaning and achievement to social life (including very specifically the aging process and commercial inducements to resist its displays). As with the international financial classes, individual settlement decisions involve resolution of bundles of time, space and money factors which apportion the costs to be assigned to transportation, commuting time and the work utilities which can be squeezed from them and the amount of life-style which can be bought as a result of varying distance/effort/time calculations. For the working classes these calculations are constrained by the necessity to trade scarce values (e.g. income) for that over which there is less commodification choice (e.g. time). In addition, however, is the value provided time within the cultural enclave which often carries with it rhythms of the society from which the immigration occurred. Spatiality is valued in part by the association within the enclave to those traditions and values which can only be performed in settings which retain their cultural integrity.

The rapid growth of gang culture in Los Angeles can be interpreted in part as a response to the tensions which occur at the intersection between the vertical domain of culture, the dominant social values of deferred gratification and acculturation, and the horizontalizing commercial/achievement messages transmitted by the dominant media. Gang organization provides a focus of identification within the ethnic/racial/culture/language group. It can be held in sharp contrast to other "primary" identifications proffered by the horizontalizing media, for example, "inclusion" in the ESPN congregation. Gang membership provides a solidity of reinforcing identifications which among other capabilities permits members to incorporate mass culture and its "inclusions" into the perspectives of their own exclusionary criteria. Membership also provides a vehicle for economic achievement with chances for success often superior to those provided by the conventional acculturation route which programs ethnic groups at the bottom of the economic ladder to remain in a wage exploitable position for a considerable period before permitting significant upward mobility.

The international drug economy for which these organizations are often as much local product outlets as Stereo Warehouse is for Sony or Pioneer, supplies them with opportunities for profit maximization and growth which rival the "formal" economy. The dynamics of this underground economy display virtually all the features of the model entrepreneurial capitalist economy in a state of rapid growth: low market entry costs, large numbers of competing suppliers, large numbers of sellers able to affect demand through price, high rates of return on investment, a plentiful and productive labor force, etc. Governmental efforts to control the traffic are treated as externalities to the market process, ultimately little different from the response of the Southern California petroleum industries to governmental environmental regulation. And, like other entrepreneurial activities, these enterprises seek constantly for technical advantage over their competitors and their would-be regulators; in this instance the technological advantage happens to be in communications equipment and armaments rather than in communications and, say, computer chips. The motives for achievement within these groups are little different from those of their international financial counterparts: power, wealth and the life-styles which money can buy. To accomplish these ends, gang entrepreneurs must reclaim the ground on which economic activity can be sustained. In doing so, they are in constant contest with the ostensible forces of political authority and the formal economy to which it gives service.

"Public Policy" in Los Angeles

As we have suggested then, to understand most of what happens in Los Angeles it is misleading to use the ordinary descriptive language of public or urban policymaking, which speaks of "policy options" and various forms of "decisionmaking." When thinking of policy in Los Angeles it is more appropriate to think in terms of "tendencies" rather than events or options, because policy in Los Angeles is more a function of the historical process through which Los Angeles has been shaped rather than a matter of local decisions.[50]

Nevertheless, the predominant orientation of most policy discourse operates within the misleading grammar that locates actors within Los

Angeles' boundaries producing policy outcomes. A recent essay in *The Atlantic* on Los Angeles is exemplary in this respect. The title of the article, "Los Angeles Comes of Age," inaugurates the "investigation" with a depoliticizing destiny narrative in which Los Angeles is seen not as something produced by spatial practices but something drawn by a future place at the top of the urban heap. Los Angeles is figured as a city competing with New York to be the "... greatest" city in the world, measured in terms of economic power, the prestige of its artistic community, and the notoriety of its political leaders.[51] The writers recognize that Los Angeles has "problems," but the grammar of their policy discourse is the traditional policy type, presenting a mythic unified actor, a set of decisionmakers who strive to cope with traffic, pollution, and political integration. There is no narrative on the production of the problems (or the production of non-problems) other than what is implied in the concept of "growth." It is thus the typical passive grammar of decisionmakers "faced with problems," rather than, for example, a more politically acute version that would inquire into the way public policy thinking tends to remain within certain narrow modes of problematization.[52] For example, "traffic congestion," which receives more space than any other "urban problem," is a middle-class problem, in that it accepts the already-produced segregation, housing, and shaping of the labor force that has arisen from the structures of real estate speculation, work force creation, city planning, etc. Traffic congestion is a "complaint" from those who are in a position to vocalize; it does not access the production and distribution of such positions.

A much more political aspect of the "reality" that is Los Angeles is that there is, as the article acknowledges, a Third World labor pool operating within the city. But the article's policy codes remain ecumenical; there is a lot of talk about banding together to solve problems, and the reasons for getting together register very little about the map of highly disparate levels of well-being and, most significantly, the produced levels of social disintegration that have been a result of a "policymaking" that has been complicit with the tendencies produced by forces that extend from inside Los Angeles to remote domains of effectivity shaping Los Angeles. What is offered as the big problem is to avoid missing opportunities assumed to be of general benefit, e.g., the opportunity to control even more of the trade in the Pacific rim than Los Angeles has already captured. ("There is no better time to build Los Angeles' role as a gateway.")[53]

To the extent that there is talk of the political space of Los Angeles it is represented as the political coalition of city council members.[54] For *The Atlantic*, finally, Los Angeles is the "second city," the Avis of the world of cities that is trying to be number one, and only cooperation by local decisionmakers can allow LA to fulfill this destiny.

There are other recent policy discourses on Los Angeles, which serve to illustrate the disenabling aspects of *The Atlantic*'s obtuse form of policy talk. First, and perhaps most important, what shapes Los Angeles life cannot be formulated without paying attention to dominant aspects of "late capitalism," which has, in Los Angeles, produced the "progressive globalization of its urban economy."[55] This is not the place for an exhaustive inventory, but, put simply, how people in Los Angeles live—and indeed what "decisionmakers" can control—is produced to a large extent outside of Los Angeles. One is foreign finance capital. There is, for example, the "Zaitech" phenomenon from Japan, which is the strategy of using financial technology to shift cash overflow from production to speculation. It is Zaitech that has been largely responsible for the financial and architectural structure of contemporary, downtown, Los Angeles.[56] Another is the modern version of warfare in the nuclear age. Much of Los Angeles' industry occupies military space in that there has been an increasing flow of money from the federal government into military-related manufacturing in the area.[57]

Related to the "outside" control of its economy is the fact that Los Angeles is one of the fastest growing manufacturing centers in the world. This is related to the dominant aspect of Los Angeles' spatial ordering, the situation—even acknowledged by *The Atlantic*—in which the inner shape of Los Angeles is constituted as a Third World labor force in a First World city.[58] In effect, Los Angeles has a domestic labor pool of Mexican and Asian workers who occupy very poor residential space, poorly remunerated labor space, and are largely excluded from effective legal and political space (for most are not represented by unions and as aliens are excluded from legal privileges). Increasingly, industry in Los Angeles operates with Third World labor conditions. In addition, the tremendous economic growth along with the highly touted emergence of this second city has not benefited another highly segregated group of the poor in Los Angeles, the black population. As Mike Davis has shown, Los Angeles' blacks have in fact been increasingly marginalized by the "internationalization of the metropolitan economy."[59]

This is not the place to elaborate on the racial segregation structure which is intimately related to the Third World within a First World labor condition. What is most disenabling from the point of view of political analysis are the predominant policy discourses, which focus on Los Angeles as a unified actor faced with problems and which see politics as the proper representation of the city's different ethnic groups. The spatial map of Los Angeles is a social map produced by the operation of various forms of power. To read the production of this map requires both a historical depth and a more politicized model of modernity. Some of the elements required have already been suggested above, particularly in reference to the brief discussion of the productive relation that obtains between law enforcement and the creation of a delinquent milieu. Let us convert public attention to problems of "law enforcement" into a brief analysis of why the production of what constitutes policy in Los Angeles cannot be understood within the traditional law enforcement discourse.

Among other things, Los Angeles' policy discourse is increasingly occupied by its "crime problem." Although much of what produces what is understood as modern crime and delinquency is what produces the modern city—the globalization of the city's economy, the marginalization of its poor, mostly "ethnic" classes, the recruitment (in LA's case) of a Third World labor force—the strategy has been reactive or, in Foucault's term, "carceral."[60] At its most concrete level, the paradigmatic carceral strategy is the prison, and Los Angeles' prison population is considerable. But, as Foucault has shown, the carceral does not end at the prison walls, for in many respects, modern social science (as well as many of modernity's disciplinary agencies) is complicit with the prison; its form of knowledge practice has contributed to an observational gridding in which all members of society occupy segments that contribute to our knowledge of their contribution to work, to delinquency, to public acquiescence to public policy, etc. Thus, for example, while Los Angeles' actual prison population is enormous, the carceral network is even more vast when broadly conceived. Of late, the vast surveillance network involves policymakers and social scientists in an attempt to react to the most recent form of delinquency, the formation of the Los Angeles gang system, which controls much of the city's drug trafficking in the poor, ethnic neighborhoods.

How are these gangs to be understood? The traditional social science approach to delinquency has fashioned a space in the grid for "predatory criminal offenders" who, as one recent study notes, are "more likely to exhibit impulsiveness and disregard for others' feelings."[61] In this kind of approach, delinquency is a "behavior," and although this disregard for others' feelings may well be essential to the success of corporate executives (e.g. Lee Iacocca by many accounts), it does not provoke investigations of its genesis in this social space. Rather, it is applied only to the behavior of "criminal offenders," as social scientists go on to theorize about what else we know about such delinquents—the coherence of their families, school performance, etc. It is noted, for example, that the family is a "promising locus of explanation for and treatment of delinquent behavior."[62] Within such a policy discourse, which refines Foucault's grid, making more dense the surveillance cross hatch, the only policy options available relate to intervention by police, welfare, or other corrections agencies belonging to the carceral network.

Now, let us imagine another frame. First, one can view delinquency not simply as a behavior of marginal types but rather as precisely a function of marginalization, of the positive, administratively driven aspect of what constitutes the spatial practices of the city. Anthony Giddens has described a process which has produced Los Angeles' tribalized set of locales from which "delinquency" springs; it is a newly formed delinquent culture.

Surveillance—the coding of information relevant to the administration of subject populations, plus the direct supervision by officials and administrators of all sorts—becomes a key mechanism furthering a breaking away of system from social integration. Traditional practices are dispersed (without, of course, disappearing altogether) under the impact of penetration of day-to-day life by codified administrative procedures. The locales which provide the settings for interaction in situations of co-presence (the basis of social integration) undergo a major set of transmutations. The old city–country relation is replaced by a sprawling expansion of a manufactured or "created" environment.[63]

Now, as noted above, Foucault has already explicated the intimate connection between policy and the delinquent milieu, but in contemporary Los Angeles, there seems to be a new level of warfare between "youth gangs" and the police, whose traditional methods for controlling and rendering delinquency usable are not effective. This has been recently represented in the film *Colors*. Whatever the explicit ideational color of the film may be, it is clear that the youth gangs are represented as being not as amenable to complicity with law enforcement practices as have been traditional "delinquents." To understand the current police-gang warfare we can have recourse to a conceptualization of urban spatial practices offered by Michel de Certeau. Distinguishing strategies from tactics, de Certeau argues that strategies belong to those (e.g. the police) who occupy legitimate or what is recognized as proper space within the social order. In this case, they are part of a centralized surveillance network for controlling the population. Tactics, by contrast, belong to those who do not occupy a legitimate space and depend instead on time, on whatever opportunities present themselves.[64]

The drug dealing and controlling of gang warfare amounts to the seizing of part of what is left of a possible economy in a greater economy controlled and policed by agents of those with legitimated spaces within which to operate. And, ironically, the very structure of modern Los Angeles—especially its high degree of racial/ethnic segregation, which has created a virtual tribalized order—has pushed "delinquency" further away from the traditional forms of law enforcement control of it. And it is clear that law enforcement officials, frustrated with their inability to operate with the old delinquency model, have increasingly adopted a warfare mentality and mode of operation. For example, recently the head of the Los Angeles District Attorney's drug unit used the Vietnam War analogy, saying, "This is Vietnam here."[65]

Thus we are back to the insight with which we began when we noted that in the case of the medieval city, it is better to speak of the city *as* policy rather than speaking of policy in the city. In important respects, this remains the case. Los Angeles is in part a city constituted as a system of internal war, a series of spaces informed by strategies and, in reaction, tactics. These actions and reactions cannot be drawn into traditional conversations about treating delinquency, cleaning up the environment, recruiting more ethnics into the city council, or strengthening the family.

The Normalizations of Policy

The discourses of urban policy and the processes through which it is produced normalize the tensions, competitions and contests of the urban landscape, masking the emergence of Los Angeles' islands of verticality. To the extent that the city is viewed as a historical result, it is as the linear product of the forces of industrialization and expansion which date from the end of the medieval period. Even as enthusiastic a future proclamation as the *Atlantic* article cited above situates Los Angeles primarily in the expansionist pattern of the industrial city. In this view those processes which had occurred as the result of national processes are now global. That which is modern to the city is its placement within the global economy. Los Angeles, the 23rd largest economic unit in the world, gains its significance by virtue of its integration into the extensive horizontalizations which the global economy represents.

The urban policy process as constructed by the terms of public policy discourse continues to function through the institutions and mechanisms of a historic liberalism, characterized by what Walzer has termed its "artful separations" and which Gottdiener sees as the product of an outdated paradigm based on unwarranted separations of those forces creating the urban environment.[66] Increasingly, it appears this liberal formula may be inappropriate to deal with what have become the "problems" of the urban environment. Let us approach our conclusion by returning to Walzer's argument in defense of the "art of separation" wrought by liberalism and its embodiment in the policy process itself.

For Walzer the great success of liberalism was its ability to separate spheres of social activity, to create a world of walls within which various liberties, not the least of which is the opportunity to pursue economic gain, could be conducted. The art of separation permits simultaneously both liberty and equality. For example, "The free market is open to all comers, without regard to race or creed. . . . The idea of privacy presupposes the equal value, at least so far as the authorities are concerned of all private lives. . . ."[67] And following familiar reasoning he concludes: "Limited government is the great success of the art of separation, but that very success opens the way for what political scientists call private government, and it is with the critique of private government that the leftist complaint against liberalism properly begins."[68]

Not surprisingly Walzer argues that the state must be the form of redress against the abuses of private power. He conceives of a

> consistent liberalism . . . one that passes over into democratic socialism. But this is still a democratic socialism of a liberal sort; it does not require the abolition of the market (nor does it require the abolition of religion) but rather the confinement of the market to its proper space.[69]

Walzer's remarks illustrate both the continued appeal of liberal formulations and their weakness as criteria for addressing the "problems" of policy. One enduring appeal of liberalism is its notion of balance. If private power grows excessive, the remedy is to utilize the democratic process to "discipline" that power, to relegate it to its "proper space." This commitment to balance proceeds from the prior commitment to separation itself wherein private and public power are by definition differentiated phenomena. This formulation begs the central question which a nonseparated view of the political economy centers, namely who controls the state?[70] Walzer, as previously noted above, dismisses this question by locating it within Marxist thought wherein it is viewed as a misguided absence of appreciation toward the benefits of separation and therefore the benefits of liberty. However, a significant number of readings of the current economy of the United States and the world, Marxist, neoMarxist and thoroughly nonMarxist, have raised as one of the central features of the emerging international economy the role of the enormously powerful transnational corporations whose behaviors are of sufficient moment to dominate the dynamics of national policy.[71] These are the sources of "private power" which more than any other force create the substance of what becomes "policy" at the domestic and local level, yet the abilities of these units of "public power" are excessively limited in two important respects. First, these forces of economic power are themselves increasingly represented as those which set national agendas with respect to a wide range of economic, social and military policy. Second, their truly international character places their actions in an international arena in which political authority and reach are poorly articulated and of a fragmented nature.

As a result national governments are confronted with a set of problems which are extremely difficult to address with national policies. Increasingly, for example, nation-states find that the sources of international capital must be courted for investment, and that the cost of this courting is a corresponding limitation in national revenue. Or, international capital markets make it extremely difficult for national authorities to control domestic interest rates. A growing perception among economists holds that internal political coloration may be of less importance to domestic policy decisions than interest rates: the bond market has come to have the status of a policy imperative. And, it must be added, this market responds very imperfectly to the actions of any single national entity.

One result is a steadfast concentration within the policy process on issues of individual behavior. Faced with "policy problems," be they in health, education, housing, traffic, drugs, gang warfare, etc., the "policy actor," especially the local policy actor, is led to the identification of individual behavior and its transformation as the appropriate response (as the traditional discourse would put it). Much of this impetus is given by the centering of the individual which continues to occur with liberal grounded policy thought. A conception of separation as an "art" treats the boundaries which separate one bureaucratic structure from another as wisdom rather than political practice. It focuses attention on isolated individuals rather than the forces encouraging alternatively cohesion and disintegration, leaving us with no effective way to figure the political consequences of boundary creation and maintenance. Further, the radical centering of the individual produces any number of epistemological subspecies in which problem causation is circumscribed in a reductionist manner. (The transformation of public health into an individual centered/behavior modification problematic is a case in point.)[72] These narrowly focussed policy problematics are both the result of the bureaucratic response to the intense pressure which is levied by the more powerful economic interests and a convenient response by the policy agency to the demand that it address a given social problem.

Finally, "the policy actor" is faced ultimately with the realization that often he/she has no effective policy response to a "problem" whose generative forces lie far beyond the confines of the political authority within which the problem is being addressed. Operating within this disenabling discursive space, those constructed as "policy actors" within the prevailing policy discourse are moved to address "the problems" with the tools made available by the imposed problematics, however inappropriate they might be to the issue of significantly affecting life in the postmodern city.

Notes

1. Paul Virilio, *L'espace Critique* (Paris: Christian Bourgois, 1984).

2. Robert Reinhold, "The Los Angeles Life on New York Time," *New York Times*, 3 June 1988, Style, pp. 1–3.

3. Paul Virilio's concept of chronospace is developed in *Pure War* (New York: Semiotext(e), 1983).

4. Jean Baudrillard, "The Art Auction: Sign Exchange and Sumptuary Value," in *For a Critique of the Political Economy of the Sign*, trans. Charles Levin (St. Louis: Telos Press, 1981), p. 122.

5. This use of the concept of the "ground plan" comes from Martin Heidegger, "The Age of the World Picture," in *The Question Concerning Technology*, trans. William Lovett (New York: Harper & Row, 1977).

6. For a discussion of the failure of contemporary social theory to treat spatialization as practice, see Edward W. Soja, "Modern Geography, Western Marxism and the Restructuring of Critical Social Theory," in Richard Peet and Nigel Thrift, eds., *The New Models in Geography* (London: Allen & Unwin, 1987).

7. This is why Gilles Deleuze has called Foucault, an analyst of discursive practices, also a cartographer. See his *Foucault*, ed. and trans. Sean Hand (Minneapolis: University of Minnesota Press, 1986), pp. 23–44.

8. Jacques Derrida, *Speech and Phenomena*, trans. David Allison (Evanston: Northwestern University Press, 1973), p. 78.

9. Anthony Giddens, *A Contemporary Critique of Historical Materialism* (Berkeley: University of California Press, 1981), p. 90.

10. Ibid., p. 93.

11. Ibid., pp. 93–94.

12. Michel de Certeau, "Practices of Space," in Marshall Blonsky, ed., *On Signs* (Baltimore: Johns Hopkins University Press, 1985), p. 124.

13. Both expressions belong to de Certeau, ibid.

14. Ibid., p. 127.

15. Edward W. Soja, "The Socio-Spatial Dialectic," *Annals of the Association of American Geographers*, no. 70 (June 1980): 210.

16. For an excellent summary of the production of merchandising space in 19th century France see Richard Terdiman, *Discourse, Counter-Discourse* (Ithaca: Cornell University Press, 1985), pp. 136–138. See also Michael B. Miller, *The Bon Marche* (Princeton: Princeton University Press, 1981), pp. 165–230.

17. Daniel Boorstin, *The Americans: The Democratic Experience* (New York: Vintage Books, 1974).

18. Aldous Huxley, *The Grey Eminence* (London: Chatto & Windus, 1944), p. 292.

19. Ibid., p. 11.

20. Michel Foucault, "Of Other Spaces," trans. Jay Miscowiec., *Diacritics* 16 (Spring 1986).

21. Huxley, *The Grey Eminence*, note 18, p. 11.

22. Foucault, "Of Other Spaces," note 20, p. 23.

23. Michael Walzer, "Liberalism and the Art of Separation," *Political Theory* 12 (August 1984): 315.

24. Ibid.

25. See Gilles Deleuze and Felix Guattari, *The Anti-Oedipus*, trans. Robert Hurley, Mark Seem, and Helen A. Lane (New York: Viking, 1977). The quotation is an application of Deleuze and Guattari's concepts of deterritorialization by Klaus Theweleit in *Male Fantasies*, Vol. I, trans. Stephen Conway (Minneapolis: University of Minnesota Press, 1987), p. 264.

26. Deleuze and Guattari, *The Anti-Oedipus* p. 35.

27. Walzer, "Liberalism and the Art of Separation," note 23, pp. 317–320.

28. Michel Foucault, "War in the Filigree of Peace," *Oxford Literary Review* 4 (Autumn 1979): 18.

29. This treatment of discursive practices as assets is suggested in Michel Foucault, *The Archeology of Knowledge*, trans. A. M. Sheridan Smith (New York: Pantheon, 1972), p. 120.

30. Walzer, "Liberalism and the Art of Separation," note 23, p. 323.

31. Foucault, "Of Other Spaces," note 20, p. 23.

32. Michel Foucault, *Discipline and Punish*, trans. Alan Sheridan (New York: Pantheon, 1977), pp. 257–292.

33. Ibid., p. 277.

34. Henri Lefebre, "Reflections on the Politics of Space," trans. Michael J. Enders, *Antipode* 8 (May 1976): 33.

35. Ibid., p. 31.

36. Jacques Attali, *Noise*, trans. Brain Massumi (Minneapolis: University of Minnesota Press, 1985), pp. 117–118.

37. Ibid., p. 47.

38. See ibid., p. 119 for a discussion of the delocalizing effect of the phonograph record.

39. See Norbert Elias, "Introduction," in Norbert Elias and Eric Dunning, *Quest for Excitement: Sport and Leisure in the Civilizing Process* (New York: Basil Blackwell, 1986).

40. See E. P. Thompson, "Patrician Society, Plebeian Culture," *Journal of Social History* 7 (Summer 1974) : 403; and "The Moral Economy of the English Crowd in the Eighteenth Century," *Past and Present* 50 (February 1971): 76–136.

41. On gambling's shaping effects on sport, see Dennis Brailford, *Sport and Society: Elizabeth to Anne* (London: Routledge & Kegan Paul, 1969), p. 213.

42. On the implications for the city of the development of broadcasting space, see Virilio, *Pure War*, note 3, p. 87.

43. The creation of a monetized world radically horizontalized the relational structures characteristic of medieval society. Note: "Money . . . functions as a concrete abstraction, imposing external and homogeneous measures of value on all aspects of human life reducing infinite diversity to a single comparable dimension, and masking subjective human relations by market exchanges," David Harvey, *Consciousness and the Urban Experience: Studies in the History and Theory of Capitalist Urbanization* (Baltimore: Johns Hopkins University Press, 1985), pp. 253–254.

44. S. Christopherson and M. Storper, "The City as Studio; the World as Back Lot: The Impact of Vertical Disintegration on the Location of the Motion Picture Industry," *Environment and Planning, D: Society and Space* 4 (1986): 305–320, 321.

45. Soja, "Taking Los Angeles Apart," note 15.

46. W. C. Baer, "Housing In An Internationalizing Region: Housing Stock Dynamics in Southern California and the Dilemmas of Fair Share," *Environment and Planning, D: Society and Space* 4 (1986): 337–339, 349.

47. Foucault, "Of Other Spaces," Ref. 20, p. 22.

48. Tom Wolfe, *The Bonfire of the Vanities* (New York: Farrar, Straus & Giroux, 1987).

49. Tom Peters reports that currency exchanges now total $80 trillion per annum, only $4 trillion of which are necessary to finance trade in goods and service. Tom Peters, *Thriving on Chaos: Handbook for a Management Revolution* (New York, Alfred A. Knopf, 1988), p. 9.

50. This use of the concept of tendency belongs to Virilio, *Pure War*.

51. Charles Lockwood and Christopher B. Leinberger, "Los Angeles Comes of Age," *The Atlantic* 26 (January 1988): 31 ff.

52. The turning of "problem" into the action "problematization" is an analytic strategy of Michel Foucault. For a good summary of how he views this strategy, see the "Introduction" in his *The Use of Pleasure*, trans. Robert Hurley (New York: Pantheon, 1985).

53. Attali, *Noise*, note 26, p. 39.

54. Ibid., p. 46.

55. On the "globalization" of the Los Angeles economy see Edward Soja, "Taking Los Angeles Apart: Some Fragments of a Critical Human Geography," *Society and Space* 4 (1986), and Mike Davis, "Chinatown, Part Two? The 'Internationalization' of Downtown Los Angeles," *New Left Review* 164 (March/April 1987), pp. 65–86.

56. "Zaitech" is discussed in Davis, ibid., pp. 72–73.

57. Soja, "Taking Los Angeles Apart," note 15, pp. 260–261.
58. The Third World labor pool theme is developed in Davis, "Chinatown, Part Two?" note 55.
59. See ibid., pp. 73–75 for an elaboration of the increasing marginalization of Los Angeles' black population.
60. Foucault, *Discipline and Punish*, note 32, pp. 293–308.
61. Glenn C. Loury, "The Family as Context for Delinquency Prevention: Demographic Trends and Political Realities," in James Q. Wilson and Glenn C. Loury, eds., *From Children to Citizens* (New York: Springer-Verlag, 1987), pp. 3–26.
62. Ibid., p. 4.
63. Anthony Giddens, *The Constitution of Society* (Berkeley: University of California Press, 1984), pp. 183–184.
64. Michel de Certeau, *The Practice of Everyday Life*, trans. Steven F. Rendall (Berkeley: University of California Press, 1984), pp. xviii–xx.
65. Quoted in Mike Davis, "Los Angeles: Civil Liberties between the Hammer and the Rock," *New Left Review*, no. 170 (July/August 1988): 38.
66. Note: "The fields of urban science require reconceptualization because the patterns of spatial organization have changed." Gottdiener's critique is directed primarily at mainstream urban science which in his view is dominated by urban ecology, economics and geography and the liberal paradigm which underlies them and produces a fundamentally depoliticized view of urban processes. His critique is equally directed at left-liberal and Marxist political economy perspectives for their inattention to the "absolute space of political and social denomination" which "reigns hegemonically over the social space of everyday life," M. Gottdiener, *The Social Production of Urban Space* (Austin: University of Texas Press, 1985), p. 290.
67. Walzer, "Liberalism and the Art of Separation," note 23, p. 320.
68. Ibid., p. 321.
69. Ibid., p. 323.
70. Again, Gottdiener on urban science—"The mainstream paradigm explains urban development as if the state did not exist. As we have seen socio-spatial development is as much a product of the state as it is of the private sector," note 66, p. 268.
71. Simply, for example, consider such diverse sources as Richard J. Barnet and Ronald E. Mueller, *Global Reach* (New York: Simon and Schuster, 1974); Creel Forman, *The Two American Political Systems* (Englewood Cliffs, N.J.: Prentice-Hall, 1984); Edward S. Greenberg, *Capitalism and the American Political Ideal* (Armonk, N.Y.: M. E. Sharpe, 1985); and Michael Moffett, *The World's Money* (New York: Simon & Schuster, 1983).
72. J. Powels, "On the Limitations of Modern Medicine," *Science, Medicine and Man* 1 (1973): 1–50.

7

The Politics of Secularism and the Recovery of Religious Tolerance

Ashis Nandy

Faith, Ideology, and the Self

A significant aspect of the post-colonial structures of knowledge in the Third World is a peculiar form of imperialism of categories. Under such imperialism, a conceptual domain is sometimes hegemonized by a concept produced and honed in the West, hegemonized so effectively that the original domain vanishes from our awareness. Intellect and intelligence become IQ, the oral cultures become the cultures of the primitive, the oppressed become the proletariat, social change becomes development. After a while, people begin to forget that IQ is only a crude measure of intelligence and that one day someone else may think up another kind of index to assess the same thing; that social change did not begin with development, nor will it stop once the idea of development dies a natural or unnatural death.

In this paper, I seek to provide a political preface to the recovery of a well-known domain of public concern in South Asia, ethnic and especially religious tolerance, from the hegemonic language of secularism popularized by Westernized intellectuals and middle classes exposed to the globally dominant language of the nation-state in this part of the world. This language, whatever may have been its positive contributions to humane governance and to religious tolerance in the past, increasingly has become a cover for the complicity of modern intellectuals and the modernizing middle classes of South Asia in the new forms of religious violence. These are the forms in which the state, the media and the ideologies of national security, development and modernity propagated by the modern intelligentsia and the middle classes play crucial roles.

To provide the political preface I have promised, I have first to describe four trends which have become clearly visible in South Asia during this century, particularly after the Second World War.

Reprinted with permission from *Alternatives: Social Transformation and Humane Governance* 13, no. 2 (April 1988).

Four Trends in South Asia

The first and the most important of these trends is that each religion in South Asia, perhaps all over the southern hemisphere, has split into two: faith and ideology. Both are inappropriate terms but I give them, in this paper, specific meanings to serve my purpose. By faith I mean religion as a way of life, a tradition which is definitionally non-monolithic and operationally plural. I say "definitionally" because, unless a religion is geographically and culturally confined to a small area, religion as a way of life has to in effect turn into a confederation of a number of ways of life, linked by a common faith having some theological space for the heterogeneity which everyday life introduces. Witness the differences between Iranian and Indonesian Islam, two cultures divided by the same faith. The two forms of Islam are interlocking, not isomorphic in relation to each other.

By ideology I mean religion as a sub-national, national or cross-national identifier of populations contesting for, or protecting non-religious, usually political or socioeconomic, interests. Such religions-as-ideologies are usually identified with one or more texts which, rather than the ways of life of the believers, then become the final identifiers of the "pure" forms of the religions. The texts help anchor the ideologies in some-thing seemingly concrete and delimited and in effect provide a set of man-ageable operational definitions.

The modern state always prefers to deal with religious ideologies rather than with faiths. It is wary of both forms of religion but it finds the ways of life more inchoate and, hence, unmanageable, even though it is faith rather than ideology which has traditionally shown more pliability and catholicity. It is religion-as-faith which prompted 200,000 Indians to declare themselves as Mohammedan Hindus in the census of 1911; and it was the catholicity of faith which prompted Mole–Salam Girasia Rajputs to traditionally have two names for every member of the community, one Hindu and one Muslim.[1] It is religion-as-ideology, on the other hand, which prompted a significant proportion of the Punjabi-speaking Hindus to declare Hindi as their mother tongue, thus bringing the politics of language to bear on the differences between Sikhism and Hinduism and sowing the seeds for the creation of a new minority. Likewise it is religion-as-ideology which has provided a potent tool to the *Jamaat e Islami* to disown the traditional, plural forms of Islam in the Indian subcontinent and to disjunct official religion from everyday life.

Second, during the past two centuries or so, there has grown a tendency to view the older faiths of the region through the eyes of evangelical European Christianity and its various off-shoots—such as the masculine Christianity associated with 19th-century missionaries like Joshua Marshman and William Carey, or its mirror image in the orthodox modernism vended by the likes of Friedrich Engels and Thomas Huxley. Because this particular Eurocentric way of looking at faiths gradually came to be associated with the dominant culture of the colonial states in the region, it subsumes under it a set of clear polarities: center versus periphery, true faith versus its distortions, civil versus primordial, and great traditions versus local cultures or little traditions.

It is part of the same story that in each of the dyads, the second category is set up to lose. It is also a part of the same story that, once the colonial concept of state was internalized by the societies of the region through the nationalist ideology, in turn heavily influenced by the Western theories and practice of statecraft,[2] the nascent nation-states of the region took on themselves the same civilizing mission that the colonial states had once taken on vis-à-vis the ancient faiths of the subcontinent.

Third, the idea of secularism, an import from 19th-century Europe into South Asia, has acquired immense potency in the middle-class cultures and "state sectors" of South Asia, thanks to its connection with and response to religion-as-ideology. Secularism has little to say about cultures—it is definitionally ethnophobic and frequently ethnocidal, unless of course cultures and those living by cultures are willing to show total subservience to the modern nation-state and become ornaments or adjuncts to modern living —and the orthodox secularists have no clue to the way a religion can link up different faiths or ways of life according to its own configurative principles.

To such secularists, religion is an ideology in opposition to the ideology of modern statecraft and, therefore, needs to the contained. They feel even more uncomfortable with religion-as-faith claiming to have its own principles of tolerance and intolerance, for that claim denies the state and the middle-class ideologues of the state the right to be the ultimate reservoir of sanity and the ultimate arbiter among different religions and communities. This denial is particularly galling to those who see the clash between two faiths merely as a clash of socioeconomic interests, not as a simultaneous clash between conflicting interests and a philosophical encounter between two metaphysics. The Westernized middle classes and literati of South Asia love to see all such encounters as reflections of socioeconomic forces and, thus, as liabilities and as sources of ethnic violence.

Fourth, the imported idea of secularism has become increasingly incompatible and, as it were, uncomfortable with the somewhat fluid definitions of the self with which many South Asian cultures live. Such a self, which can be conceptually viewed as a configuration of selves, invokes and reflects the configurative principles of religions-as-faiths. It also happens to be a negation of the modern concept of selfhood acquired partly from the West and partly from a re-discovery of previously recessive elements in South Asian traditions. Religion-as-ideology, working with the concept of well-bounded, mutually exclusive religious identities, on the other hand, is more compatible with and analogous to the definition of the self as a well-bounded, individuated entity clearly separable from the non-self. Such individuation is taking place in South Asian societies at a fast pace and, to that extent, more exclusive definitions of the self also are emerg-ing in these societies as a by-product of secularization.[3]

A more fluid definition of the self is not merely more compatible with religion-as-faith, it also has—and depends more on—a distinctive set of the non-self and anti-selves (to coin a neologism analogous to anti-heroes). On one plane, these anti–selves are similar to what psychologist Carl Rogers used to call, infelicitously, the "not–me"—and some others call rejected selves. On another plane, they, the anti-selves, are counter–points without which the self just cannot be defined in the major cultures of South Asia. It is the self in conjunction with its anti-selves and its distinctive concept of the non-self which define the domain of the self. Religion-as-faith is more compatible with such a complex self-definition; secularism has no inkling of this distinct, though certainly not unique, form of self-definition in South Asia. For everything said, secularism is, as T. N. Madan puts it, a gift of Christianity, by which he presumably means a "gift of post-medieval, European Christianity" to this part of the world.[4]

It is in the context of these four processes that I now discuss the scope and limits of the ideology of secularism in India and its relationship with the new forms of ethnic violence we have been witnessing.

The Fate of Secularism

Two meanings of secularism

I must make it clear at this point that I am not a secularist. In fact, I can be called an anti-secularist. I call myself an anti-secularist because I feel that the ideology and politics of secularism have more or less exhausted their possibilities. And that we may now have to work with a different conceptual frame, which is already vaguely visible at the borders of Indian political culture.

When I say that the ideology and politics of secularism have exhausted themselves, I have in mind the standard English meaning of the word "secularism." As we know, there are two meanings of the word current in modern and modernizing India and, for that matter, in the whole of this subcontinent. One of the two meanings you can easily find out by consulting any standard dictionary. But you will have difficulty finding the other, for it is a non-standard, local meaning which, many like to believe, is typically and distinctively Indian or South Asian. (As we shall see below, it also has a Western tail, but that tail is now increasingly vestigial.)

The first meaning becomes clear when people talk of secular trends in history or economics, or when they speak of secularizing the state. The word "secular" has been used in this sense, at least in the English-speaking West, for more than 300 years. This secularism chalks out an area in public life where religion is not admitted. One can have religion in one's private life; one can be a good Hindu or a good Muslim within one's home or at one's place of worship. But when one enters public life, one is expected to leave one's faith behind. This ideology of secularism is associated with slogans like 'we are Indians first, Hindus second' or "we are Indians first, then Sikhs." Implicit in the ideology is the belief that managing the public realm is a science which is essentially universal and that religion, to the extent it is opposed to the Baconian world-image of science, is an open or potential threat to any modern polity.

In contrast, the non-Western meaning of secularism revolves around equal respect for all religions. This is the way it is usually put by public figures. Less crudely stated, it implies that while public life may or may not be kept free of religion, it must have space for a continuous dialogue among religious traditions and between the religious and the secular—that, in the ultimate analysis, each major faith in the region includes *within* it an in-house version of the other faiths both as an internal criticism and as a reminder of the diversity of the theory of transcendence.

Recently, Ali Akhtar Khan has drawn attention to the fact that George Jacob Holyoake, who coined the word "secularism" in 1850, advocated a secularism accommodative of religion, a secularism which would moreover emphasize diversities and co-existence in the matter of faith. His contemporary, Joseph Bradlaugh, on the other hand, believed in a secularism which rejected religion and made science its deity.[5] Most non-modern Indians (that is, Indians who would have reduced Professor Max Weber to tears), pushed around by the political and cultural forces unleashed by colonialism still operating in Indian society, have unwittingly opted for the accommodative and pluralist meaning, while India's Westernized intellectuals have consciously opted for the abolition of religion from the public sphere.

In other words, the accommodative meaning is more compatible with the meaning a majority of Indians, independently of Bradlaugh, have given to the word "secularism." This meaning has always disconcerted the country's Westernized intellectuals. They have seen such people's secularism as adulterated and as compromising true secularism. This despite the fact that the ultimate symbol of religious tolerance for the modern Indian, Gandhi, obviously had this adulterated meaning in mind on the few occasions when he seemed to plead for secularism. This is clear from his notorious claims that those who thought that religion and politics could be kept separate, understood neither religion nor politics.

The saving grace in all this is that, while the scientific, rational meaning of secularism has dominated India's middle-class public consciousness, the Indian people and, till recently, most practicing Indian politicians have depended on the accommodative meaning. The danger is that the first meaning is supported by the accelerating process of modernization in India. As a result, there is now a clearer fit between the declared ideology of the modern Indian nation-state and the secularism that fears religions and ethnicities. Sociologist Imtiaz Ahmed euphemistically calls this fearful, nervous secularism the new liberalism of the Indian élites.[6]

The political hierarchy in secularism

Associated with this—what then South Asians perceive as the more scientific Western meaning of secularism—is a hidden political hierarchy. I have spelt out the hierarchy previously elsewhere but I shall nevertheless have to re-state it to make the rest of my argument. This hierarchy makes a four-fold classification of the political actors in the sub-continent.

At the top of the hierarchy are those who are believers neither in public nor in private. They are supposed to be scientific and rational, and they are expected ultimately not only to rule this society but also dominate its political culture. An obvious example is Jawaharlal Nehru. Though we are now told, with a great deal of embarrassment, that he believed in astrology and *tantra*, Nehru rightfully belongs to this rung because he always made the modern Indians a little ashamed of their religious beliefs and ethnic origins, and convinced them that he himself had the courage and the rationality to neither believe in private nor in public. By common consent of the Indian middle classes, Nehru provided a perfect role model for the 20th-century citizens of the flawed cultural reality called India. It is the Nehruvian model which informs the following charming letter, written by a distinguished former Ambassador, to the editor of India's best-known national daily:

> M. V. Kamath asks in his article "Where do we find the Indian?" My dear friend and colleague, the late Ambassador M. R. S. Beg, often used to say: "Don't you think, old boy, that the only Indians are we wogs?" However quaint it may have sounded 30 years ago, the validity of this statement has increasingly become apparent over the years.[7]

On the second rung of the ladder are those who choose not to appear as believers in public despite being devout believers in private. I can think of no better example of the type than Indira Gandhi. She was a genuine non-believer in her public life (she after all died in the hands of her own Sikh guards, rather than accept the advice of her security officers to change the guards), but in private she was a devout Hindu who had to make her 71—or was it 69?—pilgrimages. Both the selves of Indira Gandhi were genuine and together they represented the self-concept of a sizeable portion of the Indian middle classes. A number of rulers in this part of the world fit this category —from Ayub Khan to Lal Bahadur Shastri to Sheikh Mujibur Rahman. Though the Westernized literati in the South Asian societies have never cared much for this model of religious and ethnic tolerance, they have been usually willing to accept the model as a reasonable compromise with the "underdeveloped" cultures in the area.

On the third rung are those who are believers in public but do not believe in private. This may at first seem an odd category, but one or two examples will make its meaning clear and also partially explain why this category includes problematic men and women. To me the two most illustrious examples of the genre from the Indian sub-continent are Mohammed Ali Jinnah who was an agnostic in private life but took up the cause of Islam successfully in public, and D. V. Savarkar who was an atheist in private life but declared Hinduism as his political ideology.

Such people can be dangerous because to them religion is a political tool and a means of fighting one's own and one's community's sense of cultural inadequacy. Religion to them is not a matter of piety. Their private denial of belief only puts off-guard the secularist who cannot fathom the seriousness with which the Jinnahs and the Savarkars take religion as a political instrument. On the other hand, their public faith puts the faithful off-guard because the latter never discern the contempt in which the heroes hold the common run of the faithful. Often these heroes invoke the classical versions of their faiths to underplay, marginalize or even de-legitimize the existing ways of life associated with their faiths. The goal of those holding such an instrumental view of religion has always been to homogenize their co-believers into proper political formations and, for that reason, to elimi-nate those parts of religion which smack of folklore and which threaten to legitimize diversities, inter-faith dialogue and theological polycentrism.

At the bottom of the hierarchy are those who are believers in private as well as in public. The best and most notorious example is that of Gandhi who openly believed both in private and in public, and gave his belief spectacular play in politics. This category has its strengths and weaknesses. One may say that exactly as the category manifests its strength in someone like Gandhi, it shows its weakness in others like Ayatollah Khomeini in Iran or Jarnail Singh Bhindranwale in the Punjab, India, both of whom ended up trying to fully homogenize their communities. The category can even throw up grand eccentrics. Chaudhuri Rehmat Ali 50 years ago used to stand on Fridays outside the King's College gate at Cambridge and chant like a street hawker, "come and buy Pakistan—my earth-shaking pamphlet."[8]

The four categories are not neat and in real life they rarely come in their pure forms. Often the same person can move from one to the other. Thus, writer Rahi Masoom Raza, being also a scriptwriter for commercial Hindi films and at home with spectacular changes of heart, comfortably oscillates between the first two categories.

> This Babari Masjid and Ram Janambhoomi temple should be demolished.... We as Indians are not interested in Babari Masjid, Rama Janambhoomis ... as secular people we must crush the religious fanatics.

Only ten months earlier Raza had, with as much passion, said:

> I, Rahi Masoom Raza, son of the late Mr Syed Bashir Hasan Abidi, a Muslim and one of the direct descendants of the Prophet of Islam, hereby condemn Mr Z. A. Ansari for his un-Islamic and anti-Muslim speeches in Parliament. The Quran nowhere says that a Muslim should have four wives.[9]

For the moment I shall not go into such issues. All I shall add is that in India, we have been always slightly embarrassed about this modern classification or ordering in our political life, for we know that the Father of the Nation, Gandhi, does not fare very well when the classification is applied to him.

Collapse of secularism

Fortunately for some modern Indians, the embarrassment has been resolved by the fact that this classification is not working well today. It is not working well because it has led neither to the elimination of religion and ethnicity from politics nor to greater religious and ethnic tolerance. This is not the case only with us; this is the case with every society which has been put up to the Indians, some time or another, as an ideal secular society.

Thus, problems of ethnicity and secularization haunt today not merely the twin capitals of the world, Washington and Moscow, they even haunt the country which the older South Asians have been trained to view as remarkably free from the divisiveness of ethnicity and religion. For instance, for some 150 years the Indians have learned, as part of their political socialization, that one of the reasons Britain dominated India and one of the reasons why the Indians were colonized was that they were not secular, whereas Britain was. That was why the Indians did not know how to live together, whereas Britain was a world power, perfectly integrated and fired by the true spirit of secular nationalism. Now we find that after nearly 300 years of secularism, the Irish, the Scottish and the Welsh together are creating as many problems for Britain as some of the religions or regions are creating for us in India.

Why is the old ideology of secularism not working in India? There are many reasons for this; I shall mention only a few, confining myself specifically to the problem of religion as it has become entangled with the political process in the country.

First, in the early years of independence, when the national élite was small and a large section of it had face-to-face contacts, one could screen people entering public life, especially the upper levels of the public services and high politics, for their commitment to secularism. Thanks to the growth of democratic participation in politics—India has gone through eight general elections and innumerable local and state elections—such screening is no longer possible. We can no longer make sure that those who reach the highest levels of the army, police, bureaucracy or politics believe in old-style secular politics.

To give one example, two ministers of the present central cabinet in India and a number of "high–ups" in the ruling party have been accused of not only encouraging, organizing and running a communal riot, but also of protecting the guilty and publicly threatening civil rights workers engaged in relief work. One chief minister has been recently accused of importing rioters from another state on payment of professional fees to precipitate a communal riot as an antidote to violent inter-caste conflicts. Another allegedly organized a riot three years ago so that he could impose a curfew in the state capital to stop his political opponents from demonstrating their strength in the legislature.

Such instances would have been unthinkable only ten years ago. They have become thinkable today because India's ultra-élites can no longer informally screen decision makers the way they once used to; political participation in the country is growing, and the country's political institutions, particularly the parties, are under too much of a strain to allow such screening. Religion *has* entered public life but through the backdoor.

Second, it has become more and more obvious to a large number of people that modernity is now no longer the ideology of a small minority; it is now the organizing principle of the dominant culture of politics. The idea that religions dominate India, that there are a handful of modern Indians fighting a rear-guard action against that domination, is no longer convincing to many semi-modern Indians. These Indians see the society around them—and often their own children—leaving no scope for a compromise between the old and new and opting for a way of life which fundamentally negates the traditional concepts of a good life and a desirable society. These Indians have now come to sense that it is modernity which rules the world and, even in this sub-continent, religion-as-faith is being pushed into a corner. Much of the fanaticism and violence associated with religion comes today from the sense of defeat of the believers, from their feelings of impotency, and from their free-floating anger and self-hatred while facing a world which is increasingly secular and de-sacralized.

This issue has another side. When the state makes a plea to a minority community to be secular or to confine itself to only secular politics, the state in effect tells the minority to "go slow" on its faith, so that it can be more truly integrated in the nation-state. Simultaneously, the state offers the minority a consolation prize in the form of a promise that it will force the majority community also to ultimately dilute its faith. What the state says to a religious community, the modern sector often indirectly tells the individual: "You give up your faith, at least in public; we also shall give up our faiths in public and together we shall be able to live in freedom from religious intolerance." I need hardly add that however reasonable the solution may look to people like us, who like to see themselves as rational non-believing moderns, it is not an adequate consolation to the faithful, to whom religion is what it is precisely because it provides an overall theory of life, including public life, and because life is not worth living without a theory, however imperfect, of transcendence.

Third, we have begun to find out that, while appealing to the believers to keep the public sphere free of religion, the modern nation-state has no means of ensuring that the ideologies of secularism, development and nationalism themselves do not begin to act as faiths intolerant of other faiths. That is, while the modern state builds up pressures on citizens to give up their faith in public, it guarantees no protection to them against the sufferings inflicted by the state itself in the name of its ideology. In fact, with the help of modern communications and the secular coercive power at its command, the state can use its ideology to silence its non-conforming citizens. The role of secularism in many societies today is no different from the crusading and inquisitorial role of religious ideologies. In such societies, the citizens have less protection against the ideology of the state than against religious ideologies or theocratic forces. Certainly in India, the ideas of nation-building, scientific growth, security, modernization and development have become parts of a left-handed technology with a clear touch of religiosity—a modern demonology, a *tantra* with a built-in code of violence.

This can be put another way. To many Indians today, secularism comes as a part of a larger package consisting of a set of standardized ideological products and social processes—development, mega-science and national security being some of the most prominent among them. This package often plays the same role vis-à-vis the people of the society—sanctioning or justifying violence against the weak and the dissenting—that the church, the *ulema*, the *sangha*, or the Brahmans played in earlier times.

Finally, the belief that values derived from the secular ideology of the state would be a better guide to political action and to a more tolerant and richer political life (as compared to the values derived from the religious faiths) has become even more untenable to large parts of Indian society than it was a decade ago. We are living in times when it has become clear that, as far as public morality goes, statecraft in India may have something to learn from Hinduism, Islam or Sikhism; but Hinduism, Islam, and Sikhism have very little to learn from the Constitution or from state secular practices. And the hope that the Indian state would give a set of values to guide a Hindu, a Muslim or a Sikh in his daily public behaviour lies splintered around us. The ideology of the Indian state and, for that matter, the deification of the state may go well with modern and semi-modern Indians, but both pall on a large number of decent Indians who are outside the charmed circle of the state sector.

In sum, we are at a point in time when old-style secularism can no longer pretend to guide moral or political action. All that the ideology of secularism can do now is to sanction the absurd search for a modern language of politics in a traditional society which has an open polity. Let me spell this out.

The long shadows of the "Western Man"

In most post-colonial societies, when religion, politics or religion and politics are discussed, there is an invisible reference point. This reference point is the Western Man. Not the Western Man in reality or the Western Man of history, but the Western Man as the defeated civilizations in this part of the world have construed him. This Western Man rules the world, it seems to the defeated, because of his superior understanding of the relationship between religion and politics. To cope with this success, every major relig-ious community in the region has produced three responses—I should say two responses and one non-response. These responses have rather clear-cut relationships with the process of splitting religions described at the beginning of this paper; in fact, they derive from the process.

The first response—it is not easy to capture the spirit of the response, but I shall try—is to model oneself on the Western Man. I do not want to use the work "imitation" because something more than mimicking is involved. The response consists in capturing, within one's own self and one's own culture, the traits one sees as the reasons for the West's success on the world stage. Seemingly it is a liberal, synthesizing approach and those responding to the West in this fashion justify it as a universal response. A recent and very neat example of this response is mathematician and philosopher Raojibhai C. Patel's essay in which the analysis is almost entirely in terms of Western experience with religion and politics, and the conclusions are all about India.[10]

The second response to Western Man is that of the zealot. The zealot's one goal is to somehow defeat Western Man at his own game—the way Japan, for instance, has done in economic matters. This is a crude way of describing a complex response, but it does convey that what passes as fundamentalism or revivalism is often only another form of Westernization becoming popular among the uprooted middle classes in India and, to judge by some of the Sri Lankan writings on ethnic issues, in Sri Lanka. A recent newspaper interview of nuclear physicist A. Q. Khan of Pakistan is a copybook instance of the same response seeking expression in the political culture of Pakistan.[11]

In India at least, the heart of the response is the faith that what Japan has done in economy, one can do in the case of religion and politics. One can, for example, decontaminate Hinduism of its folk elements, turn it into a classical

Vedantic faith, and then give it additional teeth with the help of Western technology and secular statecraft, so that the Hindus can take on, and ultimately defeat, all their external and internal enemies, if necessary, by liquidating all forms of ethnic plurality—first within Hinduism and then within India, to equal Western Man as a new *übermenschen*. The zealot judges the success or failure of his or her own religion only by this one criterion.

Historian and Sinologist Giri Deshingkar loves to give the example of a book written by one of the Shankaracharyas on the Mantrashastra. The book not merely pathetically justifies the Mantrashastra by claiming that its premises are justified by the discoveries of modern science, as if that made the text more sacred, the title page of the book says—remember, it is an exposition of an ancient *shastra* by a much venerated traditional religious preceptor—that its author is a BA, LLB. If a guru of the world, a *jagadguru*, needs to justify his commentary on Indian sacred texts by referring to his second-rate Western degrees and by seeking endorsement from an alien science, then of course we know where we are and what the state of India's cultural self-confidence is. No wonder, every other day we see full-page advertisements by Maharishi Mahesh Yogi in the newspapers, suggesting that Vedanta is true because quantum physics says so.

Such responses are characteristic of the zealot as well as the ultimate admission of defeat. They constitute the cultural bed on which grows the revivalism of the defeated. Japan in a sense has admitted such defeat by deciding to model itself on the West. Once it probably had other options, as the Japanese scholar M. Kasai would have us believe, but it chose to ignore them and tried to defeat the West at the West's own game. I am not concerned here with Japan's success or failure as an imitation West; I am concerned with the zealot and with the so-called revivalist movements in South Asia, based on the zealot's instrumental concept of religion as an ideological principle useful for political mobilization and state formation.

Usually, modern scholarship tends to see zealotry as a retrogression into primitivism and as a pathology of traditions. On closer examination it turns out to be a by-product and a pathology of modernity. For instance, whatever the revivalist Hindu may seek to revive, it is not Hinduism. The pathetically comic, martial uniform of khaki shorts, which the RSS cadres have to wear, tell it all. Unconsciously modelled on the uniform of the colonial police, the khaki shorts are the final proof that the RSS is an illegitimate child of Western colonialism. If such a comment seems trivial, one can point out the systematic reform movements under colonialism, on the dominant Christian and Islamic concepts of religion (one Book and one God, for instance) and on the modern Western concept of the nation-state. Once such concepts of religion and state are imported into Hinduism, the inevitable happens. One begins to judge the everyday life-style of the Hindus, their diversity and heterogeneity negatively—usually with a clear touch of hostility and contempt.

Likewise, there is nothing fundamentally Islamic about the fundamentalist Muslims. As we see in Pakistan today, they are the ones who are usually first to sell their souls at a discount to the forces which seek to disenfranchise the ordinary Muslims on the pretext that the latter do not know their Islam well. And we are today witnessing the same process within Sikhism and Sri Lankan Buddhism, too.

Tolerance as a pre-secular tradition

There is, however, the response of a third kind. It usually comes from the non-modern majority of a society, even though to the middle-class intellectuals it may look like the response of a minority. This response does not keep religion separate from politics, but it does say that the traditional ways of life have, over the centuries, developed internal principles of tolerance and these principles must play a part in contemporary politics. This response affirms that religious communities in traditional societies *have* known how to live with each other. It is not modern India which has tolerated Judaism in India for nearly 2,000 years, Christianity from before the time it went to Europe, and Zoroastrianism for more than 1,200 years; it is traditional India which has shown such tolerance. That is why today, as India gets modernized, religious violence is increasing. In the earlier centuries, according to available records, inter-religious riots were rare and localized; even after Independence we used to have less than one event of religious strife a week; now we have about one and a half incidents a day. And more than 90 per cent of these riots begin in urban India, and within urban India, in and around the industrial areas. Even now in the 1980s, Indian villages and small towns can take credit for having avoided communal riots. Thus we find that after four years of bitterness, the Punjab villages are still free of riots. They have only seen assassinations by small gangs of terrorists and riot-like situations in the cities. Obviously, somewhere and somehow, religious violence has something to do with the urban-industrial vision of life and with the political processes the vision lets loose.

It is awareness of this political process which has convinced a small but growing number of Indian political analysts that it is from non-modern India, from the traditions and principles of religious tolerance encoded in everyday life associated with the different faiths of India, that one will have to seek clues to the renewal of Indian political culture. This is less difficult than it at first seems. Let us not forget, the great symbols of religious tolerance in India over the last 2,000 years have not been modern, though the moderns have managed to hijack some of these symbols.

For example, when the modern Indians project the ideology of secularism into the past, to say that Emperor Ashoka was "secular," they forget that Ashoka was not exactly a secular ruler; he was a practising Buddhist, even in his public life. He based his tolerance on Buddhism, not on secularism. When the moderns say that Akbar was secular, they forget that he derived his tolerance not from secularism but from Islam. He believed that tolerance was the message of true Islam. And in our times, Gandhi derived his religious tolerance from Hinduism, not from secular politics.

Modern India has a lot to answer for. So have the cosmopolitan intellectuals in this part of the world. They have failed to be respectful to the traditions of tolerance in their societies. These traditions may have become creaky, but so is—it is now pretty clear—the ideology of secularism itself. As we are finding out to our cost, the new forms of religious violence are becoming, paradoxically, quite secular. The anti-Sikh riots which took place in Delhi in November 1984, the anti-Muslim riots in Bangalore in 1986—they were associated not so much with religious hatred as with political cost-calculations and/or economic greed.[12] The same logic had operated in the case of the riots at Moradabad, Bhiwandi and Hyderabad earlier. Zealotry has produced many riots, but secular politics, too, has now begun to produce its own version of "religious riots." As for the victims of a riot, the fact that the riot might have been organized and led by persons motivated by political cost-calculations and not by religious bigotry can hardly be a solace.

The moral of the story is this: the time has come for us to recognize that, instead of trying to build religious tolerance on the good faith or conscience of a small group of de-ethnicized, middle-class politicians, bureaucrats and intellectuals, a far more serious venture would be to explore the philosophy, the symbolism and the theology of tolerance in the faiths of the citizens and hope that the state systems in South Asia may learn something about religious tolerance from everyday Hinduism, Islam, Buddhism, and Sikhism rather than wish that the ordinary Hindus, Muslims, Buddhists and Sikhs will learn tolerance from the various fashionable secular theories of statecraft.

The Heart of Darkness

New forms of violence

The last point needs to be further clarified, and I shall try to provide this clarification by putting my arguments in a larger psychological and cultural frame. Table 7.1 gives an outline of the frame. (Though the table also shows the dangers of clarifying a live issue by casting one's argument in the schematized language of the social sciences; for the argument, as it is summarized in the table, already seems somewhat reified, if not opaque.)

The table admits that the Western concept of secularism *has* played a crucial role in South Asian societies, it *has* worked as a check against some forms of ethnic intolerance and violence; it *has* contributed to humane governance at certain times and places.

By the same token, however, the table also suggests, secularism cannot cope with many of the new fears and intolerance of religions and ethnicities, nor can it provide any protection against the new forms of violence which have come to be associated with such intolerance. Nor can secularism contain those who provide the major justifications for calculated pogroms and ethnocides in terms of the dominant ideology of the state.

Table 7.1
Classification of Violence

Sectors Involved	Typical Violence	Model for Violence	Locus of Ideology	Nature of Motives	Effective Counter-Ideology
Non-modern peripheralized believers	Religious war	Traditional sacrifice (of self or others)	Faith	Passion	Internal critiques of faith/ agnosticism
Semi-modern zealots	Riot	Exorcism/ search for parity	State	Passion and interest	Secularism
Modern, secular rationalists	Manufactured riots or 'assembly' line violence	Experimental science (vivisection), industrial management	Hegelian or Bismarckian concept of state	Interest	Critiques of objectification and de-sacralization

These new forms of intolerance and violence are sustained by a different configuration of social and psychological forces. The rubrics in the table allude both to these forces as well as to the growing irrelevance of the broad models proposed by a number of important empirical social and psychological studies done in the 1950s and 1960s—by those studying social distance in the manner of E. Bogardus, by Erich Fromm in his early writings, by Theodor Adorno and his associates working on the authoritarian personality, by Milton Rokeach and his followers exploring dogmatism.[13] The stereotyping, authoritarian submission, sado-masochism and the heavy use of the ego defences of projection, displacement and rationalization which went with authoritarianism and dogmatism, according to some of these studies, have not become irrelevant, as Sudhir Kakar shows once again in a recent paper.[14] There *are* persistent demonologies which divide religious communities and endorse ethnic violence. But these demonologies have begun to play a less and less central role in such violence. They have become increasingly one of the psychological identifiers of those participating in the mobs involved in rioting or in pogroms, not of those planning, initiating or legitimizing mob action.

This is another way of saying that the planners, instigators and legitimizers of religious and ethnic violence can now be identified as secular users of non-secular forces in the society. There is very little continuity between their motivational structures and that of the street mobs which act out the wishes of the organizers of a riot. Only the mobs now represent, and that only partially, the violence produced by the predisposing factors described in the social science literature of the earlier decades. In the place of these factors have come a new set of personality traits and defence mechanisms, the most important of which are the more "primitive" defences such as isolation and denial. These defences ensure, paradoxically, the primacy of cognitive factors in violence over the affective and the conative.

The involvement of these newly important ego defences in human violence were also first noticed in the 1950s and 1960s. But those who drew attention to these defences did so in passing (for instance Erich Fromm in one of his incarnations and Bruno Bettelheim) or from outside the ambit of empirical social sciences (for instance Joseph Conrad and Hannah Arendt).[15] Moreover, these early analyses of the 'new violence' were primarily concerned with "extreme situations," to use Bettelheim's term, and not with the less-technologized and less-extreme violence of religious feuds or riots. Even when the violence these analyses dealt with did not directly involve genocide and mass murders, they involved memories of genocide and mass murders, as in the well-known book by Alexander and Margarete Mitscherlich.[16] Only now have we become fully aware of the destructive potentials of the once-low-grade but now-persistent violence flowing from objectification, scientization and bureaucratic rationality. The reasons for this heightened awareness are obvious enough. As the modern nation-state system and the modern thought machine enter the interstices of even the most traditional societies, those in power or those who hope to be in power in these societies begin to view statecraft in full secular, scientific, amoral and dispassionate terms.[17] The modernist élites in such societies then begin to fear the divisiveness of minorities and the diversity which religious and ethnic plurality introduces into a nation-state. These élites then begin to see all religions and all forms of ethnicity as a hurdle to nation-building and state-formation and as a danger to the technology of statecraft and political management. The new nation-states in many societies tend to look at religion and ethnicity the way the 19th-century colonial powers looked at distant cultures which came under their domination—at best as "things" to be studied, "engineered," ghettoed, museumized or preserved in reservations; at worst as inferior cultures opposed to the principles of modern living and inconsistent with the game of modern politics, science and development, and therefore deservedly facing extinction. No wonder that the political cultures of South Asia have begun to produce a plethora of official social scientists who are the perfect analogues of the colonial anthropologists who once studied the "Hindoos" and the "Mohammedans" on behalf of their king and country.

This state of mind is the basic format of the internal colonialism which is at work today. The economic exploitation to which the epithet 'internal colonialism' is mechanically applied by radical economists is no more than a by-product of the internal colonialism I am speaking about. This colonialism validates the proposal—which can be teased out of the works of a number of philosophers such as Hannah Arendt and Herbert Marcuse—that the most extreme forms of violence in our times come not from faulty passions or human irrationality but from faulty ideologies and unrestrained instrumental rationality. Demonology is now for the mobs; secular rationality for those who organize, instigate or lead the mobs. Unless of course one conceptualizes modern statecraft itself as a left-handed, magical technology and as a new demonology. (One image that has persisted in my mind from the days of the anti-Sikh pogrom at Delhi in 1984 is that of a scion of a prominent family, which owns one of Delhi's most exclusive boutiques, directing with his golf club a gang of ill-clad arsonists. I suspect that the image has the potential to serve as the metaphor for the new forms of social violence in modern India.)

As I have already said, this state-linked internal colonialism uses legitimating core concepts like national security, development, modern science and technology. Any society, for that matter any aggregate, which gives unrestrained play or support to these concepts gets automatically linked to the colonial structure of the present-day world and is doomed to promote violence and expropriation, particularly of the kind directed against the smaller minorities such as the tribals and the less numerous sects who can neither hit back against the state, nor live away from the modern market.

Secularism has become a handy adjunct to this set of legitimating core concepts. It helps those swarming around the nation-state, either as élites or as counter-élites, to legitimize themselves as the sole arbiters among traditional communities, to claim for themselves a monopoly on religious and ethnic tolerance and on political rationality. To accept the ideology of secularism is to accept the ideologies of progress and modernity as the new justifications of domination, and the use of violence to achieve and sustain the ideologies as the new opiates of the masses.

Gandhi, an arch anti-secularist if we use the proper scientific meaning of the word "secularist," claimed that his religion was his politics and his politics was his religion. He was not a cultural relativist and his rejection of the first principle of secularism—the separation of religion and politics—was not a political strategy meant to ensure his political survival in a uniquely multi-ethnic society like India. In fact, I have been told by sociologist Bhupinder Singh that Gandhi may have borrowed this anti-secular formulation from William Blake. Whatever its source, in some version or the other this formulation is becoming the common response of those who have sensed the new forms of man-made violence unleashed by post–17th-century Europe in the name of the Enlightenment values. These forms of violence, which have already taken a toll of about a hundred million human lives in this century, have come under closer critical scrutiny in recent decades mainly because they have come home to roost in the heart of Europe and North America, thanks to the Third Reich, the Gulag, the two world wars, and the threat of nuclear annihilation.

Many modern Indians who try to sell Gandhi as a secularist find his attitude to the separation of religion and politics highly embarrassing, if not positively painful. They like to see Gandhi as a hidden modernist who merely used a traditional religious idiom to mobilize his unorganized society to fight colonialism. Nothing can be more disingenuous. Gandhi's religious tolerance came from his anti-secularism, which in turn came from his unconditional rejection of modernity. And he never wavered in his stand. Note the following exchange between him and a correspondent of the *Chicago Tribune* in 1931:

> Sir, 23 years ago you wrote a book *Hind Swaraj*, which stunned India and the rest of the world with its terrible onslaught on modern Western civilization. Have you changed your mind about any of the things you have said in it?
> Not a bit. My ideas about the evils of Western civilization still stand. If I republish the book tomorrow, I would scarcely change a word.[18]

Religious tolerance outside the bounds of secularism is exactly what it says it is. It not only means tolerance of religions but also a tolerance that is religious. It therefore squarely locates itself in traditions, outside the ideological grid of modernity. Gandhi used to say that he was a *sanātani*, an orthodox Hindu. It was as a *sanātani* Hindu that he claimed to be simultaneously a Muslim, a Sikh and a Christian and he granted the same plural identity to those belonging to other faiths. Traditional Hinduism or rather, *sanātan dharma* was the source of his religious tolerance. It is instructive that the Hindu nationalists who killed him—that too after three unsuccessful attempts to kill him over the previous 20 years—did so in the name of secular statecraft. They said so explicitly and declared Gandhi to be an enemy of the nascent Indian nation-state.

That secular statecraft now seeks to dominate the Indian political culture, sometimes in the name of Gandhi himself. Urban, Westernized, middle-class, Brahmanic, Hindu nationalists and Hindu modernists often flaunt Gandhi's tolerance as an indicator of Hindu catholicity but contemptuously reject that part of his ideology which insisted that religious tolerance, to be tolerance, must impute to other faiths the same spirit of tolerance. Whether a large enough proportion of those belonging to the other religious traditions show *in practice* and *at a particular point of time and place* the same tolerance or not is a secondary matter, for it is the imputation or presumption of tolerance in others, not its existence, which defines one's own tolerance in the Gandhian world-view and praxis.

That presumption must become the major source of tolerance for those who want to fight the new violence of our times, whether they are believers or not.

Notes

1. Shamoon T. Lokhandwala, "Indian Islam: Composite Culture and Integration," *New Quest* 50 (March–April 1985): 87–101.

2. For instance, Partha Chatterjee, *National Thought and the Colonial World: A Derivative Discourse* (New Delhi: Oxford University Press, 1986).

3. Donald F. Miller, "Six Theses on the Question of Religion and Politics in India Today," *Economic and Political Weekly*, 25 July 1987, pp. 57–63.

4. T. N. Madan, "Secularism in Its Place," *The Journal of Asian Studies* 46 (November 1987): 747–759.

5. Ali Akhtar Khan, "Secularism and Aligarh School," *The Times of India*, 2 December 1986.

6. Imtiaz Ahmed, "Muslims and Boycott Call: Political Realities Ignored," *The Times of India*, 14 January 1987.

7. Gurbachan Singh, "Where's the Indian?" *The Times of India*, 21 September 1986.

8. Mulk Raj Anand, "New Light on Iqbal," *Indian Express*, 22 September 1985.

9. Rahi Masoom Raza in "How to Resolve the Babari Masjid-Ram Janmabhoomi Dispute," *Sunday Observer*, 18 January 1987; and "In Favour of Change," (Letter to the Editor), *The Illustrated Weekly of India*, 16 March 1986.

10. Raojibhai C. Patel, "Building Secular State; Need to Subordinate Religion," *The Times of India*, 17 September 1986.

11. "Pak a Few Steps from Bomb," *The Times of India*, 29 January 1987.

12. A comparable example from outside India would be the untitled case study of the 1983 riots in Sri Lanka, paper presented at the workshop on New Dimensions of Ethnic Violence in South Asia, Kathmandu, 15–17 February 1987.

13. Erich Fromm, *Escape from Freedom* (New York: Farrar and Rinehart, 1941); Bruno Bettelheim, *Surviving and Other Essays* (London: Thames and Hudson, 1979); T. W. Adorno et al., *The Authoritarian Personality* (New York: Norton, 1950); and Milton Rokeach, *The Open and Closed Mind* (New York: Basic Books, 1960).

14. Sudhir Kakar, "Some Unconscious Aspects of Ethnic Violence in India (Paper presented at the Workshop on New Dimensions of Ethnic Violence in South Asia, Kathmandu, 15–17 February 1987).

15. Erich Fromm, *Anatomy of Human Destructiveness* (New York: Holt, Rinehart and Winston, 1973); Hannah Arendt, *Eichmann in Jerusalem* (New York: Viking, 1963); *On Violence* (London: Allen & Unwin, 1969); and Joseph Conrad, *The Heart of Darkness* (Harmondsworth: Penguin, 1973).

16. Alexander and Margarete Mitscherlich, *The Inability to Mourn: Principles of Collective Behaviour* (New York: Grove, 1984).

17. That is, in terms of what Tarique Banuri calls the impersonality postulate in his "A Critical Review of Modernization Theories" (Paper presented at the Meeting

on Technological Transformation in Traditional Societies: Alternative Approaches, Helsinki, July 1986). See also Ashis Nandy, "Science, Authoritarianism and Culture: On the Scope and Limits of Isolation Outside the Clinic," in *Traditions, Tyranny and Utopias: Essays in the Politics of Awareness* (New Delhi: Oxford University Press, 1987), pp. 95–126.

18. Quoted in T. S. Ananthu, *Going Beyond the Intellect: A Gandhian Approach to Scientific Education* (New Delhi: Gandhi Peace Foundation, 1981, mimeographed), p. 1.

8

Beyond Sovereignty: An Emerging Global Civilization

Mary Catherine Bateson

We live at a time when the density of interaction between states and among peoples is increasing rapidly. We are experiencing a growing sense of common dangers and an awareness of common tasks that must be addressed at the global level. International institutions continue to appear in response to the need for global cooperation. More and more individuals identify with the ecological unity of the planet and sense the emergence of a global community. For all the diversity of systems of knowledge and meaning, communication between communities is becoming even more intense as a consequence of new electronic technologies. A few systems—especially those related to science and technology, such as weather forecasting and air traffic control, and some forms of economic exchange—are already effectively shared.

These trends suggest the emergence of a global civilization. Unlike the idea of world government, the notion of an emerging global civilization suggests a loosely integrated form of world order that might have the following characteristics: it would develop gradually, and may indeed already be in the process of development; it could coexist with rich cultural and political diversity; it would not rely on the centralization of power characteristic of the modern state; and it might make a virtue of ambiguity.

Civilization is the most appropriate term now available for a commonality that might fit this description, yet the term presents many opportunities for misunderstanding. The ambiguity and flexibility that might characterize a global civilization understood in this way stand in sharp contrast with inherited accounts of political community modeled on the state. These accounts continue to inform our understanding of what a global civilization might be. Consequently, the meaning of the term *civilization* remains to be explored, both in theory and in practice.

Unless we are careful with our definitions, the use of the term civilization can prejudge the relevance of certain aspects of human experience. What is essential to a sense of shared membership is a sense of the familiar, a resilient substructure of global community that will allow flexibility in tackling the vast and urgent issues that we as a species must face together. Trust and a tolerance for ambiguity within some broader framework are built from the ordinary. At the local level, such a substructure is built up from day-to-day interactions. At the global level, it is more likely to develop by listen-ing to radio and television and walking in a marketplace that draws on worldwide resources than through formal educational programs.

Thus, in discussing the kind of integration implied by the notion of a global civilization, it is important to include a discussion of the way in which a multitude of exchanges and borrowings, each one trivial, creates a structure of familiarity. A viable form of world order must be pieced together from only partially shared systems of meaning, crossing over existing cultural diversity. Such systems of meaning will be very different from the systems developed by diplomats or philosophers, for they will be improvisational and ambiguous, with room for both contention and humor. Such a development is, I believe, already under way.

Culture and Civilization

Human communities are able to live and work together because, in addition to the common biological inheritance of all human beings, they share learned cultural systems—dynamic, and evolving over long periods of time—that are primarily systems of meaning or knowledge, implemented in institutions and artifacts and the reshaping of natural environments. Yet human groups with different cultures may think and act so differently that it sometimes seems to members of different communities as if they belong to different species, finding themselves incapable of empathy or cooperation and all too willing to turn to violence. The question of global civilization is the question of shared meanings uniting a multiplicity of communities, rather than a single community.

Historically, a strong tradition of political analysis, going back to such figures as Hobbes and Austin, and focusing on the divisive rather than cohesive aspects of human interaction, has affirmed a different necessity in order to make it possible for human beings to live and work together, the necessity for a center of power and/or authority. This view was critical in the development of the concept of the sovereign state. It also informs the popular hope that an alternative form of world order might be achieved through the development of a world government, with its own capacity for coercion and to which states might surrender some measure of power and authority.

Assumptions about the possibility of world order rest upon long-standing views of human nature. Both the academic discipline of political science and the current political organization of the world reflect a narrow sampling of human experience and often accept this as the human norm, even as logically necessary. In this way, our imagination of the future is constrained. The idea of sovereignty, the notion of the state, and the states system are barely five hundred years old, and until about two hundred years ago were largely limited to Europe. Yet they have come to seem inescapable and commonsensical. The term *civilization* allows us to focus on systems of meaning not emphasized by these other terms. It refers to a set of ideas that is more broadly and deeply applicable in human history, but it too may have a range of assumptions buried within it, assumptions about progress and evolution, assumptions about values that direct attention to some issues and ignore others.

As a cultural anthropologist, I am more concerned with patterns of communication and with value systems than with institutions and forms of government. Anthropologists began by concentrating on small, highly integrated, often isolated societies, such as have almost ceased to exist. Political analysis, too, was once concerned with the kind of society that anthropology is most often concerned with today. The Greek city-states were relatively small, homogeneous communities whose members spoke the same language and shared the same cultural tradition; their citizens had the possibility of face-to-face interaction. This commonality of tradition did not preclude either wide institutional diversity from polis to polis, or conflict and institutional change within any one of them. Indeed, it permitted the very contention that has made the Greek polis the prototype of the political process—contention framed by the possibility of communication. A common language does not create agreement, but it permits discussion. The relative homogeneity of ancient Athens inhered in a body of shared knowledge and assumptions, often unstated, that underlay the day-to-day behavior and interactions of the Athenians, just as such a common culture underlies the behavior of people in a village in Wales or among the Istmul of New Guinea, a commonality that changes over time and allows the development and expression of individual diversity and disagreement.

Culture in this sense consists of the workaday and the ordinary—bread and salt, water and rice, the knowledge that every farmer or nomad has of how to find subsistence and how to spend the day—as well as the only partly shared knowledge of specialists. It includes curse words as well as poetry, animal husbandry as well as religion, ways of walking as well as styles of dance. This is a very important distinction, because it is often true that the highly elaborated and literate elements that form a specialized part of the wider culture move more easily from place to place than those elements that provide the texture of everyday life, but commonality is also needed at the level of the ordinary. Cultural anthropologists do not use the term *culture*—as several cognate terms are used—as a value-laden term to refer only to the fruits of education and refinement. That usage is sometimes distinguished by capitalization: Culture. All too often, the concept of Culture is used invidiously, to seek division rather than to recognize emergent unity. Much of the Culture of Athens is shared by educated people today, while much of the texture of ordinary life must be guessed at. In this sense, no normal human being can be said to be uncultured or without culture.

The term *civilization* is perhaps even more muddled and value laden than the term *culture* and is therefore used gingerly by anthropologists. The least problematic meanings lie in the sphere of archeology and have to do with qualitative historical development relating to particular cultural innovations: urban settlement, increased division of labor, and sometimes writing. From the archaeological point of view, civilization has been virtually worldwide for some time. This is not the usage intended here, but it is this usage that gives the term *civilization* the connotation of a step in evolutionary progress. A comparable step might be discerned in new communicational technologies.

There are other possible and potentially confusing meanings. "Civilization" is sometimes used as a synonym for culture, without the implication of progress, as in such phrases as "Eskimo civilization." While undoubtedly intended as a gesture of respect, this relatively rare usage supplies no additional clarity. On the other hand, civilization may be used invidiously, as a synonym for Culture, with the same overtones of ethnocentrism and snobbery. Usually it turns up as an adjective: all sorts of traits may be labeled as civilized or uncivilized: beer at room temperature or, equally, beer that is served chilled; tea with milk or, equally, tea without milk. In this usage, the antonym of civilized is barbaric.

The usage I intend here, however, is a slightly different one in which it is possible to speak of multiple civilized traditions that have emerged since the urban revolution, and of the possibility that a new one might now be emerging, creating a degree of global *integration* new in human experience.

For many in the Western tradition, "civilization" is almost synonymous with Greece, simply because we admire Greece and trace so many of our roots to that source. Greek civilization met the archaeological definition of course, but it also meets the integrative definition. Not only were the Greeks civilized in the sense of building cities, but they were also the shapers of a body of ideas and institutions that wind their way through the lives of many subsequent communities. In this sense their "civilization" represents the usage of the term that transcends the merely local, however lofty the intellectual and artistic achievements of a particular place and time. Thus, we might differ in our application of the term to various stages in Greek history. Some, for example, might refer only to the "civilization" of the later periods, when Greek ideas were transported to and adapted in the Macedonian, Roman, and Byzantine empires, to become part of the common thread of cosmopolitan life around the Mediterranean, woven into the history of Christianity and Islam, right up to the present.

In this usage, civilization connotes the capacity to transcend differences. Many aspects of the Greek tradition gradually became part of the lives of people whose ordinary local culture was not Greek. The same thing may be said, for instance, of Chinese or Indian civilization. From this point of view—which I believe to be the best interpretation of the phrase "emerging global civilization"—civilization represents a second-layer phenomenon, bridging local cultural differences, and therefore often linked historically with a religious tradition or with a long period of imperial rule. The population of ancient Athens was indeed relatively small and homogeneous, but its heirs are not only numerous but also highly diverse. The Jew in Alexandria, the Roman infantryman in Gaul, the Orthodox priest, and the public schoolboy in Great Britain today, can all in various degrees lay claim to Greek civilization, without, however, losing their local particularity.

At this point, however, we should be careful to strip the term of its value-laden quality. Whether or not any one of us regards rock music as one of the high achievements of the human race, it is clearly a part of the emerging world civilization. Furthermore, we should not limit our sense of emerging commonality to aspects of culture that are accurately or completely grasped, but should include every idea or image that passes around the world creating a loose web of commonality.

Different aspects of a civilization may be integrated in different ways. Anthropologists have sometimes made a distinction between "high cultures" or "great traditions," and what Robert Redfield called "little traditions." For example, a seminarian from Mexico City, fully trained in Thomistic theology, might spend his holidays teaching in a remote community where illiterate villagers practice a form of Christianity generously mixed with preColumbian tradition. From the seminarian's point of view, the aspects of Spanish Catholic civilization grasped by the villagers may seem fragmentary. However, even though the experience of the villagers is derived from different sources—like the Anglo-Saxon and Romance vocabulary of this sentence—it is at least roughly synthesized in a single system. The villagers have been taught that their version of Christianity is inferior to the one that comes from the city, but it may be strangely resistant to the seminarian's corrections precisely because it is, for the villagers, part of an integrated whole. The Redfield approach suggests a variety of different kinds of membership in a given tradition and a variety of different types of integration. Both the rural syncretism of the peasant and the cosmopolitan expertise of the seminarian give a sense of membership in a larger whole.

Imagining Alternatives

Most political analysts have been preoccupied with the characteristics of their own polities. Today, political science is the discipline that studies forms of governance in societies too large for face-to-face interaction. The norm of political science is the society of strangers, in which commonality once derived from shared understandings and day-to-day interactions has had to be replaced by some other mechanism. One might use Aristotle's hegira to Macedon to symbolize concerns that have come to underlie so much of our thinking today. In particular, these include the politics of empire and later of the state system, large entities defined not so much by an internal process of communication as by lines—political boundaries—around the periphery, and by a concentration of coercive power at the center. Political science has focused primarily on states as they have emerged since the sixteenth century. The state is not a fact of nature, however, but the solution to a problem—a modern and Western solution, recently generalized to the rest of the world, which is, in its turn, itself a source of problems.

Anthropology, by contrast, is a product of curiosity about peoples, both neighboring and remote, whose customs are bizarre or unintelligible, peoples with whom the possibilities of interaction were so sharply limited that it is necessary to regard the recognition of common humanity as having been an achievement—and still a partial and halting one. For most of its history, anthropology has focused on the study of small, technologically less advanced societies, societies not yet civilized but rather "primitive" or "barbaric," often finding these within the boundaries of larger imperial enclaves—nomads in Iran, Indians on the Amazon, Eskimos at the northern edge of the Americas. These are peoples trapped willy-nilly in the politics of boundaries and central coercive power, no longer sovereign but often excluded from participation, dwindling and at the mercy of larger entities. They are threatened today everywhere. Like canaries in a mineshaft, they test the extent to which any system tolerates internal diversity; all around the world, the canaries have been dying.

Nevertheless, the contribution of anthropology to the debate about emerging forms of world order is not limited to a cry of alarm about the loss of diversity that occurs under the state system. Although much of the anthropological focus arises from a legacy of interest in the exotic and from an urgent need to record ways of life that may be obliterated within a generation, there have also been efforts to apply anthropological theory and method to larger societies. Such efforts have often been controversial and frustrating, for the concept of culture that has emerged as central to anthropology seems to depend on community, on the process of continuous and dense communication that sustains shared assumptions. Anthropologists prefer to study networks of identified persons, not mass samples, and to seek those elements that are shared, rather than to study the statistical distribution of differences. Such networks, for example, were the stuff of political process in the Greek polis. Against this background, the most useful role an anthropologist can play may be to pose the question of what kinds of patterns of communication and belief can emerge, as Marshall McLuhan speculated, in a very large—perhaps worldwide—population, so that it can function, in some sense, as a community.

In light of the weight of modern history and the statistics of modern populations, the kind of challenge that anthropology can mount against such notions as the state is fragile. Yet cultural possibility is not determined by statistics. We can say that things have not always and everywhere been thus, and therefore that the familiar patterns of modernity, although nearly worldwide, are not a necessity of human biology. The most useful analogs may not be those that are superficially most similar. Every isolated example of a band or tribe or island settlement that has ordered its affairs differently is an example of possibility, and only where we find no such alternatives may we have discovered a universal of human experience—but only of human experience *to date*. Critics respond to exotic examples with a Darwinian vision that emphasizes that certain forms of human organization have become dominant while others—although conceivably viable in a less selective environment—have been progressively eliminated. These comments conceal hierarchical value systems, notions of "more highly evolved" and therefore better. Yet the cetaceans evolved by a return to the sea. It remains true that the dominant pattern of a particular era may prove maladaptive under new circumstances. It may indeed represent an evolutionary cul-de-sac and prove self-destructive. We cannot assume that currently dominant forms represent either progress or maturity. If we wish to extend our imaginations to the full range of human possibility, the multitude of past experiments are a significant resource.

A few examples may be helpful. Territoriality of some sort, for instance, seems to be a human universal, but a preoccupation with boundaries or with expansion and trespass is not. It would be a mistake, given the evidence, to anticipate a totally nonterritorial form of human organization. But it is possible to look at human groups whose sense of territoriality, such as that of many nomads, is defined focally rather than by boundary lines, by use rather than by possession, by a sense of covenant with the land rather than by exclusive ownership. It is also possible to look at peoples who identify with territories that are not exclusive or united within a single polity. Moreover, even if fixed boundaries remain the primary model on the earth's surfaces, other ways of thinking about geography are becoming increasingly important in terms of our relationship to the air, the sea, or outer space. Every form of tie that crosses national boundaries, whether between "sister cities" like Erevan and Boston, or between regions of the African diaspora, or between ethnic groups living under different governments, is a potential link in an emerging sense of global civilization, providing the links are plentiful enough.

No human group functions without binding custom and expectation, although it may lack a code of law and a police force. Every human group recognizes leadership of one sort or another and uses it in making decisions, but relatively rarely is such leadership regarded as absolute and exclusive. Thus, sovereignty—in the sense of an unambiguous locus of power and authority as the basis of social organization—is by no means universal or necessary. Substantial territories and populations may be organized acephalously, i.e., without central authority. Pluralism is possible, but anarchy is not. Again, the conflict-free primitive society of total harmony is also a myth—one that is less interesting than the study of alternative expressions of conflict and alternative styles and methods of resolution, a question of far greater moment in a world where certain familiar expressions of conflict have become unacceptable. Not all conflict is resolved from above.

The monotheistic concept of an unambiguous locus of power seems to have an even more compelling logic than the concept of the state—of which it became a part—but it is not necessary. The ancient Hebrews asserted the presence and power of a single omnipotent deity. Since then, the Western religious tradition has struggled with the belief in one God, and the belief in more than one has come to seem absurd. But such a belief was apparently not at all absurd for the ancient Indo-Europeans, including the Greeks and the ancestors of present-day Hindus, and for most other human communities whose sense of the divine was more ecological, that is, more multifaceted and interdependent. The Hebrews, indeed, found monotheism a difficult belief to sustain, perhaps because it was so often dissonant with their tribal social organization, their contact with neighboring peoples, and their dispersal in the notably varied terrain of Palestine. These factors led them astray repeatedly, following multiple deities, perhaps most regularly when central political power was in question.

Can one imagine the return to a world in which a polytheism, hospitable to gods as yet unknown, would seem persuasive? Or must even postreligious societies model themselves on religious forms they no longer accept? Once formulated, the idea of the singular and omnipotent has survived as central in Christianity and Islam to this day, influencing the imagination of a great part of the world's population. The idea of divine monopoly is accompanied, logically, by the immensely costly conviction that doctrine is either true or false. However, even as political power was pluralistic and fragmented in the Middle Ages, divine absolutism was also ambiguous, delegated severally to a flock of intercessory beings—saints, angels, popes, and clerics—like a corrupt Byzantine bureaucracy. The Virgin Mary played the supreme intercessory role, and one cannot help but feel that her significance lay in her ability—perhaps—to persuade her son to do something "against his better judgment," as appears to have been the case at the wedding at Cana. While not in entire synchrony, the emergence of absolutism as a political form corresponds to the theological centralization of the Counter-Reformation.

Early theorists of the states system asserted that only with a clearly definable locus of power could the rule of law be assured, guaranteeing domestic peace and tranquillity. It is interesting today to find these intellectual arguments echoed in fundamentalist tracts about family life: it is necessary and logical, they assert, that there should be one voice able to make a final decision, and therefore any attempt at equality between men and women is *necessarily* unworkable, as absurd as the idea of multiple gods managing the universe by a system of consultation and compromise. Every ship must have a captain. There is no difficulty with delegation or with a separation of powers, providing these are unambiguously defined.

It is the viability of ambiguity that is rejected by the logics of sovereignty and monotheism. Interestingly, the idea of a central focus of power entails the idea of a boundary, and the two combine to give commonsensical force to the notion of sovereignty. Inevitably, one of the most common themes in discussions of world order has been the question of how to create an authority—monarch or proletariat—with sufficient power to enforce its will unambiguously. The intellectual traditions of the West, including those associated with Christianity, Islam, and Marx, are still in thrall to these ideas of exclusive truth and have spread them around the world.

These must be very persuasive ideas, almost certainly self-reinforcing, for they create a logic whereby any real concentration of power can argue for acceleration of that concentration, using an edge once acquired as if it were a force of nature, like a ratchet. Absolutism often seems to function like the bad currency of Gresham's law, or even like entropy—in a single direction—except that clearly, just as there are negentropic forces in biology, there are forces in human society that work against the unambiguous focus of power. The alternative to arguments for centralization of power enforcing an exclusive view of truth would be that if only conflict can be contained, a certain amount of muddle is both beautiful and creative.

Intelligibility is more important than agreement. It is important to emphasize this because of the romanticism that attends the study of the exotic—the idea that communities sharing a common culture are free of conflict or coercion or exploitation. These are pervasive elements of human society. An emerging world civilization would certainly include conflict, but it is to be hoped that conflict could be channeled into tolerable forms of expression. It is as possible for a tradition to specify rigid etiquette as brutal combat, but it can never specify forms for complete harmony. No community avoids internal conflict entirely, although some go a long way to cocoon all conflict in forms of courtesy. No community avoids exploitation, although it is perhaps most common across social divisions that limit or reduce interaction, so that it may be necessary to speak of classes as having differing cultures. But exploitation also occurs under conditions of greatest intimacy. Conflict and exploitation can be built into a culture and regarded as entirely legitimate, resting upon shared assumptions and expectations. This does not mean they are welcomed or applauded. It does mean they are experienced as intelligible and as at least partly predictable, and could be compatible with world civilization. Not all disputes need to be resolved.

The form of authority based on what is now increasingly referred to as patriarchy has seemed to many to be necessary and logical, because it provides for an unambiguous locus of authority, and has been expanding somewhat longer than the state system. It seems probable that except in technologically advanced societies the balance is still shifting toward male domination, facilitated by the role of warfare, the centralization of power, and the monetization of productive systems. Matriarchy is often imagined as a mirror image of patriarchy, yet this has probably never existed as a consistent and pervasive form of social organization, and does not seem to be a part of the human repertoire to date, although there have of course been many powerful matriarchs as well as queens and priestesses. There have, however, been examples of matrilineal or matrifocal societies in which a balanced complementarity between the sexes obtained. In our own time, the reduced reliance on sheer physical strength, the control of conception, and the extension of the life cycle, are all results of technological developments that propose changed possibilities for women. In understanding these potential changes, the available alternative model is not female domination but a more shared, more ambiguous order, of a kind that has been relatively rare but is not outside the range of human possibility. Such a society would not implicitly argue for the state system by providing an unambiguous locus of power within the family, but would instead be intimately—and perhaps internationally as well—pluralistic.

Living with Ambiguity

It is not easy to maintain a sense of commonality based on partial and ambiguous sharing, but that may be the only option for world order. If this is the case, then many kinds of contemporary efforts to move toward unequivocal rules, precise language, and verification, are misguided. We can identify little willingness to rely on unarticulated and partially shared understandings, and yet I believe that the search for fixed and explicit understandings is self-defeating.

This problem is not limited to international relations, but arises within any country where the fabric of commonality is breached or has never fully developed. In the 1970s and 1980s the United States has been engaged in a flurry of specification and regulation, trying to define exact procedures for decisionmaking to make these processes more determinate, to make the functioning of democracy less ambiguous. A police officer who fires a gun outside of a firing range can expect to spend a day filling out forms—whether someone is hit or not. This is designed, for good reasons, to constrain the decision and to reduce the doubt about the propriety of any given decision—that is, to eliminate ambiguity in a society where consensus is in doubt. The U.S. Constitution, of course, serves us because of its supreme ambiguity, but it does not satisfy us.

During this same period, most of us have had enough contact with computers to experience the process of disambiguation from another point of view. Most computers to date, unlike human beings, are incapable of dealing with ambiguity, which makes them, as they are fondly called in the U.K., TOMs: totally obedient morons. If there is even a trace of unclarity in an instruction given to a computer, it will not comply; struggling with a recalcitrant computer is the best reminder that human beings, on the other hand, often benefit from ambiguity. Even as the average number of words in drafts of new legislation is increased, and each attracts additional volumes of administrative specification, it must be clear that we are engaged in a reductio ad absurdum of the attempt to escape ambiguity.

The alternative is to embrace ambiguity, to recognize it as second cousin to creativity. Creative problem solving requires the use of a great deal of background and general knowledge. The effort toward disambiguation is directly related to the loss of background and general knowledge. It is because there is no longer a shared understanding of the role of the police that the administrative manuals and the forms get printed. Any process that increases the fund of shared knowledge, whether it be trivial or profound, can be helpful. Large numbers of people may be united in a single polity by political and economic institutions without sharing a single culture; their understandings of their society may indeed span sharply differing assumptions and ideas of legitimacy. Under these circumstances, there are a number of alternative forms of integration. Of these, direct coercion is only the most obvious. Over time, direct coercion may become less direct, through legislation backed up by the possibility of police action. Dogmatism (political or religious) may replace complex understandings with a list of unquestionable beliefs, and indoctrination may gradually convert imposed ideas into accepted wisdom. It has been traditional in states and empires with a high degree of cultural diversity held together by force to attempt to hasten the development of homogeneity and to force the adoption of a common language or a common religion.

The attempt to find noncoercive substitutes for shared understandings evolved over the centuries inevitably involves a certain shallowness and simplification. There is a large number of noncoercive devices for facilitating translation across cultural difference that share these problems. The best example of translation devices is money, whereby individuals with sharply different goals and views of the world can interact within a broader framework: money creates the illusion of commensurability. There are even shortcuts that can be used for efficient interaction in the absence of a common language. Pidgin languages develop by combining linguistic elements from several systems and are generally grammatically simple and quickly learned. At one time diplomatic French, supplemented with elaborate courtesies, provided a medium for communication lubricated by the appearance of commonality.

The affirmation of shared identities, of whatever depth of reality, can sometimes transcend the experience of cultural heterogeneity, perhaps long enough for a richer commonality to develop, but in the process such affirmations are often negative and jingoistic. During the twentieth century, peoples living in different Middle Eastern countries and often speaking mutually unintelligible dialects of Arabic tried to forge a positive common identity around the previously pejorative term *Arab*. It has proved easier, however, to unite in hostility to nonArabs such as Zionists and imperialists. Israel is a particularly interesting case study because the shared Jewish identity is at odds with the extreme differences in culture among the many immigrant groups. The necessity for Israel to mobilize against its enemies has provided a basis of unity for a society that is otherwise severely divided. Arguably, the emergence of fundamentalism in a number of transnational religions is also a form of simplified affirmation cutting across disparate local interpretations.

To the extent that a large society such as the United States, recently formed from disparate groups, can be said to have a common culture, it necessarily relies heavily on these alternative forms of integration. Herein is the source of the common criticism of U.S. society as superficial and materialistic. Superficiality, materialism, and apparent conformity are adaptations to flux and to cultural diversity. They characterize the mechanisms that allow a family transferred by a corporation from Texas to Connecticut to develop new social relationships quickly, adopt appropriate behavior, and assume a new social niche. These mechanisms coexist with much more rooted regional traditions and ethnic enclaves.

A certain difficulty has always attended the effort by anthropologists to discuss "national cultures," as in the body of work referred to as national character studies. These are inevitably coarse-grained, almost to the point of caricature, ignoring or brushing aside huge differences. But the point is that this is necessarily so. Such studies cannot tell the whole story of diverse cultures and communities within some larger entity; they can only summarize the makeshift structures of commonality. It is indeed often by self-caricature that people in the United States maintain the belief in a common culture. No better example can be found than the national political conventions.

All of us everywhere must feel a little ambivalent about the versions of our traditions that thrive abroad, for they all share the quality of portability and easy transportation, cut off from their roots: Kentucky Fried Chicken in Tokyo, Hindu gurus in California, Bruce Lee movies. Even those who believe most deeply in the importance of spreading a given system of ideas may wince when they encounter its various new incarnations. Roman prelates no doubt wince when they are trying to understand African versions of Catholicism and so, surely, do the proponents of capitalism or socialism when they see complex systems converted into simplistic slogans. Ideas that pass quickly around the world, whether they are commercial or political or even religious, are sea-changed by the process of transmission. Purists may call them debased—but one may think of them alternatively as shaped and trimmed for flight. A chain of U.S. restaurants selling sandwiches made from croissants is equally an occasion for celebration and for mourning, for lives are marginally enriched by novelty even as the old idea of a croissant is impoverished.

Conclusion

It is tempting to argue that politics necessarily becomes focused in central power and external boundaries as units become larger, with populations no longer able to interact in the ways that fascinated and obsessed the men of Athens. Implicit in this view is the expectation that the only effective route to world order would resemble the governments we know—and would be achieved by a blurring of existing boundaries and a diminution or loss of sovereignty of existing states. This approach has come to seem unrealistic. An alternative approach would suggest that changes in patterns and possibilities of communication are creating a new civilization—a pattern of commonality not necessarily expressed as sovereignty—and that the emergence of the states system was in fact a way of compensating for a paucity of interaction between, and even within, the emerging states, a level far short of the level we have to work with today. We must question the assumption that the ideas that are most widespread today are the most useful or represent the deepest truth.

Such a "new civilization" would come about if the various peoples of the world, rooted in their own local cultures, incorporated a substantial number of common elements of meaning, just as it would come about by common involvements in common tasks with shared goals—a mixture of the Beatles and the International Geophysical Year. The centralization of power and authority could come to look, in retrospect, like one of several possible adaptations to insufficient cultural integration, one that is becoming obsolete. The matter of integration, and the degree of integration, to be found in different kinds of societies must be sorted out in relation to issues of scale and issues of value.

It seems probable that an "emerging global civilization" will consist of multiple fragments and linkages differently integrated in different places. The links and fragments will not all come from the most elevated sources, and in this sense what we come to share will not look like Redfield's "great tradition," but like its echo incorporated in the understandings of the villagers. Certainly, there is a sense in which more and more people around the world have a knowledge of the "great traditions"; this is especially true of science, which is increasingly international. But in envisioning a worldwide currency of everyday understanding and in looking toward a opening up of the possibility of mutual intelligibility and empathy, it is very important that we not become mired in lofty expectations of what that commonality might be based on—that we include culture as well as Culture. Furthermore, the forms in which ideas are shared, whatever their sources, will be garbled, and continually liable to diverge—emerging from and informing patterns of pluralism and ambiguity—and will cohere not by orthodoxy but by a continual process of rapid interchange and the steady need to address practical problems.

9

Sovereignty, Identity, Community: Reflections on the Horizons of Contemporary Political Practice

R. B. J. Walker

An Essentially Uncontested Concept

Most political concepts are intrinsically controversial, "essentially contested," open to interpretation and appropriation by competing doctrines and strategies of inquiry.[1] Claims about democracy, freedom, equality, power, or interest spring readily to mind in this context. State sovereignty, by contrast, seems tame, even tedious. Its meaning might be marginally contestable by constitutional lawyers and other connoisseurs of fine lines, but for the most part state sovereignty elicits a commanding silence.[2] At least some problems of political life, it seems to suggest, are simple and settled, fit for legalists and footnotes, but not of pressing concern to those interested in the cut and thrust of everyday political struggle.

In this chapter I take the position that state sovereignty is in fact very interesting, indeed crucial, for any attempt to reconstruct our understanding of where and what political life can be at this historical juncture. It is interesting, I argue, precisely because of the practices through which it has been made to seem so incontestable for so long. Silences do command. They shape the practices and aspirations that are taken for granted, and the conditions under which alternative possibilities can be articulated. As everyone supposedly knows, state sovereignty is the primary constitutive principle of modern political life. But the manner in which this "fact" is known and treated as obvious tells us a great deal about the conditions under which claims about democracy, freedom, equality, and the rest have been constructed and deemed to be contestable. It tells us especially about the limits within which that contestability is constrained, ritualized, and fixed through a historically specific account of the possibilities of political community and human identity.

To the extent that state sovereignty has been the subject of critical debate, three sets of interrogations have been especially helpful. They provide the starting point for the analysis to be developed here.

One asks how we have so easily forgotten about the concrete struggles that have left their traces in the clean lines of political cartography and the codifications of international law. This question is concerned with how the formalization of state sovereignty as the primary constitutive *principle* of modern political life reifies the *practices* of state sovereignty—the disciplining of boundaries, the affirmation of inclusions, the defamation of foreigners, the inscription of danger, the legitimation of violence.

Another set of interrogations asks how it is possible to sustain claims to state sovereignty in a world in which temporal accelerations and global processes seem at least as significant as the capacity of states to persuade us of their ability to monopolize power and/or authority in a specific territory. In this context, claims about state sovereignty are usually challenged by claims about the need for more inclusive accounts of what it means to be human, to participate in some global political community, to be secure, democratic, or developed. These claims are then challenged in turn on the ground that they are naive—even dangerous—and that the principle of state sovereignty remains the only possible, or perhaps only desirable, context in which questions about human identity and political community can be resolved.

A third set of interrogations asks about the relationship between accounts of state sovereignty given by analysts of political life within states and those given by analysts of relations between states. From the inside, state sovereignty appears to be a matter of monopoly or centering. The primary concern is then whether sovereignty lies with the state itself or with the people who are somehow "represented" by the state. From the outside, by contrast, state sovereignty is usually taken to mean just the opposite—fragmentation, autonomous "powers," and a system of relations rather than a society, community, or polity. How has it been so easy, it may be asked, to construct accounts of political life by assuming that state sovereignty means either monopoly or fragmentation, community or anarchy, the possibility of a theory of political life guided by normative ambition or a theory of international relations guided only by hopes of pragmatic accommodation and regret at the tragic necessities of war? Why has it seemed so attractive to portray a world somehow freed from the claims of state sovereignty as a statist community writ large?

In this chapter I draw on all three of these forms of interrogation in order to show how the questions to which the principle of state sovereignty has seemed to provide an uncontestable answer for so long—questions about who "we" are, where "we" have come from, and where "we" might be going—might now be answered differently. This possibility, I argue, depends on a clear recognition of the extent to which state sovereignty is the primary constitutive principle of *modern* political life. How could it be otherwise? The connection between state sovereignty and modernity is both so obvious and so obscure—incontestable. But otherwise it surely must be.

A Discourse of Presence and Absence

It has been abundantly clear to many observers that the principle of state sovereignty is increasingly problematic. As a formalization of configurations of power and authority that emerged in a specific historical context, it has been criticized as an inappropriate guide to both theory and practice in an age of rapid transformation. It has come to seem particularly inappropriate in view of the current internationalization or globalization of economic, technological, cultural, and political processes. We are increasingly asked to think in terms of world or global politics rather than of politics within, and mere relations between competing sovereign states.

Yet this problematization continues to be resisted vigorously. Over the course of this century, influential currents of opinion have suggested that state sovereignty is, if not obsolete, then certainly due for reinterpretation and demotion in the hierarchy of major political concepts. Each time, and in whatever form the suggestion is made, it is challenged by counterassertions of the continuing vitality of state sovereignty as the indispensable constitutive principle of contemporary political life. It may be admitted that there is a certain incongruity between the claims formalized in the principle and the untidy processes of everyday politics. The boundaries drawn on maps, and guarded by soldiers and customs officials, it is acknowledged, suggest distinctions that are too sharp, too insensitive to the complex flows of international interaction. The invocations of formal equality will certainly be admitted to jar disconcertingly with the patterns of hierarchy, penetration, and domination that make such unpleasant news every day. Even so, while particular sovereignties may experience constant violation, the principle of state sovereignty itself remains inviolate. Despite clear evidence that the world is not as it was when the principle of state sovereignty was first articulated, or even when it was still the burning ambition of societies around the world struggling to escape from overt imperial control, we find the principle exceptionally difficult to renounce.

It is helpful to reflect upon the persistent pattern of debate in which claims and counterclaims about the continuing relevance of state sovereignty are articulated. For my present purposes, four variations on a central theme may be distinguished. Each variation in the sequence introduces a greater degree of ambiguity into the form of the debate by posing the historically specific character of the debate in a more and more striking way.

The most familiar variation occurs as a confrontation between two philosophies of history. The passing of the age of state sovereignty is announced in the ringing tones of nineteenth century accounts of history as Progress. But at the end of that century, we are always reminded, hopes for the withering away of the state, whether in the name of worldwide commerce, universal reason, or the universal class, were precipitously dashed by the passions of nationalism, by a widespread critique of the illusions of Progress, and by the war to end all wars. Max Weber gave a particularly influential expression to the connection between a more pessimistic intellectual outlook and the assertion of a statist power politics. Against the deceptive embrace of utopianism, idealism, or universalist aspirations of any kind, much of the conventional wisdom about international politics down to the present time has followed Weber in identifying statist power politics as the inevitable, if tragic, reality to which we all ought to submit.[3]

A second variation has grown out of widespread alarm about the magnitude and violence of war in the twentieth century, alarm that has induced widespread hopes for the establishment of supranational organizations that might ensure peace and security in a world of evident danger. These hopes were often inspired by long-standing intellectual and moral traditions, not least those that drew upon a revitalized nineteenth century vision of Progress. But the key theme here concerned the interpretation of novel institutions. From the regularized meetings of the great powers, to the League of Nations, to the UN, many claimed to find an evolutionary development that might eventually bring about a revolutionary restructuring of the international system. But the typical ambiguity of terms—an uncertainty as to whether they should be understood as "international" or "supranational" organizations—is indicative of the primary ground for contention. Against claims to supranational novelty, counterclaims were invariably made that organizations like the United Nations have remained firmly tied to the interests of states. While they may embody many novel features, it will be said, they are difficult to interpret as clear evidence of any nascent transnational or global community. Against those who argue that such organizations are nonetheless small steps in a long-term structural transformation, it has become conventional to argue that they represent an entrenchment and further formalization of state sovereignty as a constitutive principle of international order. In this counterinterpretation, international organizations are seen as giving institutional form to a properly *inter*national community. After all, Article 2, paragraph 7 of the United Nations Charter, formalizing the principle of sovereign self-determination, has been accorded much greater weight than Article 99, for example, which assigns specific powers to the secretary general as a sort of supranational actor. Even if there is more going on among international organizations than can be explained by this counterinterpretation, it remains quite unclear how significant it is or how it can be characterized.

A third variation grows out of observations about the accelerating internationalization or globalization of economic life since 1945. Considerable attention has been given in this context to the growth of transnational or multinational corporations, which are often interpreted as very significant innovations. They have global reach, great mobility, and enormous resources. They have demonstrated both the capacity and willingness to undermine the formal authority of smaller states and even pose major challenges to the dominant economic powers. It is in this context especially that we hear claims about "interdependence," about the establishment of significantly new rules for the international game. With interdependence, it is said, the relations between autonomous powers of the kind celebrated by the classic theories of international relations have begun to be overlaid or even eroded by complex patterns of mutual dependence and functional "regimes" that cut across territorial boundaries.

But again, counterarguments are no less audible. Some merely question an exaggerated account of the power and significance of these admittedly important developments. After all, most major corporations remain rooted in particular states. Most states have also learned to respond and adapt to the reconfigurations of the world economy, and to place important limits on the operations of large corporations. Arguments of this kind, however, can also turn into a much more interesting inquiry into ways in which the character of the modern state has been changing in response to processes of economic internationalization. States have been instrumental in initiating policies on investment, research, resource allocation, income distribution, and social control that facilitate rather than challenge emerging patterns of global economic relations. The internationalization of production, rapid flows of capital, integration of ownership and control in key industries, and the changing relations between states and multinational corporations are undoubtedly major features of the modern world. Yet it is far from clear that any of these things imply a withering away of the state as that aspiration has so often been articulated. They do seem to suggest a transformation in the character of the state—the historical transformation of a historically constituted form of political community. Similarly, recognition of the significance of novel processes of internationalization, and even of nonterritorial forms of economic organization, does not necessarily imply the obsolescence of the principle of state sovereignty, although it may suggest the need for a radical reinterpretation of its meaning.

A final variation has become increasingly significant since the late 1960s. It grows out of a variety of claims about the multidimensional dangers that now confront all human beings, no matter which state they call home. Attention has focused variously on the threat of nuclear weapons technologies, on environmental damage, on the global production of weapons of mass destruction, and on global patterns of systematic brutality on the part of established political authorities.

The significance and urgency of these dangers is widely acknowledged. They scream out past those who have learned to read only the trends of improvement and to ignore the contradictions of the age. Yet again the debate invariably turns toward a set of counterclaims that insists on the continuing vitality of the principle of state sovereignty. Global patterns there may be, but there exists a vast disjunction in the modern world between the global scope of the problems and dangers before us and established forms of political identity, community, and authority. Perhaps this discrepancy is unfortunate, it is acknowledged, but "that's the way it is." However seriously we may take specific global problems, political life remains organized within sovereign states. After all, without the formal claims of state sovereignty, most of our accounts of what it means to engage in political life would make little sense.

What do we understand by political community? Where are power and authority located? How is power legitimized? All these questions find their conventional resolution in the claims of state. These claims are formalized and encoded in the principle of state sovereignty. Debate about global problems, it is said, must come back to an affirmation of state sovereignty precisely because we do not have any other credible resolution of the fundamental questions about the possibility of political life, any other political ground on which to respond to the questions of the age.

A Resolution of Universality and Particularity

These four ways of speaking about the significance of state sovereignty in the modern world are variations on an exceptionally rich and complex theme. This theme is intricately woven into the fabric of what is conventionally understood as the Western tradition of political theory. Some may find resonances with passages in texts from Classical Greece, especially those passages in which citizens of the polis are distinguished from the barbarians outside. Others may suggest that a clearer picture emerges if we consider the theoretical problems posed by the collapse of the hierarchical forms of authority and overlapping jurisdictions characteristic of the feudal era. The emergence of the state in the late Renaissance and early-modern Europe was accompanied by attempts to articulate alternative accounts of the possibility of political community. Where the feudal order encouraged accounts of political life rooted in universalist claims about participation in a community of humankind (or at least of Christendom), theorists of the state speculated about how political life could be organized on the basis of the particular claims of a particular community. Put in its simplest form, political debate focused on the relative claims of "men" and "citizens."[4]

Elements of this debate were prefigured not only by the inheritances from Classical Greece and Republican Rome, but also by theological distinctions between finitude and infinity.[5] In the conventional political reading of the story, the point at which the claims of citizens begin to take priority over universalist claims about people in general is marked by Machiavelli's refusal of a universalist Christian ethic as an appropriate guide to public life. By the time of Bodin and Hobbes, now seen as the theorists of sovereignty par excellence, the priority of citizenship was assured. The typical task then assumed by political theory came to be understood as reconciling political life within particular states with accounts of the good, the true, and the beautiful that were assumed to have a universal validity.

Conventional accounts of political life have thus come to express a fundamental paradox or contradiction. Inside the particular state, concepts of obligation, freedom, and justice could be articulated within the context of universalist accounts of Revelation, Reason, and History. Yet these claims to universal values and processes presumed, implicitly or explicitly, a boundary beyond which such universals could not be guaranteed. Beyond the boundary, beyond the borders of the sovereign state, lay a world of difference: a world of others who were both spatially outside and usually presumed to be temporally backward; and a world of international relations, even of international anarchy, in which different rules applied.

The precise historical contours through which the competing claims of universality and particularity were resolved in this specific way at the level of the state are indeed long and involved. The contemporary significance of the form this resolution has assumed is measured less by the extent to which it has become a matter of controversy than by the way in which it has come to silently define both an account of political community and a division of intellectual labor. Acceptance of this resolution has come to be a precondition for speaking about political life at all. It informs distinctions between contemporary academic disciplines, notably those between sociology and anthropology and between politics and international relations. It sets severe constraints on those who try to make sense of the rapid transformations and global processes that are at once so readily apparent and so difficult to capture convincingly within prevailing conceptual categories.

For, again to reduce the problem to its simplest terms, claims about the obsolescence of the principle of state sovereignty, or about the significance of processes and forces that are identified as somehow global in scale and significance, amount to a fundamental challenge to the resolution of the claims of universality and particularity at the level of the state. Claims about global problems, global processes, or even a global civilization may easily be interpreted as latter-day manifestations of earlier claims about the priority of people as people rather than as the citizens of particular states. As such, claims about global processes come to be articulated within a series of already existing categories and expectations. They fit into an established discourse in which aspirations for the universal already have their proper place: the state.

The Limits of Political Community

It is in this context that it is necessary to understand the persistent tendency for claims about the problematic character of state sovereignty to be countered by claims about its continuing vitality. This tendency has become ritualized in what is often referred to as a "great debate" between idealist and realist theories of international relations. Understood as a serious attempt to engage in the history of political thought, the subsumption of most of the classic texts in Western political theory into representatives of one or the other of these competing positions leaves a great deal to be desired. But if we situate this sort of debate in the context of early-modern struggles to reconcile the claims of human beings as such with the claims of the citizens of particular states, its characteristic form becomes more readily understandable, though perhaps still not excusable.

Even so, the four different variations on this persistent theme suggest a crucial destabilization of familiar categories. As a greater sensitivity to historical trajectories is introduced with each new variation, the historically constituted nature of the familiar categories of analysis becomes more evident.

The first variation has been the most susceptible to reification, to the fixing of historically specific categories as if they are eternal. Expressed as a debate between competing philosophies of history, it draws upon cultural traditions and philosophical options that are deeply ingrained in modern societies. Fixed within the horizons of reified philosophical options, the state and the state system appear as permanent features of the political landscape. Attempts to suggest otherwise are said to arise from the illusions of Progress, illusions that have been punctured time and time again by states seeking to assert their own interests through an uncompromising power politics. This has been the message taken from writers like E. H. Carr and Hans J. Morgenthau.[6] Their texts have achieved paradigmatic status as expressions of a clear-headed willingness to confront the tragic imperatives of power politics without lapsing into naive longings for a different form of political community. From this point of view, there is really no point in thinking about the concept of state sovereignty. It appears as a given, as a foundational moment of a political universe that repeats itself but never changes.

In the second variation, historical change becomes more significant. The claim that international organizations such as the United Nations represent the beginnings of a new supranational community may be strongly resisted. Yet, it will be admitted, the structure of the international system has been undergoing significant modification and development. The most important effect of this admission is to begin to undermine the sharp contrast—between a community within states on one hand and international anarchy on the other—that has been understood to be the practical consequence of resolving the choice between the citizens of states and human beings in general. For some observers, this contrast was always overdrawn in any case. States, they argued, have long learned how to cooperate with each other, to devise rules of accommodation, conform to tacit agreements, even establish laws and institutions like the United Nations. The creation of international order, they suggested, did not imply the need for any imposition from above. Historical change is not to be ignored, or reduced to a cyclical repetition of the same old story, but it cannot be understood to be effecting any erosion of sovereignty or a new supranational source of power and authority. Rather, it suggests both the need for and the possibility of encouraging still further cooperation among responsible states. Sovereignty, it is claimed, has long been compatible with international cooperation.[7] There is no reason to suppose that it is incompatible with the cooperative behavior required by patterns of complex interdependence or the establishment of functional regimes. Some reinterpretation of the precise meaning of sovereignty might well be necessary, but, this variation suggests, such a reinterpretation is well within the evolutionary capacities of international law.

With the third variation, matters become more complicated. We begin to move beyond the limits within which most policymakers and even scholarly analysts feel comfortable. A sense of historical change becomes more and more evident. The capacities of multinational corporations and the rapidity of financial transfers suggest a more profound alteration in the conditions of human existence than organizations like the United Nations. The gradual evolution of international cooperation is one thing, but it provides little help in understanding the flux of contemporary economic life or the implications of ongoing technological innovation.

Sometimes, the interpretation of these processes seems to engage in yet another replay of the old debate: sovereignty forever or sovereignty farewell. This tendency has been especially prevalent in accounts of interdependence that draw on a narrowly utilitarian account of economic life. If all social processes are amenable to the same kind of explanation—one based on a utilitarian reduction of social action to the clash of individual self–interests—then the distinction between life inside and outside the state is effectively dismissed as trivial. States become just another group of actors on a uniform field. The concept of state sovereignty likewise becomes uninteresting, even irrelevant. As the expression of historically constituted political communities, it is erased in favor of an account of a single community, an interdependent world subject to the universalizing principles of modern life.

Historically constituted political communities, however, have not been erased. States have not disappeared in the face of spectacular transformations of economic processes internationally. Thus the most interesting accounts of the internationalization of production and patterns of interdependence speak not of the erasure of the state but of its transformation under specific historical conditions. States begin to appear less as a permanent and unchanging feature of international life than as historically determinate and variable expressions of power and authority.[8] From some theoretical perspectives, of course, this is hardly a novel conclusion. It is taken as an obvious assumption by influential schools of political economy, particularly those influenced by Marxist accounts of the state within capitalist modes of production. Even so, political economy has not obviously freed itself from a deep longing for the abolition of the state, an abolition more imagined outside of history than explained as a historical process.

In the second variation, accounts of historical change come to focus primarily on the evolution of the structural condition of the *inter*state system. Systemic relations may be understood as extraordinarily complex, but they do not seem to undermine the general validity of the principle of state sovereignty. In the third variation, patterns of interdependence and internationalization are understood in terms of the changing character of the modern state. The status of sovereignty becomes rather unclear, but at least the tendency to assume that it must be either present or absent is resisted. Yet if a sense of the rapidity of contemporary transformations begins to break through in this third variation, it is even more evident in the fourth. If the third variation establishes a link between sovereignty and the transformation of the state under conditions of internationalization and interdependence, the fourth variation establishes a connection between sovereignty and challenges to what we have come to understand as political community.

Here things get very difficult indeed. We have learned how to speak about the changing form of the state, despite the influence of those who persist in treating it as an ahistorical black box, Newtonian atom, or rational actor in the utilitarian mode. But in speaking about challenges to our understanding of political community, we run into the limits of our own ability to speak about politics at all. Evolutionary adjustments in the mechanisms of international cooperation are relatively straightforward, at least in principle. Policymakers are engaged in this process all the time. Even the radical restructuring of the state in response to structural transformations of economic life is well within the bounds of practical politics. But a rearticulation of what we mean by political community? It is here, we might say, that the concept of state sovereignty seems both most problematic and yet most indispensable. We cling to it because all other accounts of political community seem so unconvincing. The destabilization of the persistent way to speak about state sovereignty on the ground of history comes to a disconcerting halt.

Sovereignty as Reification

The discussion so far has drawn attention to a persistent way of speaking about state sovereignty. The rhythms of the conversation can be heard in the writings of academic analysts, the clichés of policymakers, and the most characteristic forms of popular debate. According to this way of speaking, state sovereignty appears to be something that is ever present or about to disappear.

This discursive ritual of presence and absence, I have suggested, can be understood in the context of a particular resolution of questions about the character and location of political community as these were articulated in early-modern Europe. These questions were answered through a specific account of the relationship between universal and particular mediated at the level of the state. Contemporary research on and speculation about the principle of state sovereignty occurs largely—though not exclusively—within discursive horizons that can be traced back to this historically specific resolution.

Important destabilizations of this resolution are also visible in contemporary debate, especially among those who have been concerned with the historicity of both the state and the state system. However, even these destabilizations have failed to upset the overall equilibrium of our understanding of political life. They are kept in check by the more or less successful claims of state, formalized by the principle of state sovereignty, to monopolize both the theory and practice of political community. A more radical destabilization of the prevailing political categories is resisted finally on the ground that there is no other resolution of the relationship between universality and particularity that has any substantial political plausibility in the modern world, despite the accumulating evidence of global processes and universal dangers. The particular form and functions of the state may change. The patterns of cooperation between states may also change. But when it comes to the suggestion that global processes or universal dangers imply a fundamental transformation of political community, the conventions of established discourse take on a renewed vitality.

It is important to listen carefully to the rhythms and cadences of the established rituals of speech in this context, because ways of speaking about state sovereignty reproduce certain assumptions and resolutions of philosophical and political questions that are constitutive of the principle of state sovereignty itself. To speak about state sovereignty is to engage in forms of political practice, to become caught up in immensely powerful forms of political action that appear to be mere abstractions or ideologies. Perhaps the most telling indicator of just what is at stake is that the principle of state sovereignty—whose meaning, however we define it, can be understood as a consequence of massive transformations in social, cultural, economic, and political practice—has become a seemingly innocuous, even boring political concept, of interest primarily to international lawyers and constitutional experts. Any attempt to come to terms with the principle of state sovereignty seems to become a tiresome interrogation of the obvious. But why, exactly, does it seem so obvious?

There is, to begin with, the well-known conventional history of the concept. Once upon a time, so this story goes, there were overlapping jurisdictions and hierarchical arrangements. Then there was the coming of capitalism, modernity, and the state system. Jurisdictions became separated, and authority was distributed in space to autonomous territorial communities.

The process was slow and uneven, accelerating only over the past century, and, despite formal claims, not yet complete.

Contemporary political practice confirms the authenticity of the story. State sovereignty has been encoded into law. Cultural diversity has been distributed according to the boundaries of sovereign territoriality. And whether we ask "Why should we obey?" or "What should be done?" the answer, we presume, must refer to the established sovereign authority of state power. Political practice has been given a location in which to occur: the centered space of the territorial state. And it has been given a temporal project: the mediation of differences—of interests, cultures, values, and classes—within the unified apparatus of the national political community. Moreover, as a story confirmed through practice, it can prove enormously satisfying. It is a story of grand achievements. It contrasts the progressive and democratic impulses set in motion with the emergence of the modern state with the hierarchical orderings of feudal society and the dominations of empire.

As a story confirmed through practice, it also has a powerful moral. The search for the good life, it suggests, is indeed desirable and necessary, but the search must not turn into an imposition from outside. All peoples have the right to self-determination, to find their own way forward. The resolution of questions about political community in early-modern Europe has proved to be enormously satisfying. It offers scope for both the diversity of human experience, and for the pursuit of universality within a particular community. The problem posed by the principle of state sovereignty is thus not that it gives license for states to pursue their own self-interest in an anarchical system. That may, or may not, be a consequence of a more fundamental question: whether the early-modern European resolution of questions about political community remains persuasive in the modern world. As an account of history, as a guide to political practices that we have not only come to take for granted, but can still see as liberating in many parts of the world, as a formalization of deeply satisfying answers to questions about who we are, where we are, and where we should be going, the principle of state sovereignty carries enormous political and moral weight. It will not be easily shifted by instabilities introduced by the historicity of the state or the international system.

But even recognizing that the principle of state sovereignty carries enormous political and moral weight, it is always necessary to be deeply suspicious of concepts that have come to seem obvious. It is especially important to be wary of the conventional history of the principle of state sovereignty, and to think about the extent to which that history has been subject to conventionalization and, indeed, mythmaking. For the most striking thing about most accounts of the history of state sovereignty is that they seem eerily bloodless. A legal norm has become codified and amended, but the relationship between legal processes and the transformation of social forces over several centuries remains rather obscure. In this respect, histories of state sovereignty are written in a significantly different tone than histories of the state.

As codification of the principle of equality between members of the international community, the claim to state sovereignty deflects attention from the inequalities and dominations that remain so characteristic of the world in which we live. As a codification of the relationship between universality and cultural diversity, it has fixed the possibility of cultural diversity within the more limited and spatially circumscribed diversity of nation-states. As a legal principle, it has become encoded within a particular legalistic discourse, subject to the institutionalization of specialized intellectual traditions and ways of speaking. As a political principle, it has become encoded within a specific reading of the history of Western political thought, a reading that is largely constituted through the division between political community within and mere relations without—a division that is formalized in the principle of state sovereignty itself.

Thus we have a tradition of political theory that tends to celebrate those who have taken the account of political community within the sovereign state as a given, making it possible to proceed to discussions of justice, freedom, and progress. Conversely, we also have a tradition of international relations theory that also takes the principle of state sovereignty as a given, but then proceeds to read the consequences negatively, as requiring a concern with the management of order in a system bereft of overarching power or authority. The point of intersection, the fixed boundary separating community within from relations between states, provides a seemingly static point of origin from which accounts of the history of political life can be written. We may read the history of the principle of state sovereignty from either the inside or the outside, but the point of intersection seems timeless. Yet it is, I have suggested, a point that can and must be understood in its historical specificity. The conventional history of state sovereignty, while confirmed by practice and offering a persuasive resolution of the most basic political and philosophical questions about the nature and location of political community, must also be understood as a reification.

Sovereignty, Space, and Time

If the persistent rituals of debate about state sovereignty have been subject to important destabilizations as a consequence of attempts to understand the historicity of the state and the state system, then it is also helpful to understand how the principle of state sovereignty was itself stabilized through a certain forgetting of history. In this respect, it is instructive to consider how the emergence of the state in early-modern Europe has come to be fixed within the canons of the history of political thought. The differences between

Machiavelli and Thomas Hobbes are particularly striking in this respect, not least because they have been placed so often in the same category of writers judged to have a special, and essentially similar, insight into the operation of international relations.[9]

With Machiavelli, we can see a hypersensitivity to the problem of change. He is fascinated by the founding of new states. His images and concepts are primarily temporal. He speaks of the coming of *fortuna*, and develops a notion of political *virtù* in which the capacity to read and respond to the contingencies of the temporal world becomes the most crucial moment of political judgment. Machiavelli takes time seriously. He reverses the conventional Augustinian valuation of time and eternity, insisting that political life cannot be understood as a mere staging post or preparation for the eternity to come, but as a struggle for glory in the here and now. Machiavelli's temporal politics are also rooted in a conception of political space, a reworking of the classical vision of the polis as a home for men. But as a reworking of classical themes, it is one that is more sensitive to the cycles and contingencies of political community than to the possibility of an unchanging and perfect order maintained by philosopher-kings.

At least in his best-known writings, Hobbes provides a sharp contrast with the Machiavellian preoccupation with politics as an activity occurring in time. Critical of the language and of the metaphysical assumptions of the Scholastics, he demands precision and definition in his concepts. He wants to fix meanings, to capture the vagaries of political dispute within the categories of a presumed universal logic. Hobbes' sensitivities, we might say, are primarily spatial. He draws on Galilean mechanics, which in turn draws on Euclidean geometry. His conclusions are consistent with his spatial and rationalist metaphysics. They call for law, for an unchanging sovereign power, not for a prince—or a republic—able to rise to the challenge of the times knowing that what can be achieved can only be temporary, except perhaps as it might be remembered at another time.

Hobbes' spatial sensitivities are part of a broader cultural trend. From Descartes' philosophy to Mercator's cartography, from Galilean mechanics to the magnificent constructions of Isaac Newton and Immanuel Kant, we can see the tremendous impact of a new spatial consciousness in early-modern European intellectual life. It is in this context that the concept of state sovereignty became formalized. Much more could be said about the particular conception of space—absolute, Euclidean—that became so influential, but for my purposes here it is sufficient to note that our contemporary understanding of state sovereignty reflects a spatial understanding of the possibility of political community, an understanding that necessarily gives priority to the fixing of processes of historical change in space. Not only does the principle of state sovereignty reflect a historically specific resolution of questions about the universality and particularity of political community, but it also fixes that resolution within categories that have absorbed a metaphysical claim to timelessness.[10]

The principle of state sovereignty codifies a historically specific answer to historically specific questions about political community. Moreover, this answer is articulated in the context of an attempt to fix political community within spatial categories, categories in which time and change are understood as dangers to be contained. But there is another dimension to the reifying tendencies immanent within the principle of state sovereignty, one that occurs as a crucial ambiguity in the fixing of the principle of state sovereignty in space. If we ask where state sovereignty is located, we inevitably receive a double answer. Both parts are necessary in order to define the modern state, but the connection between them poses a range of pressing political problems.

In one part of the answer, the state is understood as territory, as geography, as extension across the physical surface of the earth. Here we have the territorial state, the state as understood by geographers, regional specialists and geopoliticians. In another part of the answer, however, the state is defined less in terms of the lines of spatial extension than of the fixed point from which spatial extension is measured. Here we have the monopoly on the legitimate use of violence, in Weber's terms, a monopoly that may be deployed within a territory, but that is understood primarily as a fixed point of power and legitimacy. Here we also have the state as understood by students of political institutions and constitutions, as the sovereign center around which society, polity, culture, economy, and territory may be circumscribed.[11]

Both parts of this answer can be understood as essentially spatial in character. They refer to the location of political activity. But the second part is more open to temporalization, to accounts of the changing character of forms of state. The theory of the state in this second sense has gradually become absorbed in philosophies of history, while the analysis of everyday politics has become preoccupied with ongoing struggles to claim sovereign power, focusing on the sequences of regimes seeking to occupy the center. But the principle of state sovereignty itself remains rooted firmly in a spatial account of territory, fixed boundaries, and geopolitics.

Viewed from the outside, from the perspective of international politics, the ambiguity of this description of the location of state sovereignty is of relatively little consequence. The claim to power and authority at the center may be treated as more or less coextensive with the claim to control a piece of territory. The state is the territorial state. The theory of the state in this sense remains rooted in early-modern European assumptions about political space. Viewed from the inside, however, the ambiguity has been highly problematic. The question inevitably arises as to whether sovereignty lies with the center or with the inhabitants of the territory. Sovereignty is thus always seemingly in motion from the state to civil society. For, although the formal principle of state sovereignty provides a constitutional account of the state as somehow (abstractly) synonymous with society, there remains the rather serious difficulty of specifying precisely how the relationship between state and civil society is to be understood or achieved in practice. This provides one of the core themes of European political thought since the early-modern period, although it is usually addressed less as a problem of sovereignty as such than of the relationship between state and nation on the one hand and the democratic participation of the people in the affairs of state on the other.

It is possible to take the significance of this ambiguity one step further. When we examine the two parts of the answer to questions about the location of state sovereignty, we can specify the relationship between them both in terms of spatial configurations and of fundamental theoretical and philosophical principles.

Spatially we see the conventional relation between center and periphery. This may be specified in geographical language—national government or local government, national concerns or regional concerns. It may also be specified in the language of political hierarchies of power and influence, ranging usually from the national, to the federal, to the local "levels"—a term that combines both spatial and hierarchical principles of organization.

This spatial ordering has a theoretical analogue, in which the principles of universality and diversity are understood to be (spatially) separate, with the principle of universality having a higher status. Here we are on the well-known ground of the primary categories of Western reason, at least as these categories have become institutionalized in the received histories of what constitutes serious—that is modern—philosophical and scientific analysis. We are also back on the terrain occupied by the early-modern answer to questions about political community. This answer, we might say, takes the form of a double contradiction.[12]

Within states, the difficulty is understood as the need to resolve the claims of the many (primarily individuals) with the claims of the one, the unified national or statist community. These resolutions may tend to preserve the autonomy or freedom of the many as far as possible, but they ultimately favor the claims of state. Hence the significance of the limits placed on all theories of democracy by the claims of "national security." Political life is organized almost exclusively around the capture of state power, with the capacity to exercise the claim to universality within the state. The great differences between the different methods that are used to this end—electoral politics or violent revolution—should not obscure the common vision of political life as the capture of the state, understood as the point at which power is centered and deployed. In the end, the conviction that political life is about taking the center is the fundamental guarantee that one's politics are serious and realistic.

Relations between states, by contrast, are understood to arise from the simultaneous presence and absence of a sovereign identity. The difficulty is understood as the impossibility of any lasting way of resolving the claims of the many—the many claims to sovereign identity—within an account of one universal community. As political life is understood to be possible only among a community of citizens—among a community in which difference is subsumed into a sovereign identity—and as relations between states are understood as the absence of a community in this sense, international relations can only be a clash among the many. This clash may lead to accommodations, temporary alliances, and tacit agreements, but not to a community in which differences are resolved in a more encompassing principle of universality.

Pursuing this line of analysis, it becomes clear that the problematic identified by the principle of state sovereignty is an effect of a more encompassing principle of sovereign identity. To come to terms with state sovereignty, to understand the limits of the way we speak about it and to ask what kind of sovereignty is possible or desirable now, is necessarily to come to terms with deeply entrenched philosophical principles, of which state sovereignty is only one expression. The more encompassing philosophical principles rest on a claim to be able to fix a point of identity—a universality in space and time—against which all differences in space and time can be measured, judged, and put in their place. The principle of state sovereignty organizes this historically specific resolution into a spatially differentiated double contradiction or dialectic. Within states, the relation between universality and particularity may be resolvable. It may be understood as a dialectical interaction between state and civil society, a dialectic amenable to both a totalizing closure or a democratic opening. Between states, irresolvable contradiction is guaranteed.

Consequently, challenges to the principle of state sovereignty cannot be understood only as challenges to a historically specific account of what it means to engage in political community. They must also involve a questioning of the grounds on which that account of political community has become reified within a historically specific understanding of space-time relations. More crucially still, they must lead to a questioning of the processes through which the spatiotemporal claims of state sovereignty both reify and are guaranteed by a historically specific resolution of the relationship between universality and diversity.

This resolution, it is no exaggeration to say, has been constitutive of modern consciousness, and has been shared by all modern political ideologies. To take the problematic character of the principle of state sovereignty seriously is necessarily to come to terms with the need to rework what we have come to think of as serious politics.

Beyond Presence and Absence

The argument so far can be summarized in the form of ten propositions:

1. Given the evidence before us about the prevalence and significance of global processes, and the plausibility of hypotheses about an emerging

"global civilization," it is necessary to rethink the meaning of state sovereignty, the central category in which the primary principles of contemporary political life are expressed.

2. To begin to rethink this principle is to become caught up in a persistent pattern of speech about the presence or absence of state sovereignty.

3. Both the principle of state sovereignty and the persistent patterns of speech about it can be understood in the context of an historically specific response to questions about political community in early-modern Europe.

4. This response depended on a historically specific resolution of the relationship between universality and diversity.

5. This resolution occurred in the context of an historically specific account of space-time relations, one in which a particular account of space (Euclidean, Galilean, Newtonian) offered a way of delineating both political and philosophical options.

6. Politically, this primarily spatial consciousness informs three crucial moves:

- The fixing of temporally constituted historical communities in space;
- The formalization of the state as the spatial container in which political community can occur;
- The formalization of a fundamental spatial differentiation between community within states and noncommunity outside and between states.

7. Philosophically, both the primacy of space over time and the specific account of space are articulated in terms of a resolution of the relation between universalist identity and spatiotemporal difference in favor of the former; that is, in favor of a timeless rationalism.

8. The problematic character of the principle of state sovereignty necessarily leads us to the problematic character of both the philosophical resolutions that are constitutive of modernity and of the articulation of political space in which these resolutions are fixed by the sovereign borders of state.

9. Both the philosophical resolutions and their reification in political space are subject to significant instabilities on the ground of time and history. For the most part time is contained. Within states, time is conventionally understood as linear progress, while between states, time is understood as contingency and repetition. But relations between states are increasingly understood in terms of temporal progression, while the form of states is also understood to be as much a subject of temporal transformation as it is a place where historical change can occur.

10. Questions about history, about ongoing practices, are nevertheless constrained by the spatial categories—and the philosophical principles that

in turn sustain them—through which questions about political practice have already been resolved historically in a spatial account of political community.

Together, these ten propositions suggest that questions about the kind of sovereignty appropriate in a world plausibly characterized as an emerging civilization will have to resist the discursive strategies in which the relation of universality and particularity are reified spatially through claims to a sovereign identity. These questions will have to pursue the destabilizations already visible in analyses that challenge spatial reifications on the ground of time and history. We can characterize such questions, as well as those that remain fixed in orbit around the presence or absence of state sovereignty, in terms of (1) the degree to which time and history are taken seriously, and (2) the degree to which the historically constituted principles that constrain the possibilities of political practice within spatial reifications are challenged. In short, if we ask about the future fate of the principle of state sovereignty, it is already possible to imagine the range of possible answers. They fall into six primary groups. The first three affirm and the last three challenge the early-modern understanding of human identity and political community formalized by the principle of state sovereignty.

First, it seems safe to predict that much of the discussion of state sovereignty will continue to fix the options before us within the more general paradigm of a sovereign identity; that is, within a spatiotemporal metaphysics governed by a logic in which universality is both distinguished from and privileged over difference and diversity. Here we will continue to see a persistent oscillation of claims that state sovereignty will either continue to exist or that it is about to disappear from view.

Claims about the *persistence* of state sovereignty will occur through an affirmation of difference as the negation of a claim to sovereign identity or universality. This affirmation may occur as a cultural ascription of otherness to a specific object, as the construction of the enemy whose very being—as the opposite of one's own virtue, or "development"—guarantees one's own status as the paragon of universal community. Or it may occur as a political ascription of anarchy to the generalized other, the realm of contingency and violence outside that legitimizes the priorities of national security within. In either case, the early-modern solution to questions about political community are reproduced. Primary concern can then be focused on whether the accommodations symbolized by the Treaty of Westphalia can be maintained so as to prevent the politics of otherness from turning to a war against the infidels.

Claims about the imminent *disappearance* of sovereignty will occur through a denial of difference and the affirmation of identity. These claims will also take one of two forms.

The simplest move is to deny the spatial difference between life inside and life outside statist political communities. This is in part a claim about the essential homogeneity of space, and in part a claim about the universal character of all human behavior, or, if temporalized, a claim about the universalizing character of modernity. Here, problems of state sovereignty are rendered trivial through a utilitarian account of rational human behavior as such—an account presumed to be valid for all actors, states, organizations, or individuals, and, given the presumed eventual accommodations to "development" and "modernization," for all parts of the world. Here the principle of state sovereignty disappears into accounts of a global civilization understood as the erasure of difference in favor of unity, or more precisely, in favor of an understanding of difference as the essential similarity of all "sovereign individuals" competing in a global market. The theory of international relations disappears into a utilitarian-liberal theory of international political economy, a highly specific theory that successfully carries off a presumption of universality through a systematic suppression of the historicity of all human practices.[13]

In another version of this move, the claim about the homogeneity of space is retained, but becomes a way of articulating movement through time. Things change, but time merely brings a change in scale. Jonathan Swift already offered a well-known critique of this move in *Gulliver's Travels*.[14] In the present context, it occurs as an account of the centralization of authority in global institutions by analogy with an account of the centered state. Political community retains the form we have come to understand through the historical experience of states. Jurisdictions may be divided into varying levels of authority, as in federalism, for example, but authority is eventually fused into a sovereign center. Transcending the system of states— supranationality—then comes to be interpreted as the construction of a similar kind of community, but on a larger scale.

These four versions of the analysis of the problem of state sovereignty within the more general paradigm of sovereignty converge to confirm the persistent patterns of debate in which state sovereignty is understood to be permanently present or soon to disappear. They simultaneously confirm an account of what a world politics or global civilization must be if state sovereignty is indeed to be thrown onto the scrap-heap of history. In this account, global civilization is interpreted as a combination of the thesis of universal modernization and the construction of a supranational authority on the model of the state. Precisely how the claims of temporal change, cultural diversity, or the existing sovereign claims of state can be reconciled with a notion of global civilization in this sense remains unclear. Indeed they remain puzzles that permit no resolution except for still further oscillations of presence and absence, modernity and tradition, community and anarchy, the universal and the different.

Second, considerations of time and history will enter into this seemingly timeless play of alternatives insofar as questions are raised about who gains and who loses from how the options are framed. Debates about state sovereignty will thus continue to engage with broader concerns about the legacies of empire, colonialism, and underdevelopment, and the continuing disparities between rich and poor societies. Although the resolutions of the early-modern era may be understood as historically and culturally specific, their meaning comes to be reinterpreted in the light of contemporary patterns of global inequality. In this context, the discussion of state sovereignty merges with the discussion of nationalism. While some point to the emergence of global civilization, others still aspire to an effective sovereign state. While some point to the dangers of international anarchy, others point to the oppressions of hegemony and inequality. Time and history enter to destabilize the sense of a single way of speaking, constantly repeated by the same people, and to suggest that how one speaks within the established discourses about state sovereignty depends largely on where one is. Nevertheless, the way of speaking itself remains familiar. Resistance occurs as both a challenge to, but also a corroboration of, modernist political community.[15]

Third, the meaning of state sovereignty will continue to be reinterpreted in the light of the experience of international cooperation. As institutionalization of cooperation proceeds, the boundaries guaranteeing the absolute exclusions characteristic of the early-modern resolution of universality and diversity will dissolve still further. The criteria of exclusive jurisdictions will be relaxed, and modified claims of state sovereignty will be treated as fully compatible with shared participation in joint projects and regional responsibilities. The criteria of monopoly over power and legitimacy will also be relaxed. If the experience of the European community can be generalized, both relaxations may be taken rather a long way. But then, if the European community turns out to be a rather larger state, the essential logic of state sovereignty will be confirmed once again. Indeed, insofar as the challenge of state sovereignty is understood as the need simply to relax the absolutist character of state sovereignty, state policy toward international cooperation can proceed according to traditional principles. Only the sharpness of the boundary is put in question, not the spatial articulations of political life that place the boundaries where they are. Difficulties arise only when one of two conditions are met. On the one hand, the absolutist character of the boundaries, both territorial and authoritative, may be relaxed beyond a point at which the distinction between inside and outside makes little sense. Here we may speak of integration within the conventional logic. On the other hand, the politics of boundaries may become rather more complex than is allowed for in a metaphysics of presence and absence. The relaxation of boundaries may occur as part of a more fundamental rearticulation of political space, a rearticulation that simply cannot be understood or forced into the categories in which we have come to think about international cooperation. In this case, attention must necessarily shift away from the policy challenges such events present to the state and toward the analysis of the state as an historically variable form of political community. Questions about state sovereignty thus move beyond the categories of policy analysis to a more far-reaching attempt to probe the possible meaning of political practice at a time when the conventional guidebooks seem uninspiring.

Thus, *fourth*, the meaning of state sovereignty will continue to be reinterpreted in light of the transformation of the state in response to transformations in economic, social, and technological processes, especially in relation to the internationalization or globalization of economic production. Analysis of the state in this sense is exceptionally difficult, not least because of the way in which so many analytical traditions have insisted on seeing the state as either completely determined by or completely autonomous from economic processes. Nevertheless, in order to make any sense at all of the principle of state sovereignty in the modern world, it will be necessary to understand it in relation to an account of states as participants in large–scale patterns of global economic restructuring. If the key theme in the context of international cooperation involves the dissolution of the absolutist boundaries that have defined the conventional account of state sovereignty, then it may be suggested that the key theme in this context can be understood as a restructuring of the patterns of inclusion and exclusion along nonterritorial lines. I would venture to suggest that three insights will prove to be especially significant here:

1. The recognition (crucial, for example, to Marx's economic analysis) that capital both occurs as a universalizing relation or global process and also becomes manifest at a particular time and place. That is, capital resolves the relationship between universality and particularity or difference in a way that is sharply at odds with the resolution offered by the claims of state sovereignty. It should also be noted, however, that the interpretation of the valence of the relation between universal and particular that informs this alternative account remains defined by the philosophical options of the paradigm of sovereignty. The theory of the state often associated with this alternative resolution reflects a similar inheritance.

2. The recognition of novel patterns of participation in and exclusion from global economic processes, patterns in which relations of class and power are being restructured both within all societies and on a nonterritorial basis between societies. Neither the spatial boundaries of the territorial state nor the geographical points of the compass (North-South) provide much help in understanding how patterns of stratification, inclusion, and exclusion are being transformed on a global basis. The conventional opposition between class and nation has become yet another false dichotomy.

3. The recognition of the historically variable character of forms of state in relation to the transformation of productive forces. Where the paradigm of sovereignty encourages the claim that a state is a state is a state, to be understood in terms of an ahistorical account of the consequences of statehood (international anarchy, pursuit of national interests, and so on), it

becomes possible to distinguish the historical practices of states from the formal claims of territorial sovereignty.

In this context, the possible meaning of state sovereignty becomes quite unclear, primarily because it becomes increasingly apparent that the character and even the location of political community are being transformed in ways we barely understand. It becomes even more unclear to the extent that particular forms of state, understood as institutional forms and apparatuses, are becoming even more powerful as a consequence of their participation in global economic processes, despite the undermining of the state as a territorial entity.

Fifth, if boundaries are dissolving, if patterns of inclusion and exclusion are shifting, and if the politics of boundaries is becoming more and more complex as political space is being rearticulated in response to large-scale structural transformations, then one should expect to find a loosening of the claims of state sovereignty in response to the demands of cultural diversity. Thus it is common to note that there are more "nations" than there are nation-states. Many states now experience dissent in the name of ethnic or cultural autonomy. But whether the puzzling complexity of contemporary cultural politics can be resolved into the political accommodations of nationalism is increasingly doubtful. The politics of "patriotism" may need to be grasped in a rather different way. State sovereignty may remain the most powerful expression of participation in a political community, but the connection between state sovereignty and cultural identity does not come with a very long guarantee. Thus, in addition to the rearticulation of political space generated largely by global economic and technological processes, it seems reasonable to expect as well a rearticulation generated by struggles to rethink the possibilities of "local" identity on the basis of novel cultural explorations and community practices. This implies a rather different understanding of "local" politics than the one associated with the paradigm of sovereignty.

Sixth, in the context of both global processes and local explorations, it is possible to attempt to identify significantly novel forms of political practice. One would expect them to be responding to broad structural transformations. One would also expect them to be caught between an affirmation of forms of political life constituted through the principle of state sovereignty (that is, after all, how power and the opportunities for political action are conventionally understood) and a recognition of the need to challenge the principles that make those forms of political life possible.

It is in this context, I think, that it is possible to interpret the practices associated with many social movements that have become visible in many different societies. These movements are notoriously difficult to analyze, but at least in the case of what some call "new social movements"—and what I prefer to call "critical social movements"—the limitations of analytical categories formulated in the context of a paradigm of sovereignty seem fairly clear. Such movements seem to converge on at least five groups of explorations:[16]

1. They explore new political spaces, particularly those formerly relegated to "civil society," and they do so in relation to emerging global dangers.
2. They explore novel political practices, especially those that resist fetishizing the capture of state power.
3. They explore new ways of knowing and being, especially those that resist a metaphysics of inclusion and exclusion.
4. They explore new forms of political community, especially those that resist spatial reification.
5. They explore new ways of acting across borders, so as to make connections between the claims of humanity as such and the claims of particular peoples.

As explorations on the margin, yet responding to global processes experienced as dangers, they are no doubt exceptionally difficult. But they are not obviously more difficult than struggles to improve the world by taking or influencing the centers of a sovereign identity.

Conclusion

It seems to me that contemporary debate about the fate of state sovereignty will continue in at least these six forms, each of which, it might be said, has a clear appeal to different groups and interests. They can be fleshed out within different intellectual traditions and in relation to different political aspirations. But the significance of the sequence is fairly clear. It moves from positions that affirm the philosophical codes of modernity, to positions that understand these codes to be subject to critique on the grounds of historical change and the rearticulation of political space, to positions that understand the need for—as well as the difficulty of—challenging the resolutions of universality and diversity that now establish our expectations of what a political community must be.

If claims about the rapidity and scope of the transformation of the contemporary era are to be taken seriously, then so must the rearticulation of spatiotemporal relations. So too must resistance to a logic through which a sovereign identity defines all difference as the negation of itself. Thus questions about the presence or absence of state sovereignty must dissolve into questions about what political community can be now. And these in turn must lead us to question what democratic participation or political prudence can possibly mean in a world in which the guarantees of a sovereign identity are visibly expiring.

As long as we stay within the paradigm of a sovereign identity, it remains fairly easy to say what state sovereignty is, or is not. As we move away from it, all the interesting questions begin to open up. Questions about state sovereignty then cease being tiresome interrogations of the obvious and turn into struggles to speak of things that now escape our capacity of speech. To some, this will appear as a threat of the abyss, the terror of all those who can see no options beyond the paradoxes of modernity. For others, it will appear as a return to questions about political practice to which the resolutions of modernity have ceased to provide plausible answers.

Notes

1. W. B. Gallie, *Philosophy and the Historical Understanding*, 2nd ed. (New York: Schocken Books, 1968); Stuart Hampshire, *Thought and Action* (London: Chatto & Windus, 1959); William E. Connolly, *The Terms of Political Discourse*, 2nd ed. (Princeton: Princeton University Press, 1983).

2. In several senses, only one of which is pursued consistently here. The notion of a *commanding* silence recalls Carl Schmitt's account of sovereignty in terms of the capacity to decide on the exception, an account that had a tremendous impact on forms of so-called political realism associated with Hans J. Morgenthau, for example. See Carl Schmitt, *Political Theology: Four Chapters on the Concept of Sovereignty* (1922), trans. George Schwab (Cambridge, Mass.: MIT Press, 1985) and Alfons Söllner, "German Conservatism in America: Morgenthau's Political Realism," *Telos* 72 (Summer 1987): 161–172. Attention might also be drawn to those who are silenced, to the way in which the principle of state sovereignty codifies an account of otherness in relation to the authoritative claims of self-identity. See, for example, Edward Said, *Orientalism* (New York: Random House, 1979); Tsvetan Todorov, *The Conquest of America: The Question of the Other* (New York: Harper & Row, 1982); and Johannes Fabian, *Time and the Other: How Anthropology Makes its Object* (New York: Columbia University Press, 1983). I give these themes slightly greater attention in a parallel reading of the same problematic, "Security, Sovereignty and the Challenge of World Politics," *Alternatives* 15, no. 1 (1990): 3–28. Here I am more concerned with the silences engendered by the discourse of presence and absence—with both spatial and temporal variations—that has characterized so much analysis of structural and historical transformation in the literature on international relations, a discourse in which the legitimation of authoritarian politics and the reification of otherness are nevertheless quite unmistakable.

3. See especially Max Weber, "Politics as a Vocation," in *From Max Weber: Essays in Sociology*, trans. and ed. H. H. Gerth, and C. Wright Mills (New York: Oxford University Press, 1946), pp. 77–128. This theme has also passed into contemporary forms of political realism through the writings of Hans J. Morgenthau; see Stephen P. Turner and Regis A. Factor, *Max Weber and the Dispute over Reason and Value* (London: Routledge & Kegan Paul, 1984); Michael Joseph Smith, *Realist*

Thought from Weber to Kissinger (Baton Rouge: Louisiana State University Press, 1986); and Raymond Aron, "Max Weber and Power Politics," in Otto Stammer, ed., *Max Weber and Sociology Today*, trans. K. Morris (Oxford: Basil Blackwell, 1979), pp. 83–100.

4. For a succinct account of this debate, see Andrew Linklater, *Men and Citizens in the Theory of International Relations* (London: Macmillan, 1982). For accounts of how the tension between claims to citizenship and claims to humanity have been resolved through the principle of state sovereignty see R. B. J. Walker, *State Sovereignty, Global Civilization and the Rearticulation of Political Space*, World Order Studies Program Occasional Paper No. 18 (Princeton: Princeton University Center of International Studies, 1989); and Walker, "Ethics, Modernity and the Theory of International Relations." More generally, see Otto Gierke, *Political Theories of the Middle Ages*, trans. F. W. Maitland (Cambridge: Cambridge University Press, 1900); Quentin Skinner, *The Foundations of Modern Political Thought*, 2 vols. (Cambridge: Cambridge University Press, 1978); F. H. Hinsley, *Sovereignty*, 2nd ed. (Cambridge: Cambridge University Press, 1986); Kenneth Dyson, *The State Tradition in Western Europe* (Oxford: Martin Robertson, 1980); Andrew Vincent, *Theories of the State* (Oxford: Basil Blackwell, 1987); and David Held, *Political Theory and the Modern State* (Cambridge: Polity Press, 1989).

5. See especially Ernst Cassirer, *The Individual and the Cosmos in Renaissance Philosophy*, trans. Mario Domandi (New York: Harper & Row, 1963); and Pierre Duhem, *Medieval Cosmology*, ed. and trans. Roger Ariew (Chicago: University of Chicago Press, 1985).

6. E. H. Carr, *The Twenty Years Crisis* (London: Macmilian, 1946); Hans J. Morgenthau, *Politics Among Nations* (New York: Knopf, 1948).

7. See, e.g., Hedley Bull, *The Anarchical Society* (London: Macmillan, 1977) and Friedrich Kratochwil, *Rules, Norms and Decisions* (Cambridge: Cambridge University Press, 1989).

8. See, e.g., Robert W. Cox, *Production, Power and World Order* (New York: Columbia University Press, 1987); Stephen Gill, *American Hegemony and the Trilateral Commission* (Cambridge: Cambridge University Press, 1989); Stephen Gill and David Law, *The Global Political Economy: Perspectives, Problems and Policies* (Baltimore: The Johns Hopkins University Press, 1988); Michael Mann, *States, War and Capitalism* (Oxford: Basil Blackwell, 1988); Mann, *The Sources of Social Power*, Vol. 1 (Cambridge: Cambridge University Press, 1986); and Kees Van der Pijl, *The Making of the Atlantic Ruling Class* (London: Verso, 1985).

9. See R. B. J. Walker, "The Prince and the 'Pauper': Tradition, Modernity and Practice in the Theory of International Relations," in James Der Derian and Michael J. Shapiro, eds., *International/Intertextual Relations: Postmodern Readings of World Politics* (Lexington, Mass.: Lexington Books, 1989): 25–48; and Walker, "Realism, Change and International Political Theory," *International Studies Quarterly* 31, no. 1 (March 1987): 65–86.

10. R. B. J. Walker, "The Territorial State and the Theme of Gulliver," *International Journal* 39, no. 3 (Summer 1984): 529–552.

11. On the significance of this distinction for the absence of much sustained analysis of the state by theorists of international relations, see Fred Halliday, "State and Society in International Relations: A Second Agenda," *Millennium: Journal of International Studies* 16, no. 2 (Summer 1987): 215–229.

12. See Richard K. Ashley, "Living on Border Lines: Man, Poststructuralism and War," in Der Derian and Shapiro, eds., *International/Intertextual Relations*; Ashley, "The Geopolitics of Geopolitical Space: Towards a Critical Social Theory of International Relations," *Alternatives* 12, no. 4 (October 1987): 403–434; Ashley, "Untying the Sovereign State: A Double Reading of the Anarchy Problematique," *Millennium: Journal of International Studies* 17, no. 2 (Summer 1988): 227–262; and Walker, *State Sovereignty, Global Civilization and the Rearticulation of Political Space*.

13. For critical discussion see Richard K. Ashley, "The Poverty of Neorealism," *International Organization* 32, no. 2 (Spring 1984): 225–281; R. B. J. Walker, "History and Structure in the Theory of International Relations," *Millennium: Journal of International Studies* 18, no. 2 (Summer 1989): 163–183; and Fred Halliday, "The Origins of the International," *Economy of Society* 18, no. 3 (August 1989): 346–359.

14. Pierre-Maxime Schuhl, "Le thème du Gulliver et le postulat de Laplace," *Journal de Psychologie et Pathologie* 40 (April–June 1947): 169–184; and Walker, "The Territorial State and the Theme of Gulliver."

15. Partha Chatterjee, *Nationalist Thought and the Colonial World: A Derivative Discourse?* (London: Zed Books, 1986).

16. R. B. J. Walker, *One World, Many Worlds: Struggles for a Just World Peace* (Boulder, Colo.: Lynne Rienner, 1988). See also Saul Mendlovitz and R. B. J. Walker, eds., *Towards a Just World Peace: Perspectives from Social Movements* (London: Butterworths, 1987); Warren Magnusson and R. B. J. Walker, "Decentring the State: Political Theory and Canadian Political Economy," *Studies in Political Economy: A Socialist Review* 27 (Summer 1988): 37–71; Carl Boggs, *Social Movements and Political Power: Emerging Forms of Radicalism in the West* (Philadelphia: Temple University Press, 1986); John Keane, *Democracy and Civil Society* (London: Verso, 1988); Charles Maier, ed., *Changing Boundaries of the Political* (Cambridge: Cambridge University Press, 1987); Alberto Melucci, *Nomads of the Present: Social Movements and Individual Needs in Contemporary Society* (Philadelphia: Temple University Press, 1989); and Rajni Kothari, *State Against Democracy: In Search of Humane Governance* (New Delhi: Ajanta Publications, 1988). I prefer to refer to "critical" rather than "new" social movements on the grounds that questions about the nature and possibility of critique are more interesting, important, and difficult than questions about novelty.

Index

Adorno, Theodor, 139
Agh, Attila, 30–31
Akbar (Mughal emperor), 137
Ali, Chaudhuri Rehmat, 131
Alternative social structures, 149–154; ambiguity in, 154–157
Aquino, Corazón. *See* Philippines
Arendt, Hannah, 92, 140
Ashoka (king of Magadha), 137
Attali, Jacques, 107
Austin, John, 19, 22

Baer, W. C., 110
Baudrilland, Jean, 98
Bentley, Arthur, *The Process of Government*, 50
Bernstein, Richard, 88
Bettelheim, Bruno, 140
Bodin, Jean, 15, 17, 23; *De la République*, 16
Bradlaugh, Joseph, 129
Brucan, Silviu, 26, 29

Carr, E. H., 166
Certeau, Michel de, 100, 118
Christopherson, S., 109
Civilization, definition of, 145–146. *See also* Culture and civilization
Communities of resistance, 91–93. *See also* Welch, Sharon
Conrad, Joseph, 140
Constantino, Renato, 86
Cox, Robert, 32
Culture and civilization, 146–149

Davis, Mike, 116

De la République, 16
Deleuze, Gilles, 104
Democracy, 45–50. *See also* Popular politics; Social movements
Derrida, Jacques, 99
Deshingkar, Giri, 136

Elias, Norbert, 107
Evasions of sovereignty, 8–9, 70–77

Foucault, Michel, 90, 92, 102–105, 112, 116–117
Frank, Andre Gunder, 89
Friere, Paulo, 91
Fromm, Erich, 139–140
Fuentes, Marta, 89

Gadamer, Hans Georg, 85, 90
Gandhi, Indira, 130
Gandhi, Mohandas, 129, 131–132, 141–142
Gellner, Ernest, 46
Giddens, Anthony, 100, 108, 117
Global city, 9; as policy, 108–114; historical forces shaping spatialization of, 102–103; normalization of policy in, 118–121; sacred spatialization in, 103–106; spatialization of, 97–102; urban policy in, 106–108, 114–118
Global civilization, 9, 61–70, 157–158; definition of, 145–146. *See also* Alternative social structures; Culture and civilization
Globalization, 25–33; implications

of, for state sovereignty, 33–39.
    See also Evasions of sovereignty;
    Global city; Global civilization;
    Secularism
Gottdiener, M., 119
Great Peace Journey (GPJ), 71–72
Greenpeace, 73
The Grey Eminence, 102
Guattari, Felix, 104
Gulliver's Travels, 178

Habermas, Jürgen, 91
Hegel, Georg W. F., 15, 18
Heilbroner, Robert L., 38
Hinsley, F. H., 13–14, 21, 24–25
Hobbes, Thomas, 15, 18, 172; The Leviathan, 17–18
Holyoake, George Jacob, 129
Huxley, Aldous, The Grey Eminence, 102–103

Ileto, Reynaldo, 86
Interdependence, 2–4. See also Globalization; State sovereignty

Jinnah, Mohammed Ali, 131

Kakar, Sudhir, 139
Kaldor, Mary, 31
Kant, Immanuel, 18
Kasai, M., 136
Khan, A. Q., 135
Khan, Ali Akhtar, 129

Lapham, Lewis, 61
Laski, Harold, 15, 23
Lefebre, Henri, 106
The Leviathan, 17–18
Locke, John, 17

Machiavelli, Niccolo, 4–5, 172
McLuhan, Marshall, 150
Madan, T. N., 128
Maritain, Jacques, 16, 23
Marx, Karl, 19–20
Mendlovitz, Saul H., 92
Mitscherlich, Alexander, 140

Mitscherlich, Margaret, 140
Morgenthau, Hans J., 166

Nationalism, 21. See also Democracy; Global civilization; Globalization
Nation-state. See Political community
Nehru, Jawaharlal, 130
New York Times. See Global city

Offe, Claus, 89
Olalia, Rolando, 82

Patel, Raojibhai C., 135
Philippines, 9; legitimacy and authority in, 83–88; transformation of sovereignty in, 81–83, 88–91
Polis. See Culture and civilization; Democracy; Political community
Political community, 8, 45, 67; democracy and, 45–50; limits of, 165–168. See also Alternative social structures; Communities of resistance; Global city; Popular politics; Social movements
Popular politics, 54–56
The Process of Government, 50

Raza, Rahi Masoom, 131–132
Redfield, Robert, 149
Rees, W. J., 15
Rogers, Carl, 128
Rokeach, Milton, 139
Rosenau, James N., 25
Rousseau, Jean-Jacques, 15; Social Contract, 18

Savarkar, D. V., 131
Secularism, 9; religious faith and, 125–128. See also South Asia
Singh, Bhupinder, 141
Social Contract, 18
Social movements, 50–54, 88–90, 181–182. See also Communities of resistance; Globalization; Popular politics
Soja, Edward, 100
South Asia: collapse of secularism in, 132–135; idea of "Western Man"

in, 135–137; intolerance and violence in, 138–142; meaning of secularism in, 128–130; political hierarchy of secularism in, 130–132; religious tolerance in, 137–138; secularizing trends in, 126–128

Sovereignty: as reification, 168–171; space, time, and, 171–175. *See also* State sovereignty

State sovereignty: criticism of, 159–160; development of theory of, 15–19; in historical perspective, 13–15; in the global civilization, 61–70; legitimacy, authority, and, 83–88; possible meanings of, 10, 175–183; principle of, 5–8; problematic aspects of, 160–164; theoretical rationale of, 20–25; transformations of, 79–81; transformative practices and, 88–91. *See also* Alternative social structures; Evasions of sovereignty; Globalization; Sovereignty; Universality

Storper, M., 109

Structural transformations, 1–2. *See also* Alternative social structures; Global city

Swift, Jonathan, *Gulliver's Travels*, 178

Taylor, Charles, 91
Thompson, E. P., 37

Universality, 164–165. *See also* Political community

Vanunu, Mordechai, 69, 74
Virilio, Paul, 97–98

Walker, R. B. J., 79
Wallerstein, Immanuel, 29–30
Walzer, Michael, 104–105, 119
Weber, Max, 161–162, 173
Welch, Sharon, 89
Williams, Howard, 18
Wolfe, Tom, 112
World politics, 2, 4–5. *See also* Globalization